THE
FRAGILITY OF
THINGS

For Ken,
with respect,
Bill Conly

THE
FRAGILITY OF
THINGS

self-organizing processes, neoliberal fantasies, and democratic activism

WILLIAM E. CONNOLLY

DUKE UNIVERSITY PRESS :: DURHAM AND LONDON :: 2013

Printed in the United States of
America on acid-free paper ∞
Designed by Amy Ruth Buchanan
Typeset in Minion by Tseng
Information Systems, Inc.

Library of Congress Cataloging-in-
Publication Data
Connolly, William E.
The fragility of things : self-organizing
processes, neoliberal fantasies, and
democratic activism / William E. Connolly.
pages cm
Includes bibliographical references and index.
ISBN 978-0-8223-5570-0 (cloth : alk. paper)
ISBN 978-0-8223-5584-7 (pbk. : alk. paper)
1. Neoliberalism. 2. Economic policy.
3. Social policy. I. Title.
JC574.C654 2013
320.51′3—dc23
2013018960

:: *prelude*
     1755 · *1*

CHAPTER 1
Steps toward an Ecology
of Late Capitalism · *20*

:: *first interlude*
     Melancholia and Us · *43*

CHAPTER 2
Hayek, Neoliberalism,
Freedom · *52*

:: *second interlude*
     Modes of Self-Organization · *81*

CHAPTER 3
Shock Therapy, Dramatization,
and Practical Wisdom · *98*

:: *third interlude*
     Fullness and Vitality · *140*

CHAPTER 4
Process Philosophy and Planetary
Politics · *149*

:: *postlude*
     Role Experimentation and
     Democratic Activism · *179*

acknowledgments · *197*
notes · *201*
bibliography · *225*
index · *233*

CONTENTS

prelude :: 1755

It happened on a beautiful morning in November. It was All Saints Day in Lisbon; the faithful were gathered in churches across the city. The ground heaved. A minute later a more powerful and longer shock arrived, rumbling, tossing, and shaking the city in waves. By the third shock most of the structures in the city had been destroyed, including the palace and churches. Thousands of people were dead. Lisbon, a jewel of Europe and home to immense riches of gold and diamonds secured through colonial exploitation, lay in ruins. A short time later a huge tsunami poured into the city, just when thousands of survivors had run to the harbor and river shore to escape the devastation. Thousands more were killed. And then a massive fire roared through the city, started mostly by timbers in church ceilings falling onto candles designed to honor God on this special day. It took thousands more victims with it, in the most agonizing way. One captain, observing the events before the fire and from a distance in the harbor, described the events this way:

> Almost all the palaces and large churches were rent down. Or part fallen, and scarce one house of this vast city is left habitable. Every body that were not crushed to death ran out in large places, and those near the river ran down to save themselves by boats, or any other floating conveniency, running, crying, and calling to the ships for assistance; but whilst the multitude were gathered near the river side, the water rose to such a height that it overcome and overflow'd the lower part of the city, which so terrified the miserable and already dismayed inhabitants, who ran to and fro with dreadful cries, which we heard plainly on board, it made them believe the dissolution of the world was at hand; every one falling on his knees, and intreating the almighty for his assistance.[1]

There was no science of tectonic plates available to those who survived or heard about this catastrophic event. They did not know that Lisbon, on the edge of the ocean, sat close to the conjunction of two large plates. There was no knowledge of how such plates rub together as they move slowly, setting up the probability of a future huge quake and tsunami. Indeed the science of tectonic plates did not advance very far until the 1930s. Yet it is doubtful how much difference such knowledge would have made to the populace, given what we know about the behavior of populations today in California, Chile, Haiti, and Japan.

The interpretations and actions that followed this searing shock were different from those that later accompanied the Kobe quake, the Haitian disaster, the Japanese tsunami, and recurrent events along the San Andreas fault, though a listener might hear some similar chords. John Wesley, the renowned Protestant theologian in England, publicized the event eagerly as the punishment God imposed on carriers of a derelict Catholicism and a city wallowing in ill-gotten opulence. Many Jesuits treated the event as a dark harbinger of the Final Judgment, which would, they said, occur on the same date the next year. The local prime minister, a man soon to be named Lord Pombal, had the leading Jesuit propagator of this view imprisoned, tortured, and eventually hanged. Pombal himself favored a naturalistic reading, though he had little idea what that would involve. He was hell-bent on rebuilding the city with structures that could withstand future quakes and in convincing the king, who had taken flight with his entourage, to live there again. The king did eventually return, but he insisted on setting up a royal village of tents where his palace had been, and he lived in those tents for the rest of his life. He had lost trust in stone structures. Many believers were disturbed that God could have allowed so many people to die who were honoring Him in church at that very moment, particularly when a bevy of criminals had escaped as they fled a damaged prison after the first shock and the prostitution district was largely spared.

The quake, estimated today to have been between 8.5 and 9.0 on the Richter scale, was felt in northern Europe and northern Africa, the latter being hit hard by a tsunami. The aftershocks lasted months. The cultural aftershocks lasted a century, involving controversies between the Vatican, Protestant leaders, and new devotees of the Enlightenment. The debate was less securely contained by the Church than previous debates had been; each party found something in the shock of this massive suffering that called upon it to either modify its previous thinking or to intensify it to protect its creed from a disturbance that had shaken it. Kant himself wrote an early essay on it, and his later philosophy of the sublime is touched by the shock of this event.[2]

Voltaire, a leading figure of the burgeoning Enlightenment who had faced exile from and imprisonment in France for his unorthodox views, dramatized the quake in a way that assaulted, first, Catholic and Protestant theologies and, second, the philosophy of Leibniz that, as he saw it at least, comprehends all evils in this world as necessities serving a higher purpose. The event had provided a jolt to the earlier cosmic optimism he himself had felt.

Voltaire's poem "On the Lisbon Disaster," written shortly after the event, expresses revulsion against both of these interpretations. Theological readings of the event as an instance of divine punishment aroused his indignation:

Say ye, o'er that yet quivering mass of flesh:
"God is avenged; the wage of sin is death?"
What crime, what sin, had those young hearts conceived
That lie bleeding and torn, on mother's breast?
Did fallen Lisbon deeper drink of vice
Than London, Paris, or sunlit Madrid?

The philosophy of this as the best possible world replete with necessary evils because of "the iron laws that constrain the will of God" fared no better:

> Come you philosophers who cry, "All's well"!
> And contemplate this ruin of a world.
> Behold these shreds and cinders of your race.
> This child and mother heaped in common wreck,
> These scattered limbs beneath the marble shafts —
> A hundred thousand whom the earth devours . . .
> To that appalling spectacle of woe,
> Will ye reply, "You do but illustrate
> The iron laws that chain the will of God."[3]

Voltaire may have concluded that his direct plea was insufficient to shock ingrained theodicies out of their ruts. So he responded with a satire, published in 1759, barely four years after the quake.

In *Candide* the servant Candide is smitten by the beautiful, pure Cunegonde, daughter of the Westphalian nobleman he serves. She is drawn to him too. Both are also dedicated to Pangloss, a Leibnizian of sorts and philosopher in residence, who repeatedly proves to them how each untoward event is a necessary part of a universe that makes this the best of all possible worlds. Every evil is functional. Stones are scattered around the earth so that they could be gathered to build opulent palaces. Even the nose, not always so beautiful, was placed on the face so that we could wear glasses to improve our vision when literacy became widespread.[4] Pangloss may remind you of football players today who are convinced that every setback they suffer serves a higher purpose — for them. After Cunegonde's chance observation of the noble Pangloss applying his philosophy directly to a serving maid, she and Candide are moved to follow the great philosopher's lead. Candide is summarily dismissed, just before the family is attacked by villains. Two more evils with a purpose.

The worldwide adventure begins. Cunegonde, after observing the brutal killing of her parents by villains, is raped by them. She escapes, only to live a life punctuated by attacks, rape, enslavement, joint service to an Inquisitor and a Jew who take regular turns with her as their concubine, and apparent death. Candide, thinking only about reuniting with the fair Cunegonde, encounters similar adventures, being beaten, enslaved, robbed, and betrayed innumerable times, often just before or after encountering a stroke of good luck. Each event of the latter type convinces him once again of the wisdom of Pangloss. But the optimist also displays an inveterate tendency to publicize his plans to strangers. Each act of publicity sets up the next betrayal.

Pangloss also goes through merciless adventures, seeming to be executed once or twice and then returning for reunions with Candide. Each time, he is saved at the last moment by a most improbable event. His philosophy is tested by such events, but his survival encourages him to retain it.

You may chuckle at the cultural variety on the face of the earth when Candide lands in the exotic land of "Eldorado," seeing two naked girls running in the field as monkeys nip gently at their buttocks. And laugh again when Candide, who shoots the monkeys to save the girls, is rudely told that he has interfered with a mode of foreplay beyond his ken. Or maybe not. You laugh when he and his companion discover that gold and diamonds are plentiful enough in Eldorado to be treated as dirt. The two pile huge amounts of both onto goats and prepare to sail back to Europe to become rich men. Nothing can impede Candide's search for Cunegonde now.

On the trip to Lisbon the good doctor is demonstrating yet again to Candide and an Anabaptist how "individual misfortunes create general welfare so that the more individual misfortunes there are, the more all is well."[5] The Anabaptist squints as he hears an assault on his cherished doctrine of free will, as the sky begins to darken and the winds become severe at the entrance to the port of Lisbon. Just in time for the quake.

> Half the passengers, expiring from the indescribable agony which the rolling of a ship inflicts on the nerves and humors of the body, shaken in different directions, were so weakened that they lacked even the strength to become alarmed at their danger. The other half were shrieking and praying. . . . The Anabaptist was topside helping a little to handle the ship. A frenzied sailor struck him violently and laid him out flat on the deck, but his own blow threw him off balance and he fell overboard head first. . . . The good James [the Anabaptist] . . . helped him climb back on board but in the course of his efforts he was thrown into the sea in full view of the sailor, who let him perish without deigning to look at him. Candide came over and saw his benefactor reappear on the surface for a moment before sinking forever. He tried to leap into the sea after him; Pangloss the philosopher stopped him by proving to him that the Lisbon

harbor was formed precisely for the Anabaptist to drown in. As he was proving this *a priori*, the ship split open and everyone drowned except Pangloss, Candide and the brutal sailor.[6]

They are soon caught in the aftershocks, the "boiling up of the sea," and the fire cascading through the city, leading even Pangloss to wonder briefly what the "sufficient cause" could be.

A contemporary reader of *Candide* may be moved to compare the philosophy of Pangloss with that of neoliberalism, since the latter both acknowledges many evils and treats them as necessary effects of impersonal markets when the markets are allowed to rip and irrational state interference is not allowed.

Eventually the aging Pangloss, Candide, and Cunegonde are again united. They decide to leave philosophy, the restless pursuit of adventure, and the quest for reputation, resting content to cultivate their own gardens. Whenever Pangloss is moved to pontificate, the others help him turn to less abstract pursuits. Voltaire knows that this decision too expresses a philosophy of life, one encouraged but not required by the adventures, rapid turns, and suffering that preceded it.

:: :: ::

I prefer Voltaire's philosophy to several that he was contesting, though I know that some versions of each can be filled with a spirituality of presumptive generosity to others. I also admire his willingness to address juxtapositions between natural events and the vicissitudes of life. But can the wisdom the deist commends at the end work today? Put otherwise, it may be that to cultivate our gardens today means to engage the multiform relations late capitalism bears to the entire planet. It may be that Candide's response, which is once again tempting, must give way today to a multiform activism in a world that is very fragile, an activism that folds an ethos of *cultivation* into political practices set on several intercoded scales: local, familial, workplace, state, theological, corporate, global, and planetary. At any rate, I do not embrace the deism of Newton and Voltaire, in which a God winds up the universe and allows it to unfold according to a law-like plan. I embrace a post-Voltairian cosmology, one that fixes attention on recurrent moments when a shock or event disrupts some of the ingrained habits and assumptions that preceded it. I concur with him in calling into question both providential and mastery images of the world, though it seems clear that he himself tended toward a mild version of the former.

I believe the human estate is both imbricated with and periodically over-matched by a cosmos composed of multiple, interacting force fields moving at different speeds. We are today at least as closely implicated in several nonhuman force fields as the city of Lisbon found itself to be with that earthquake, tsunami, and fire. [In a world more scientifically and technically advanced, we are not that much better equipped culturally, philosophically, politically, or spiritually to address these entanglements.]

I have attended to precariousness and the fragility of things before.[7] But advances in the exploration of self-organizing systems and the hegemony of neoliberalism both suggest the need to do so more relentlessly now. Indeed neoliberalism has become a recent incarnation of the idea that the best of all possible worlds out of a relatively bad lot comes into being when its ideology is in charge. The term *neoliberalism* does not refer to that tattered American liberalism that supports labor union activism, unemployment insurance, the modest reduction of inequality, public medical care, and Keynesian policies of growth—though some differences between my view and that philosophy will also become clear. *Neoliberalism*, particularly in its American version, projects inordinate confidence in impersonal market rationality as it resists such policies. The evils that issue from a neoliberal economy are said by its proponents to be necessary to clear markets, or to promote future growth, or to discipline recalcitrant segments of society, or to prevent the state from becoming too large, or to protect the essential character of freedom. As neoliberalism proceeds it diverts attention from multiple conjunctions between capitalism and a variety of nonhuman force fields with differential powers of self-organization. It also obscures how it itself requires a very large state to support and protect its preconditions of being.

What about those rapid, strange turns that Voltaire takes so much pleasure in recording in *Candide*? Are they all reducible to a classical notion of efficient causality? It seems doubtful, even though that is the alternative already in place to consider when people overturn the idea of a final cause infused with divinity. The bizarre repetition of many fateful accidents in his story calls attention both to the bumpiness in our relations to the larger world and to a persistent human tendency to import an inner rationality or a final purpose into them. If you contest such tendencies, should you conclude that we periodically encounter accidents? Well, perhaps the ideas of chance and accident need to be reworked too to help us to move beyond both mechanistic and finalist readings of the world. What is an "accident"? What is an "event"? I don't claim to answer those queries definitively, but they are engaged in this text.

Sometimes an accident is understood by observers epistemically, as an event with natural causes that have so far escaped our ability to delineate them. Like the Lisbon earthquake, according to Pombal at the time. At other times people may hear a whisper of something beyond both the philosophies of definitive explanation *and* the theologies of final purpose in these events. Two force fields, following different trajectories, collide or intersect in a surprising way. Does at least one of them sometimes enter into a process of *self-organization* that helps to bring something new into the world for good or ill, without the result either having been intended from the start or entirely reducible to an aggregation of blind causes or serving a preordained purpose? Some complexity theorists in several of the human and nonhuman sciences think so. Here *self-organization* means a process by which, say, a simple organism restlessly *seeks* a new resting point upon encountering a shock or disturbance. Such activity may periodically help to bring something new into the world. Self-organization often involves a rhythmic interaction between two entities, when one or both has been disrupted. It subsides, to a degree at least, if and when a new equilibrium is established. Sometimes the process issues in a new, unplanned plateau of stability: a teleological element in a searching process that issues in a result not reducible to finalism as a preordained final purpose toward which things tend.

There are simple and complex versions of self-organization, as we shall see. The most complex version is perhaps best described as having a "teleodynamic" element in it: it exceeds blind causality without being tethered either to *simple* intentionalism or to ontological finalism. A cosmos composed of innumerable, interacting temporal force fields with varying degrees of self-organizational capacity subtracts from it both finalism and the sufficiency of blind, efficient cause. The sufficiency of simple intentionality bites the dust too. There are efficient causes, but they do not suffice to explain the most critical events. That is because in some of these events a creative result emerges out of the conjunctions between blindness and self-organizational processes.

A process of self-organization can be marked and identified in specific cases; it can even be experimentally induced and observed on occasion, as we shall see. But the process does not conform neatly to any model of classical explanation. The imputation of differential capacities of self-organization to heterogeneous processes may help us to grasp, up to a point, an element of real uncertainty and real creativity that periodically courses through processes and beings. A residue of mystery may still cling to our understanding of self-organization, however. At least, there is no cosmic guarantee that the puny human estate will someday grasp fully everything that happens or even elaborate a framework sufficiently capable of doing so in principle. The more you identify an element of real creativity in human life, in some nonhuman processes, and in the relations between them, the more such a suspicion grows. For the reality of creativity and the demands of complete explanation do no mesh together neatly.

So the version of speculative realism embraced here folds a fungible element of mystery into its philosophy. Some mysteries may be reduced or eliminated, but it seems unlikely that all will. This is a *speculative* realism, then, a philosophy that welcomes exchanges with theologies, seeking to engage the latter's adventures even as it respectfully contests some elements in this or that version.

At any rate, the adventure pursued here is irreducible simultaneously to eliminative materialism, to mechanistic theories of causation, to grand teleologies pulled by a final purpose, to simple human intentionalism, to the most familiar notions of progressive time, to any notion of complete explanation, and to the sharpest lines of division between nonliving nature and human agency. Being so, it seeks to render us more sensitive to a variety of nonhuman force fields that impinge upon politico-economic life as it too impinges upon the force fields. It seeks to *extend* our political and cosmic sensibilities.

The ontocosmology within which such an adventure is set is replete with dark spots, including its preliminary renderings of self-organization and distributed creativity. But it is not unique in these respects. When you engage other perspectives closely you also run into places where the future promise of the theory rests upon past achievements and future hopes more than the current sufficiency of its concepts, experiments, and explanations.

Indeed whenever you speak of the promise of a theory, a purposive or teleological notion is invoked. Often a cloudy promise is projected into the future in a way that supports several experiments and rules out others. To speak of such a promise, as we all do, is to pose the question of whether the pursuit seeks to solidify the unique powers of human beings created in the image of God, or to follow a "postulate" that creatures like us can't avoid making about ourselves and the world if we are to be moral and self-consistent, or to perfect an evolutionary power folded into human life alone, or to consolidate a power that humans share to differential degrees with some other beings and forces. The experiment here is to pursue the last promise, to see where it leads.

That is part of the adventure. Here is another aspect with which it stands in a relation of interdependence and tension. If you join attention to differing degrees of creativity in the domains of human culture, nonhuman force fields, and culture-nature imbrications to a critical account of the expansion, intensification, and acceleration of neoliberal capitalism, you may be brought face-to-face with the fragility of things today—that is, with growing gaps and dislocations between the demands neoliberalism makes upon several human activities and nonhuman fields and the capacities of both to meet them. These pressures set off boomerang processes as the demands intensify. Almost paradoxically, I contend, an educated sense of the fragility of things today solicits a more refined sensitivity by us to dangers attached to several contemporary institutions and role definitions *and* that the inculcation of such sensitivities must be linked to a more militant democratic politics. A difficult combination.[8]

Certainly enhanced sensitivity to what is most fragile about ourselves and our place on the planet does not go smoothly with militancy. The combination may seem like carefully laying a mirror down on the ground and then trampling on it as you ride a horse into battle. Cultivation of sensitivity to the subtlety of tradition, for instance, meshes well with the kind of cultural conservatism associated with a Burke or a Tocqueville. And enhanced sensitivity to nonhuman processes—such as to the seasons, or to changes in a climate pattern, or to the musical capacities of whales, or to bird-human disease crossings, or to delicate soil processes of self-renewal, or to the two pounds of bacteria of innumerable types carried around by adult human beings, or to the precarious habitats of crocodiles—often fits with a desire to slow down human processes so as to commune with a holistic nature that moves slowly.

I am pursuing, with some trepidation, a different experiment. The intuition is that we must simultaneously *slow down* at key points and moments as we enhance sensitivity to the course of things outside our habitual modes of perception, expectation, and security and *speed up* a series of changes in contemporary role definitions, identities, faiths, public ethos, state priorities, and economic practices. To do the latter requires a politics of democratic activism situated on several sites. What's more, the contention is that the tensions within such an unruly combination do not merely testify to tensions in my perspective; they express a torsion folded into the contemporary condition. If you ignore any of the relevant dimensions—the differential distribution of real creativity in the cosmos, the acceleration of pace in some domains of contemporary life, the hegemony of neoliberal capitalism, the fragility of things, the need for an expanded image of the human sciences, heightened patterns of sensitivity and experimental shifts in role redefinition, and the imperative to democratic activism—you deny something essential to our engagement with the contemporary condition. We are, as it were, under water in the grip of a hungry crocodile at the onset of its death roll. Moreover we are surrounded by many who fail or refuse—for reasons rooted in conceptions of science, religious faith, or economic activity—to be moved by the situation. Luckily I met a woman in Australia ten years ago who had been caught in a crocodile death roll and escaped.

:: :: ::

Here, then, is a map of the study. Chapter 1 begins with a critique of neoliberalism, first interrogating its assumptions about market self-rationality in relation to its less publicized demands upon the state to engineer the preconditions of existence for neoliberal power. This leads to an account of why neoliberal states are so large, active, and disciplinary today, even as the supporters of neoliberalism repeatedly call for the contraction of the state. We also explore some of the reasons so many citizens are drawn to neoliberal ideology again and again, often only a short time after it has ushered in the latest economic meltdown. It is a powerful political formula and a dangerous political movement.

As those critiques are advanced, a more basic turn is taken. While I appreciate points Keynesians, Marxists, Foucauldians, and others make against neoliberalism, another dimension is accentuated here. It is that markets are not unique systems. The cosmos itself is composed of innumerable force fields, several of which possess some characteristics of impersonal self-organization that neoliberals tend to reserve to markets. When you place the expansionary demands of neoliberalism into relation with other systems conveying differential degrees of self-organizational capacity, your awareness of the fragility of things becomes heightened. Some examples of nonhuman forces with self-organizational powers are pursued in the first chapter, and others are considered later. This chapter closes with preliminary thoughts on how to respond to this fragility by politico-economic means. The initial focus is on changing the ethos of consumption in relation to changes in the state-supported infrastructure of consumption.

The principal version of neoliberalism addressed here is that now expressed in the United States and pressed upon other countries both by it and by international organizations attached to it. That is because I know that version best, because it poses significant barriers to coming to terms with the fragility of things in both the United States and elsewhere, and because its focus on markets as unique modes of self-organization crystallizes tendencies at work less extremely in other versions. It would be pertinent to offer a comparative account of neoliberal regimes, but the focus adopted here does allow me to concentrate on the relations between neoliberalism almost as an ideal type and nonhuman force fields. I also do not argue that neoliberalism poses the only obstacle to coming to terms with the fragility of things. As I discussed in a recent book, the right edge of evangelcalism does so as well, and other orientations and regimes also pose serious obstacles.[10] The claim, rather, is that neoliberalism does pose *one* of the major barriers, both when in official power and when deploying corporate and financial initiatives, lobbying and filibustering, and media power to insinuate its objectives. It is when you explore its double drive to overemphasize the rationality of impersonal markets and to deflect attention from the self-organizing powers of other systems that the fragility of things comes into focus.

The interludes in this book are insertions that either dramatize some themes in a different tone to fix them on the visceral register or introduce points pertinent to the perspective that I am not yet prepared to elaborate more closely. The idea—or hope—is to enact through punctuations in the textual organization the ways heterogeneous subsystems in econopolitical life become imperfectly bonded into larger assemblages. The book itself is an assemblage of elements that lean upon and infuse each other, but they neither fuse together into a tight system nor express a dialectical dynamic.

The hope is that such a textual mode of organization can help to dramatize how a political economy is a moving assemblage of interconnected subsystems marked by loose joints, disparate edges, redundant noises, and somewhat open possibilities. Neither methodological individualism nor organic holism is sufficient to such a world. You can think of noise, on a first take, as a dissonance that arises when a visual image does not fit neatly with the words through which it is articulated. Noise arises in film, and it also accompanies political struggles. It is even installed at protean moments in species evolution, when a mutation is born and an unfolding organism searches to read it as a sign. Without noise, no real creativity. With it, no tight system or consummate human control.

The first interlude, "*Melancholia* and Us," seeks to dramatize our attachment to the human estate and the larger world with which it is entangled, crystallizing a mode of attachment readily buried to some degree under the joys, routines, and burdens of daily life. Those joys, injuries, and routines are an essential part of life, but they need to be infused with an enlarged sense of the planetary entanglements of the species.

While critical of the sufficiency of "exclusive humanism" in both its humanist and theological strains, this interlude also expresses wariness of any version of "posthumanism" susceptible to the charge that it does not give *any* significant priority to the human estate in its multiple entanglements with other beings and processes. The idea, again, is to amplify a subliminal mode of attachment that already infiltrates life, without rendering the image of humanity so unique that the appreciation of multiple entanglements and affinities is lost.

Some readers of chapter 1 may contest the accuracy of the report on neoliberal ideology. Fair enough. Part of the reason may be that we bring different comparisons into play as well as different assumptions about the character of the nonhuman systems with which human culture is entangled. A related reason, however, is that it is insufficient to examine a theory of neoliberalism generically, given the diversity of creeds rumbling under this banner. In lieu of examining several regimes comparatively, then, chapter 2 examines the work of a paradigmatic figure in the history of neoliberal theory. That examination allows us to crystallize tendencies at work to differential degrees in several regimes and to see what neoliberalism would become if these tendencies were given full power. Friedrich Hayek is the figure chosen, both because of his importance to the history of neoliberal practice in several states and because of the oblique ways he makes contact with themes advanced in this study.

One fascinating trait of Hayek is that he himself locates an element of *spontaneity* in human conduct as he also postulates impressive powers of unconscious *self-organization* in economic markets. The first Hayek thesis speaks to a general theme of this book too—to the uncanny experiences of spontaneity and creative power in the human condition. Several things he says thus make him a good candidate to compare to the mode of complexity theory defended here. His second thesis about impersonal self-organization, however, goes awry: first, it confines human creativity too restrictively to entrepreneurial market activity; second, it fails to distinguish sharply enough between impersonal organization and impersonal rationality; third, it does not really address differential degrees of self-organizational power in a number of nonhuman systems with which capitalism intersects; and fourth, it downplays too radically modes of self-organization that are found in democracy and those uncanny modes of creativity periodically emerging out of social movements.

The critique of Hayek, in a sense, rests upon the claim that he is too restrictive about the sites of impersonal organization identified and too confident about the equation between self-organization and impersonal rationality. An awareness of multiple sites of self-organization brings us face-to-face with the fragility of things today. It now becomes more apparent how the neoliberal recipes Hayek embraces are apt to increase this fragility more than to diminish it. It also may become clear how those outside the neoliberal tradition need to rethink the images of self-organization, creativity, and human freedom they bring to political economy too.

Hayek *emphasizes* the role neoliberal ideology must play in sustaining a neoliberal economy. I both explore that role and counter his thesis by emphasizing the pertinence of another ideology to public life today, one that engages nonhuman force fields more closely, appreciates the creative element in social movements and democracy, and explores positive affinities of spirituality across creedal difference between multiple constituencies.

In the closing section of chapter 2 I think about what it means if an element of creativity is lodged within human freedom. The element of creativity compromises notions of masterful agency; it even involves sinking periodically into uncanny processes to allow new thoughts, concepts, tactics, or judgments to emerge, if they will, as candidates for action or further reflection. We are not the masters, individually or collectively, of our own creativity. It is, in a sense, impersonal.)

The chapter closes with a brief engagement with the interdependence and tension between the value of creativity and that of folding appreciation of the fragility of things more deeply into life.

The second interlude, "Modes of Self-Organization," pulls on a thread in Hayek about the creative role of self-organization in markets. It reviews several modes of self-organization, replete with differing degrees of complexity. A walker's bridge, a thermodynamic system, a mode of species evolution, and the intensification of class differences in state-market relations are the four modes chosen. Sometimes the idea of *metamorphosis* is the best way to describe the mode of self-organization at play; at others, real *creativity* may be triggered by the excitation of "teleodynamic searching processes" in complex processes, whereby a new formation arises out of a disturbance without being entirely caused by it.

When a variety of such processes is engaged, it becomes clear that self-organization does not always or necessarily express what neoliberals would call impersonal market rationality. For instance, the collective self-amplification process by the walking traffic on the Millennium Bridge in London would have led to a disastrous break in the bridge if left alone, plunging hundreds of pedestrians to their deaths. So just as the limitation of self-organization to economic markets is abridged, the equation between impersonal self-organization and impersonal rationality is also broken. It is particularly important to challenge that equation in a world composed of multiple, interpenetrating human and nonhuman systems with differing degrees of self-organizing power.

This interlude then turns to the process by which class differences, already finding a strong presence in the regime under scrutiny, can be exacerbated by processes of self-organization in financial markets. That example, too, sharpens the break between self-organization and impersonal rationality.

Chapter 3, "Shock Therapy, Dramatization, and Practical Wisdom," engages Kant to deepen and historicize the themes now under way. The first idea is to expose selective Kantian presuppositions within which many contemporary theorists operate to a series of disturbances.

A series of micro-shocks is delivered to the "apodictic" starting points from which Kantian arguments proceed. These shocks are delivered by an image of causality, the cosmos, and ethical life promulgated by the ancient Greek visionary Hesiod. When you place Kant and Hesiod into a series of dissonant conjunctions, the noisy starting points of Kantian arguments become more detectable. We may be jolted out of thinking of them as apodictic starting points for definitive arguments about morality, a necessary, subjective faith, and the subjective necessity to project a benign telos into human existence. To loosen up the Kantian starting points is to create room, not for alternative demonstrations but for other alternative experiments and explorations.

As the chapter proceeds we explore just why Kant found himself "compelled" to treat both natural processes and the self-serving inclinations dividing nations "as if" they express benign, impersonal market-like processes that both extend well beyond the human powers of moral agency and enable moral agency to progress indefinitely toward its true end. We also address how Kant first opened a door to rethink nonhuman organisms with his brilliant discussion of their self-organizing capacities, only to close it with the postulates projected upon making that discovery. The thing to remember, however, is that Kant did open that door.

The governing idea of the chapter is that philosophy, theory, and thinking involve much more than showing in tight argument the upshot of starting points we cannot avoid making. Thinking exceeds argument and knowing, even while it includes them. Thinking, in individual instances and collective modes, is also involved in those uncanny processes by which new ideas, strategies, tactics, and ethical sensibilities emerge that were not simply implicit in what preceded them. Politics is like that too. At any rate, the apodictic starting points identified by Kant now emerge as flashpoints, replete with pluripotentialities that could be *dramatized* in this way or that. Each dramatization works on cloudy processes on the way, crafting them into a consolidation that exceeds the antecedent determinants. The uncanny link between creativity and dramatization may now become a bit more visible, as the need of participants in the human sciences to dwell creatively from time to time in artistic and literary practices becomes more palpable too.

Kant's "necessary postulates" of unconscious market-like processes in nature and the temporal relations between nations may identify one affinity across radical differences between his philosophy and the neoliberal ideology of today. To exaggerate, neoliberalism adopts Kantian instrumental reason, captures his postulates of impersonal rationality for its own purposes, and subtracts the Kantian idea of morality from its program. It also ignores Kant's exploration of what "we" must postulate *nature* to be in order to sustain the Kantian philosophy of morality, deflecting ideological attention from the corollary image of nature *it* needs to sustain itself. The thoroughness of the sublime Kant thus helps to pinpoint dark spots in neoliberal ideology.

This all suggests to me how much Kant himself sensed the fragility of things. He was, at any rate, moved to generate an impressive list of "postulates" and "hopes" to ward off a fragility that would otherwise become palpable. However you slice into his work, Kant emerges as a prescient genius to be engaged.

As with the chapters preceding it, chapter 3 does not close with mere critique. It first expresses appreciation of the love of this world with which Kant's philosophy is imbued and then pulls upon subordinate strains in his work to articulate maxims of "practical wisdom" appropriate to the fragility of things, the limits of official Kantianism, and the displacement of neoliberalism. These involve steps toward an alternative articulation of freedom of the will, an earthy ethic of cultivation, a revised ethos of responsibility, the cultivation of situational judgment in a world that shifts significantly on occasion, and appreciation of the contemporary need for democratic militancy. The idea is to track the Kantian themes of practical reason with a corollary set of maxims of practical wisdom, drawing upon subordinate strains in the master as you proceed. It is also to bring out how an ethic of cultivation set in a world of becoming shows us both how fragile the ethical life is and how important it is to cultivate it.

The task is not, however, to replace one failed system of putatively tight arguments with another set that purports to succeed. It is to forge a positive alternative without attributing necessity to it. These reflections draw sustenance from the testimonials of both Hesiod and Kant without being reducible to either.

The third interlude, "Fullness and Vitality," highlights a theme already under way. The idea is to come to terms with the creative element in human life in its bumpy relations, both internally and externally, with nonhuman forces. To do so it may be wise to spend less time pursuing the wisp of human "fullness." Such a positive pursuit solicits divine grace when it is most at home with itself, but the frustrations accompanying such a pursuit can also lead disappointed suitors to a theophilosophy of negative dialectics whereby transcendence must always be pursued and must always fail. These two complementary alternatives are resisted in this interlude.

I thus work critically upon the end of fullness itself, as it finds expression in the admirable work of Charles Taylor, comparing and contrasting it to the cultivation of vitality. It turns out that fullness and vitality express some affinities, but the priorities of each are inflected differently. While seeking to enter into ethicopolitical alliances with many who pursue fullness, such alliances are best consummated if the potential allies comprehend how and why some of us give priority to the pursuit of vitality.

Vitality is linked to the creative element in human freedom introduced in chapter 2. If we participate modestly in larger processes of periodic creativity that extend to varying degrees beyond the human estate, the pursuit of human vitality may provide a viable competitor to both fullness and failed transcendence. Vitality and belonging to the world now stand in a relation of interdependence and tension, in which each deserves priority at different moments. Our feeling of attachment to this world is enhanced by the feeling of vitality, even as the latter experience encourages us to come to terms more positively with the noise, breaks, rifts, and gaps that make creativity possible.

The last chapter, "Process Philosophy and Planetary Politics," sinks into these issues by placing two protean thinkers into conversation. Each asserts that an element of speculation, though its sites may shift historically, is probably ineliminable from the human condition. For our minds are limited *and* we seem to live into futures not entirely determined by the past. Nietzsche and Whitehead *affirm* such a double condition, as each comes to terms with differential degrees of real creativity within and beyond human practices. Both are also philosophers of vitality, though each reads it in a distinctive way. Their speculative philosophies, indeed, once they are linked to late modern sciences and experiences that enhance their plausibility, also help us to grasp why several spiritualities of existential resentment have intensified today.

My task in this chapter is to forge a position that draws selectively upon both thinkers as it places them into negotiations with each other. The chapter closes with a reading of some of the factors involved in the simultaneous growth of hubris, *ressentiment*, and studied complacency in contemporary politics, as it also explores how each of these orientations can bleed into the others.

The postlude probes subterranean flows between belief, sensibility, role experimentation, and political activism. The idea is to spur positive movements back and forth between them. The postlude also attends again to the bumpiness and frictions by which the open subsystems in which we participate are consolidated into larger assemblages with their own bumps, uncertainties, sharp edges, and fragilities. Role experimentation and democratic activism are appropriate to such a world. The activism available today requires a large constellation of interinvolved minorities more than a core class surrounded by a series of fellow travelers.

The postlude, like the -ludes and chapters before it, speaks to a time when the dilemma of electoral politics has become intense, the human-nonhuman entanglements that mark contemporary life are replete with energetic remainders and uneven edges, the fragility of things has become palpable, and political activism is needed at several interinvolved sites. It explores a few strategies that might help to loosen the dilemma of electoral politics and to infuse the palpable sense of fragility more actively into state politics, role experimentations, and cross-state citizen movements. I do not wish to claim too much for the specific explorations launched in this postlude, only that they give voice to an urgent need to think and act in ways that activate the subterranean links between beliefs, role performances, social movements, electoral politics, state actions, and cross-state citizen movements.

CHAPTER 1 :: steps toward an ecology of late capitalism

Neoliberalism, let us say, is a socioeconomic philosophy embedded to varying degrees in Euro-American life. In its media presentations, it expresses
inordinate confidence in the unique, self-regulating power of markets as
it links the freedom of the individual to markets. At a lower decibel level
and high degree of intensity, it solicits modes of state, corporate, church,
and media discipline to organize nature, state policy, workers, consumers,
families, schools, investors, and international organizations to maintain
conditions for unfettered markets and to clean up financial collapses, eco-
messes, and regional conflicts created by that collusion.

Neoliberalism and laissez-faire capitalism are thus not exactly the same
thing, at least since neoliberalism displaced the latter in Euro-American
thought between 1935 and 1960. Neoliberals, as Michel Foucault has shown,
often do not think that markets are natural; they think markets are delicate mechanisms that require careful protection and nurturance by states

and other organizations.[1] The state does not manage markets much directly, except through monetary policy, but it takes a very active role in creating, maintaining, and protecting the preconditions of market self-regulation. The most ambitious supporters want the state to inject market processes into new zones through judicial or legislative action, focusing on such areas as academic admissions, schools, prisons, health care, rail service, postal service, retirement, and private military organizations. Note how such shifts will implicate more and more citizens in the vicissitudes of nonstate, corporate practices, where the ability to discipline and channel conduct increases.

So neoliberalism solicits an active state to promote, protect, and expand market processes. And political leaders espousing neoliberal economics the most fervently—such as Margaret Thatcher, Ronald Reagan, the two Bushes, and David Cameron—often turn out also to be bellicose defenders of conservative Christianity, moralism, and/or a specific image of the nation. Neoliberalism, a selectively active state, a conservative brand of Christianity, and a nation of regularized individuals surrounded by marginalized minorities often complement one another, even if periodically they are at odds with one another.[2]

What, then, are some of the political movements and modes of state activism supported by neoliberalism? They include, with varying degrees of support from different leaders, laws to restrain labor organization and restrict consumer movements; corporate participation on school and university boards; corporate ownership and control of the media; a jurisprudence and court decisions that treat the corporation as a person with unlimited rights to lobby and campaign; court policies that treat money as a mode of speech to be protected by the state; demands for bankruptcy laws that favor corporations at the expense of those working for them;[3] special corporate access to state officials to maintain inequality and restrain unemployment benefits; extensive discipline of the workforce; legal defense of corporate financial power to limit consumer information about the policies that affect them; the ear of state officials who regulate credit and the money supply; use of the state to enforce debt payments and foreclosures; huge military, police, and prison assemblages to pursue imperial policies abroad and discipline the excluded and disaffected at home; meticulous street and institutional security arrangements to regulate those closed out of the neoliberal calculus; huge state budgets to promote the established infrastructure of consumption in the domains of highway expenditure, the energy grid, health care, and housing codes; state cleanup of disasters created by underregulated financial and corporate activity; and state or bureaucratic delays to hold off action on global climate change.

The corporate, media, state, evangelical, and think-tank cheerleaders of neoliberalism also deflect attention from ways state or neoliberal capitalism strives to order workers, consumers, localities, and international institutions to fit the neoliberal dictates of market behavior. It is an effective ideological strategy and a destructive and dangerous organization of private and public energies. The activist, neoliberal state becomes most transparent during an emergency or meltdown, but it is always operative.

Perhaps the quickest way, then, to dramatize the difference between classical market liberalism and contemporary neoliberalism is to say that the former wanted the state to minimize interference with "natural" market processes as it purported to leave other parts of civil society to their own devices, while the latter campaigns to make the state, the media, schools, families, science, churches, unions, and the corporate estate be ordered around neoliberal principles of being. This version of state activism provides a brand of statism that helps to draw together into one political assemblage, at least in America, differential priorities among neoliberals, evangelicals, neoconservatives, and the Vatican. There are others.

The Subjective Grip of Neoliberalism

Several angles of criticism have been brought against neoliberalism. Marxists focus on how its celebration of the market covers up exploitation and crisis tendencies internal to capitalism.[4] Keynesians and Social Democrats focus on how it overplays the self-regulating power of markets and underplays the recurrent need of states to seed growth after a downturn, to provide unemployment support, and to spur consumer demand by a tax system that dampens inequality. Liberal Christians, atheists, Muslims, and Jews berate its heartlessness and readiness to leave those on the bottom out in the cold. Maverick market theorists such as Fred Hirsch focus on how the combination of consumer sovereignty and unconscious market processes regularly generate severe consumer binds, until it becomes more difficult to make ends meet for people of low and middle income, people become less satisfied with the products they receive, and the middle class responds to these pressures by demanding tax reductions and the further contraction of social democracy.[5] Hirsch's book, published in 1977, is still highly relevant. Deep ecologists focus on how the state-neoliberal combine treats nature as standing reserve and depreciates the urgent need to adjust market blindness to a wholeness of nature that precedes economic life.

Several of these critiques converge on the conclusion that neoliberal capitalism is the most inegalitarian capitalism of all. To them, and to me, the identification by Georg Simmel of a general tendency in complex societies to impose the most severe burdens and sacrifices on those already on the bottom tiers of the order applies in spades to neoliberalism. One need only think of the slow fallout from the September 2008 world economic crisis when Simmel says, "Every new pressure and imposition moves along the line of least resistance which, though not in its first stage, usually and eventually runs in a descending direction. This is the tragedy of whomever is lowest. . . . He not only has to suffer from the deprivations, efforts, and discriminations, which, taken together, characterize his position; in addition every new pressure on any point whatever in the superordinate layers is, if technically possible at all, transmitted downward and stops only at him."[6]

I thus share a thing or two with each of these critiques. But the center of gravity advanced here may differ from most of theirs. First, most may not come to terms sharply enough with the subjective grip the state, media, and neoliberal combine exerts on the interpretations and desires of large sections of the populace even after it has been rocked by a meltdown, problems in securing medical care, structural unemployment, a tsunami, an oil spill, or new evidence in favor of climate change. Many white working- and middle-class males, amid the decline of social democracy, find themselves pulled in two directions at the same time: they support neoliberal promises of corporate growth to cope with the squeeze the state-market collusion has placed them in, and they demand decisive leadership from the state to resolve any fallout created by this legacy.[7]

We need to understand better the pressures on so many constituencies to reinstate faith in neoliberal ideology a short time after the latest meltdown. These are the pressures that encourage so many to translate experiences of fragility in a neoliberal world into attacks on state efforts to respond to those very troubles. Of course, many young people of affluence are pushed in this direction by pressure to *believe* in the stability of the system in which they are preparing to forge specific careers. And in the United

States at least, there is a sense among many corporate and financial elites of special world and income entitlements, which can easily be translated into neoliberal hubris if and when critics make calls for shifts in the ethos and state regulation of the economy.

But what about others? I have contended in *Capitalism and Christianity, American Style* that many anxious white males in the working and middle classes seek models of masculinity with whom to identify in a world of uncertainty. Corporate elites, sports heroes, financial wizards, and military leaders project images of independence, mastery, and virility that can make them attractive models of identification, whereas state welfare programs, market regulations, retirement schemes, and health care, while essential to life, may remind too many of the very fragilities, vulnerabilities, susceptibilities, and dependencies they strive to deny or forget. This double logic of masculinization of market icons and feminization of state supports and regulatory activities takes a toll on the polity, particularly when it is overcoded with race and immigration issues. Neoliberal heroes, TV talking heads, and evangelical publicists further incite these very vulnerabilities as they feed off the struggle of many white males to conceal them from their families and themselves through hyperidentification. Check out the *Rush Limbaugh Show* sometime. It is difficult to occupy the subject position of the white working-class male.[8]

There may be another element here, though its importance is difficult to weigh. And indeed its weight probably varies among different constituencies. If you are stuck in circumstances in which it takes Herculean efforts to get through the day—doing low-income work, obeying an authoritarian boss, buying clothes for the children, dealing with school issues, paying the rent or mortgage, fixing the car, negotiating with a spouse, paying taxes, and caring for older parents—it is not easy to pay close attention to larger political issues. Indeed you may wish that these issues would take care of themselves. It is not a huge jump from such a wish to become attracted to a public philosophy, spouted regularly at your job and on the media, that economic life would regulate itself automatically if only the state did not repeatedly intervene in it in clumsy ways. Now underfunded practices such as the license bureau, state welfare, public health insurance, public schools, public retirement plans, and the like begin to appear as awkward, bureaucratic organizations that could be replaced or eliminated if only the rational market were allowed to take care of things impersonally and quietly, as it were. Certainly such bureaucracies are indeed often clumsy. But more people are now attracted to compare that clumsiness to the myth of how an impersonal market would perform if it took on even more assignments and if state regulation of it were reduced even further. So a lot of "independents" and "moderates" may become predisposed to the myth of the rational market in part because the pressures of daily life encourage them to seek comfort in ideological formations that promise automatic rationality.

Self-Organizing Processes and Political Economy

I focus here, however, on a related issue. Many critics of neoliberalism criticize it as they downplay the self-regulatory powers of economic markets. For instance, they may say, correctly in my view, that markets don't work that way nearly as much as their defenders say they do. I agree that economic markets can be very unstable because of, say, elite collusion, self-amplifying bubbles, actions by other states, a war, and several of these in conjunction. But I further treat economic markets *as merely one type of imperfect self-regulating system in a cosmos composed of innumerable, interacting open systems with differential capacities of self-organization set on different scales of time, agency, creativity, viscosity, and speed.* These open systems periodically interact in ways that support, amplify, or destabilize one another. It is partly *because* economic markets operate in a larger world of multiple, self-organizing systems that they are much more volatile than the advocates of neoliberalism pretend. The theme to be pursued here, then, is not that markets are always efficient and rational. They are not. It is, however, that they do possess varying degrees of self-organizing power *and* that a lot of other human and nonhuman processes with which they interact do too. Such a combination changes everything.

The theme of a cosmos of open, interacting force fields may press against some assumptions in neoliberalism, socialist productivism, Keynesianism, and classical Marxism alike, though there are important variations here. So we can speak only of tendencies. Where the latter types may diverge from the theory projected here is either in the assumption that cultural theory can concentrate its attention on the internal dynamics of social, state, and economic formations without close reference to movements of natural systems of multiple sorts, or in a tendency to think that capitalism constitutes an absorbent system that automatically returns the shocks and dissenting

Science

pressures applied to it as enhanced drives to its own expansion and intensification, or in a tendency to treat nonhuman force fields as reducible to
simple law-like patterns without significant powers of metamorphosis.

When you come to terms more closely with interacting, nonhuman systems with differential capacities of metamorphosis you also come to terms
more thoughtfully with the volatile ecology of late modern capitalism and
the contemporary fragility of things. You may thus call into question assumptions about temporal progress tied to the ideas of either human mastery or a predesign of being. From the perspective advanced here, these
two competing visions are also complementary in that while proponents
of each tend to oppose the other, _they both act as though the nonhuman
world were predisposed to us_, either in being designed for us or in being
highly susceptible to mastery by us. Challenging the anthropocentric hubris in both of these images, you now _extend_, as the case requires, the reach
of politico-economic inquiry to specific noneconomic, nondiscursive systems that penetrate and impinge upon econocultural life. You thus allow
the shocks that these impingements periodically pose to open up new patterns of thinking, interpretation, and intervention.[9]

Those theorists who complain repeatedly about the "externalities" that
have messed up their model by fomenting this or that untoward event,
before returning to the purity of the model, suffer from a debilitating disease: they act as if the models would work if only the world did not contain
so many "outside" factors that are, in fact, imbricated and entangled in a
thousand ways with the practices they study. A subset of theorists on the
left who tend to construe capitalism as a closed system that automatically
recaptures and absorbs bumps in its own operations may present a mirror
image of that picture. Both parties underplay, though in different keys and
degrees, the role of noise and loose remainders _within_ the markets they
study, the ways capitalism _alters_ nonhuman force fields, and the independent power of nonhuman forces _acting upon_ capitalism.

Casting to the side these ploys, we may become better equipped to respond sensitively to the fragility of things today, as seen from the broadly
defined interests of the human estate in its complex imbrications with a
variety of human and nonhuman systems. We may then embrace the need
to infuse a new ethos inside markets, voting, consumption, investment,
churches, work, schools, the media, state action, and cross-state citizen
movements as we attend to the resonances back and forth between these

subsystems. Feedback loops between established schemes of interpretation, new social movements, markets, state and interstate organization, nonhuman force fields, and novel modes of role experimentation all attain significant standing in this image of political economy.

Capitalist-Nonhuman Entanglements

Such a theory of political economy, if and when developed, will be as different from the thought of Hayek, Friedman, Greenspan, Summers, Geithner, and Keynes as the cosmo-philosophies of Hesiod and Sophocles were from those of Augustine, Kant, Adam Smith, Hegel, and Marx. Hesiod and Sophocles indeed grasped how cultural and cosmic (or divine) forces are interwoven and how the latter can sometimes change in dramatic ways over a short period with profound effects on the human estate. Lift the gods from their stories—no small move, I grant—and the universe becomes conceived as a colossus of highly diverse force fields, each periodically flowing over, through, and around others.

Many force fields, on this interpretation, are susceptible *both* to impingement from others and to variable degrees of interpenetration with them. That combination is part of what makes their relations so complex. An example of the latter is the infusion of new rock into old, dense rock formations under conditions of intense pressure and high temperature. Another is the diverse ways microbes enter human tissue, helping to compose our tendencies and moods. Most fields are also vulnerable to periodic bouts of radical disequilibrium, partly because of unavoidable intersections with heterogeneous fields and partly because they themselves contain energetic excesses, remainders, noise, and incipiencies that, particularly when triggered by a new event, can promote collapse or inspire a new bout of self-organization. Thus one of those early single cells, upon being invaded by DNA swimming from another cell, creatively organized itself into a nucleated cell, accidentally fomenting a basis from which future biological evolution proceeded. It is called *symbiogenesis*.[10] This mode of self-organization can for now serve as a template for diverse modes in several domains, even though different types and degrees of self-organization themselves deserve close attention.[11]

In a world of becoming, periods of relative stability may emerge in this or that zone, but a zone may later slide or career into a period of rapid change. Here slowness or rapidity is defined relative to the human time-scale on which each process is set: a long scale for the evolution of geological formations, a shorter one for biological evolution, a lot shorter for the evolution of civilizations, and shorter yet for the evolution of a hurricane, with each also undergoing abrupt changes from time to time, measured, again, on a human scale. The ten-year period of rapid reheating after the last Ice Age is an instance of the latter; it occurred so fast, by the way, without intervention from the human estate. Most force fields have some self-regulatory power, interinvolvement with other fields, and periodic susceptibility to radical disruption, though there are important variations between them. Each, you might say, is a kind of impersonal market. All of these forces together help to explain how fragile and volatile economic markets can become at particular moments.

The world of temporal force fields includes solar energy fields; radioactive decay in the interior of the earth that periodically activates volcanoes; flows of molten metal in the lithosphere that periodically erupt on the crust as mountains, earthquakes, and volcanoes; slow movements of tectonic plates that change the composition of continents and oceans and occasionally generate earthquakes and volcanoes; ocean current systems with a degree of self-maintaining power and susceptibility to change by tectonic plate activity, atmospheric changes, changes in the ratio of ice to water, changes in water temperature, and differentials of salt density between sections of the ocean; a climate system with both impressive powers of self-maintenance and susceptibility to feedback loops with other systems, including capitalist expansion, shifts in ocean currents, and changes in the ratio of ice to water in oceans; a system of species evolution, periodically modified by asteroid showers, aesthetic tastes, climate change, gene and disease transfers across species, changes in the pace and scale of world travel, and capitalist evolution; a magnetic field providing the Earth with its atmosphere, connected to several other systems; systems of soil self-maintenance, imbricated with species evolution, climate change, capitalist agriculture, and oil spills; a civilizational system with internal rhythms of change that can accelerate, turn, or become overwhelmed by a perfect storm of changes in climate, soil quality, disease transmission, volcanic eruptions, military invasion, and new intensities of regional and/or class resentments; regional religious systems, fluctuating in their degree of affirmation or resentment of the most fundamental terms of human existence, intercoded at various times with several of the systems noted above; bacterial and viral disease species jumps, some enabling human life and others threatening it through interaction with systems of plane transportation, livestock, droughts, soil erosion, and so forth; a few hundred years of capitalist expansion, tethered by a thousand threads, pulleys, and osmotic processes to these other systems; and interacting secular, theological, and philosophical cultures, many of which have heretofore been organized around contests over whether an omnipotent God dominates creativity, a benign *telos* governs things, or human beings can master the forces around them to become supreme.[12]

And that tick resting quietly for eighteen years in the tree above you? It too exudes simple powers of perception, desire, and mobility, sensing you as heat when you stroll beneath it and dropping onto your warm flesh to feed upon your blood, perhaps infecting you inadvertently, as it were, with Lyme disease. And the Lyme disease? It possesses internal powers of maintenance and growth, which can in turn be diverted or amplified by a change in another system, such as the eruption of a volcano that darkens the sky for a decade, or the extinction of more mammals, or the appearance of a new Ice Age, or the human invention of a new vaccine.

Yes, science is a human force field with some degree of relative autonomy. Indeed it is partly because of advances in complexity theory in the domains of biology, oceanography, neuroscience, geology, and climatology that it is now possible to draw into close communication a philosophy of becoming, the trajectory of political economy, and appreciation of the fragility of things.

Ecology, Economy, and Becoming

If we scope down to recent thought in the West, we can identify several theologians and philosophers who articulate various interpretations of a multitiered cosmos of becoming. They include Nietzsche, William James, Henri Bergson, Alfred North Whitehead, Catherine Keller, Stuart Kauffman, Karen Barad, Ilya Prigogine, and Gilles Deleuze.[13] Some of them (such as Keller, Bergson, and James) fold faith in a limited god into their theophilosophy, a god that operates as a force field *within* the cosmos rather than hovering above or outside it. Others confine themselves either to the idea of impersonal transcendence (Whitehead) or to mundane transcendence, conceived as those processes that are outside this or that force field but do not possess the powers of divinity. Nietzsche, Deleuze, Kauffman, Barad, and I head in that direction. Others yet could be noted who touch some of these cosmological themes, including Foucault, Donna Haraway, Proust, Judith Butler, Jane Bennett, Brian Massumi, the later Althusser, Kafka, Merleau-Ponty, and Gregory Bateson. Indeed I have stolen two-thirds of the title of this essay from Bateson. Even Hannah Arendt discusses these themes with respect to the politics of enactment in history and cultural life, though her rich conception of cultural time may be adulterated by the regularized vision of bodies, nature, and the cosmos within which it is set.

Herein resides the problem. Those thinkers most attuned to a cosmos of becoming set on multiple scales of chronotime, viscosity, powers of self-regulation, and capacities for metamorphosis have been rather inactive in bringing these insights to the ecology of late capitalism. And those most involved with political economy either tend to treat the market as the only self-regulating system in the universe, or criticize market autonomy without coming to terms sufficiently with numerous intersections between economic life and other force fields with differential powers of metamorphosis, or come to terms with the latter but tend to treat capitalism as an amazingly self-absorbent system, or reduce economic life to a "discursive system" without thinking closely about its innumerable imbrications with nondiscursive systems with impressive powers of their own.

I am not saying that few political economists are interested in environmental issues; I am saying that too few bring a philosophy of becoming to the inquiry. Deleuze is a notable exception to this generalization. So are Althusser and Foucault to some degree. Stuart Kauffman provides a notable exception too, before he nearly succumbs to the attractions of automatic economic growth through market processes. Immanuel Wallerstein moves cautiously in this direction late in the day, but his shift is limited to an exploration of the future trajectory of capitalism rather than to a corollary study of its past.[14] There are surely others who have escaped my attention.

Could the implacable force of climate change provide an impetus to transform this intellectual condition during the late stages of the Anthropocene—the two hundred years during which human activity has affected several nonhuman force fields the most? Perhaps. To come to terms with looping relations between capitalist production, carbon and methane emissions, state policy, consumption practices, glacier movements, and climate change sets the stage to link political economy regularly to the behavior of nonhuman force fields. These same imbrications may also challenge some of the assumptions of deep ecologists, for they expose tendencies to morph in several systems that upset the idea of a natural, prehuman equilibrium.

Many of us, with respect to this issue, are now in something like the position of Whitehead during that fecund period in the early twentieth century when he glimpsed how the collapse of the Newtonian system he had heretofore taken to be apodictic required a radical overhaul of his cosmology and was not yet ready to launch the overhaul. Political economy is perhaps now at such a juncture, stammering and stuttering as it proceeds. Such a judgment certainly applies to me, as I begin to study processes and intersections that stretch my previous training and knowledge.

Fragility and Militancy

Today we inhabit a world in which the fragility of things—from the perspective of the endurance and quality of life available to the human estate in its entanglements with other force fields—becomes apparent, while the categories and sensibilities with which we habitually come to grips to the world make it difficult to fold that sense deeply into theory and practice. Sixty-five million years ago, bodysurfing on a few favorable force fields, two smart dinosaurs, interpreting the world through an efficient concept of cause and a simple metric of probability within a fixed set of possibilities, examined past trends and tendencies to gauge the probable future of their species. Their favorable assessment missed the huge asteroid hurtling toward them, set on its own tier of time. Nor did they realize that a massive volcano was about to erupt in India. Dinosaurs were smarter and more adaptable (more brightly colored too) than they were said to be when I studied them as a young boy, but still not perhaps sensitive enough to the planet and cosmos in which they were set. Is neoliberal political economy a dinosaur science?[15]

Neoliberal ideology is drawn to the simplicity of a two-slot system: self-organizing markets with beautiful powers of rational self-adjustment and states as clumsy agents of collective decision. *It thus inflates the self-organizing power of markets by implicitly deflating the self-organizing powers and creative capacity of all other systems.* And it treats the state as necessarily clumsy and inept by comparison to a singular, utopian image of markets. It protects this ideological combination in part by downplaying the self-organizing powers of multiple other systems highly relevant to the performance of economic markets and states.

Other familiar theories of political economy also deflate the importance of nonhuman force fields. True, Marx flirted with an aleatory image of nature in Epicurus before scrapping it.[16] And some post-Marxists now reach in that direction. But still, the *fragility* of the late modern order seems insufficiently articulated in radical theory today. Is that because radical theorists fear that coming to terms with *fragility* would undercut the political *militancy* needed to respond to it? Perhaps. At any rate, the issue is real, since a focus on the fragility of things is often associated with a drive to conserve what we already have. My sense, however, is that the contemporary condition requires both appreciation of the real fragility of things and political action on multiple fronts to act with resolution upon our patterns of identity, investment, consumption, energy use, health care, spirituality, and the like. This, to me, is a living paradox of our time to engage and negotiate rather than a contradiction in one reading of the contemporary condition.

What, more closely, are examples of that fragility mostly alluded to so far? One instance resides in the tension between the growing global dimension of capital, regional inequality, and territorially anchored intensities of religious faith that increasingly issue in state and nonstate modes of terrorism.[17] Another resides in the necessity of late capitalism to drill oil in ever more treacherous zones, triggering destructive eco-events that career out of control. The 2010 BP disaster in the Gulf, for instance, was triggered by the explosion of a gas bubble that exceeded available safety devices and the capacity of the company to repair it. It has created havoc in wetlands and waterways with delicate ecologies and has thrown tens of thousands out of work as the dispersants dispensed by BP endanger the general ecology and human health. There are at least 3,500 other wells in the Gulf capped temporarily without being closely monitored by corporations or the state. The fragility is dramatized by those "fracking" technologies that squeeze natural gas out of sand shale as they generate adverse effects on the water supply and perhaps induce future earthquakes. The fragility resides also in the perverse relation between the established terms of expanding capitalism and the acceleration of climate change, with implications for world temperature increase, the swamping of low-lying land areas with large populations, the desolation of fertile soil in some areas, the increasing energy demands imposed by increasing temperatures, the increase of extreme weather events, and a *possible* diversion of the Gulf Stream that could trigger a new "little" Ice Age in Europe. A further instance resides in regional economic asymmetries, exacerbated by the differential effects of climate change on soil and habitable areas, finding potential expression in massive migrations, imperial pressures, the intensification of regional religious resentments, and new regional wars. It also finds indirect expression in the shrillness often adopted by defenders of neoliberalism, discernible in journals, the Republican caucus, Fox News, and Tea Party hostility. It resides too in the rapid border crossings of people, arms, drugs, ideas, music, and goods that challenge the terms of territorial order upon which neoliberal state capitalism rests and generate bellicose internal drives to reinstate those borders. It resides in the complex loops between bees, viruses, and pesticides that derange the brains of bees, leading to rapid decline in bee population and decline in the pollination of crops and fruits.[18] It resides in those periodic flu virus jumps from birds and pigs to human beings in a world in which the overuse of antibiotics makes it more difficult to manage a global epidemic. It resides in intensified efforts to discipline and control the populace as the effects of periodic economic instability become widespread and the neoliberal drive to impose austerity on the middle and impoverished classes becomes urgent. It finds expression in the extended droughts, storms, and floods connected to climate change that press upon the agricultural capacities of the world in the face of rapid population growth. And, as recently seen, it resides in the potential ramifications between earthquakes, tsunamis, dense populations close to the sea, and nuclear power plants in sites of seismic instability, a combination that could become amplified into volatile clashes between citizen activists and neoliberal forces. The list goes on.

At a specific juncture several of these systems could intersect, as already suggested. Let's focus a bit more closely on one actual instance of conjunction. If all the glaciers in Greenland melted, the world's ocean level would rise about twenty feet, creating havoc in its train. If the same thing happened in Antarctica, it would rise about two hundred feet.

No one expects either to happen soon. The usual predictions are a rise in sea level of between three and seven feet by 2100, already enough to create a real mess. But these assessments do not take into account a new "factor" discovered as recently as 2003 and studied closely only more recently. As warmer water, promoted by climate change, moves into the Helheim glaciers in Greenland—and elsewhere too—it induces enhanced calving events, that is, the release of huge icebergs that hurtle down the Sermi-lik Fjord, apparently creating massive vibrations as they do. In a world of becoming, the devil resides in the vibrations. These vibrations, in turn, may unleash earthquakes at a much faster rate than heretofore observed in the area. The earthquakes would further destabilize the glaciers, increasing their rate of flow and tendency to spawn new calves. A dynamic process of mutual amplification is set into motion.

Not all geologists agree that a dynamic involving iceberg calving, vibra-tions, and earthquakes is critical to this acceleration; some focus mostly on the movement between ocean warming and glacier flow. And some have recently concluded that sludge formed in the fjord by the accelerated ice-berg calving process may be slowing down the dynamic process. The whole process is thus filled with real uncertainty at the moment (2011).[19] The geo-physicist Meredith Nettles, who believes the earthquake dynamic is im-portant, says, "Now for an individual glacier it's not clear that they can continue to speed up indefinitely. Will it continue . . . until it has some cata-strophic collapse, or will it stabilize itself at some new equilibrium level? So these are the kind of questions that a lot of people are working very hard to understand right now. That's the unknown."[20]

Indeed there may be different types of "unknowns" in play, depending very much upon the type of force field in question. There are those we know to be unknowns; there are those we do not know to be unknowns (as the glacial generation of earthquakes was not known until very recently, and the flow of tectonic plates was not known until as recently as the 1930s); and there are onto-unknowns that in some systems flow from dynamic bifurca-tions generated at key moments that could lurch in either of two directions. The last kind of unknown may be lodged in an element of real uncertainty in specific processes of metamorphosis: known unknowns, unknown un-knowns, and onto-unknowns. The third type does not represent creation ex nihilo at key moments; it embodies an element of conditioned creativity that emerges in some types of systems periodically. I *suspect* that we inhabit a world in which all three types of unknowns come into play on occasion, though I have not proven it. Even though that is my suspicion, the first two, in conjunction with the expansion and intensification of capitalism, suffice on their own to sustain the thesis of the real fragility of things today.

What we do know, however, is that the discovery of an amplification system involving climate change, glaciers, icebergs, ground vibrations, and earthquakes, could increase the rate and volume of sea level rise beyond those officially expected, even if the uncertain possibility of self-deceleration makes the precise amount uncertain. And those rises, if not stymied, could themselves enter into volatile connections with a set of tendencies already discernible in specific human constituencies, as when evangelical congregations treat such an amplification system as the sinful desert of earthly punishments rather than a result of neoliberal capital, climate, glacier, and earthquake imbrications, as when the pressures among populations in low-lying areas to escape to other areas accelerate, as when regional resentments grow as the regions that suffer most react against those who have historically generated the greatest climate change, and as when calls intensify within privileged states to secure their borders by any means necessary and to discipline internal minorities by draconian means.

I know that these examples mix human and nonhuman forces. That is because, first, while the forces convey different capacities and degrees of self-organizational power, they are not completely different in kind as many like to pretend and, second, because human and nonhuman systems regularly infuse and impinge upon one another—both at the microscopic level within human bodies and at the macroscopic level between disparate systems. We can start with how Neanderthals and Homo sapiens probably entered into reproductive relations across species lines and move to innumerable intersections between heterogeneous beings and systems operating at different levels of self-organizational power.

It is not that all the modes of fragility enumerated above require the same kind of response. Neoliberalism requires detailed exposés and militant opposition, as it defers responsive political action to the ecology of late capitalism and excites militant opposition against such efforts. Border issues require modes of cross-border economic development that involve investors, workers, and consumers on both sides of the borders. The decline in bee pollination requires radical reduction of pesticides joined to greater protection of habitat. Climate change requires radical restructuring of established priorities of production and the infrastructure of consumption tethered to them, joined to cultural negotiation of a positive frugality of material desire. Oil spill degradation requires extensive public-private assemblages to create a sustainable energy grid as the established infrastructure of consumption is also reconstituted to mesh with the new grid.

What about earthquakes and volcanoes? As Japanese geologists decided after the devastating Kobe quake of 1995, the best strategy may be to shift from a search for precise predictions of where and when they will occur (those have not been successful) to the identification of areas of greatest risk over the long term joined to programs to reinforce bridges, utilities, and travel-ways while adjusting building codes.[21] Now, of course, they have to add the potential earthquake-tsunami dynamic to inform those projects. With respect to volcanoes, the focus could be on identifying probable sites and preparing alternative modes of travel and communication for periods of extensive ash dispersal. And nuclear power? It must be dismantled and replaced by other power sources because of the dangers it promotes in a volatile world and the long-term storage issues created by radioactive waste.

Could it be possible to harness the immense power of the Gulf Stream, as its flow becomes compressed between Florida and Cuba, to reduce our dependence on oil in conjunction with needed adjustments in consumption practices? I don't know. But a philosophy of multiple force fields with differential powers of self-organization and metamorphosis does not exude an automatic presumption against technological innovation. It assesses each innovation within the larger context of human need, the fragility of things, and a cosmos of becoming.

The point now, however, is not to examine closely what must be done in each of these zones. It is to foment appreciation of the innumerable links among markets, states, hegemonic ideologies, cultural movements, and nonhuman force fields with variable powers of self-organization. It is to enact a new ethos of economic life closer to the cosmic sensitivity of Sophocles than to that of theorists, philosophers, talking heads, preachers, financial experts, and citizens who insulate extant images of social life from volatile, interacting force fields with which they are imbricated. Check out those implacable plagues the next time you read the wise Sophocles.

Strategic Sites of Action

A philosophy attending to the acceleration, expansion, irrationalities, interdependencies, and fragilities of late capitalism suggests that we do not know with confidence, in advance of experimental action, just how far or fast changes in the systemic character of neoliberal capitalism can be made.

The structures often *seem* solid and intractable, and indeed such a semblance may turn out to be true. Some may seem solid, infinitely absorptive, and intractable when they are in fact punctuated by hidden vulnerabilities, soft spots, uncertainties, and potential lines of flight that become apparent when they are subjected to experimental action, upheaval, testing, and strain. Indeed no ecology of late capitalism, given the variety of forces to which it is connected by a thousand pulleys, vibrations, impingements, dependencies, shocks, and threads, can specify with supreme confidence the solidity or potential flexibility of the structures it seeks to change.

The strength of structural theory, at its best, was in identifying institutional intersections that hold a system together; its conceit, at its worst, was the claim to know in advance how resistant such intersections are to potential change. Without adopting the opposite conceit, it seems important to pursue possible sites of strategic action that might open up room for productive change. Today it seems important to attend to the relation between the need for structural change and identification of multiple sites of potential action. You do not know precisely what you are doing when you participate in such a venture. You combine an experimental temper with the appreciation that living and acting into the future inevitably contain a shifting quotient of uncertainty. The following tentative judgments and sites of action may be pertinent.

1) Neither neoliberal theory, nor socialist productivism, nor deep ecology, nor social democracy in its classic form seems sufficient to the contemporary condition. This is so in part because the powers of market self-regulation are both real and limited in relation to a larger multitude of heterogeneous force fields beyond the human estate with differential powers of self-regulation and metamorphosis. A first task is to challenge neoliberal ideology through critique and by elaborating and publicizing positive alternatives that acknowledge the disparate relations between market processes, other cultural systems, and nonhuman systems. Doing so to render the fragility of things more visible and palpable. Doing so, too, to set the stage for a series of intercoded shifts in citizen role performances, social movements, and state action.

2) Those who seek to reshape the ecology of late capitalism might set an interim agenda of radical reform and then recoil back on the initiatives adopted to see how they work. An *interim agenda* is the best thing to focus

on because in a world of becoming the more distant future is too cloudy to engage. We must, for instance, become involved in experimental micropolitics on a variety of fronts, as we participate in role experimentations, social movements, artistic displays, erotic-political shows, electoral campaigns, and creative interventions on the new media to help recode the ethos that now occupies investment practices, consumption desires, family savings, state priorities, church assemblies, university curricula, and media reporting. It is important to bear in mind how extant ideologies, established role performances, social movements, and commitments to state action intersect. To shift some of our own role performances in the zones of travel, church participation, home energy use, investment, and consumption, for instance, that now implicate us deeply in foreign oil dependence and the huge military expenditures that secure it, could make a minor difference on its own *and also lift some of the burdens of institutional implication from us* to support participation in more adventurous interpretations, political strategies, demands upon the state, and cross-state citizen actions.

3) Today perhaps the initial target should be on reconstituting established patterns of consumption by a combination of direct citizen actions in consumption choices, publicity of such actions, the organization of local collectives to modify consumption practices, and social movements to reconstitute the current state- and market-supported infrastructure of consumption. By the *infrastructure of consumption* I mean publicly supported and subsidized market subsystems such as a national highway system, a system of airports, medical care through private insurance, agribusiness pouring high sugar, salt, and fat content into foods, corporate ownership of the public media, the prominence of corporate 403 accounts over retirement pensions, and so forth that enable some modes of consumption in the zones of travel, education, diet, retirement, medical care, energy use, health, and education and render others much more difficult or expensive to procure.[22] To change the infrastructure is also to shift the types of work and investment available. Social movements that work upon the infrastructure and ethos of consumption in tandem can thus make a real difference directly, encourage more people to heighten their critical perspectives, and thereby open more people to a more militant politics if and as the next disruptive event emerges. Perhaps a cross-state citizen goal should be to construct a pluralist assemblage by moving back and forth between experi-

ments in role performances, the refinement of sensitive modes of perception, revisions in political ideology, and adjustments in political sensibility, doing so to mobilize enough collective energy to launch a general strike simultaneously in several countries in the near future. The aim of such an event would be to reverse the deadly future created by established patterns of climate change by fomenting significant shifts in patterns of consumption, corporate policies, state law, and the priorities of interstate organizations. Again, the dilemma of today is that the fragility of things demands *shifting and slowing down intrusions* into several aspects of nature as we *speed up* shifts in identity, role performance, cultural ethos, market regulation, and state policy.

4) The existential forces of hubris (expressed above all in those confident drives to mastery conveyed by military elites, financial economists, financial elites, and CEOs) and of *ressentiment* (expressed in some sectors of secularism and evangelicalism) now play roles of importance in the shape of consumption practices, investment portfolios, worker routines, managerial demands, and the uneven senses of entitlement that constitute neoliberalism. For that reason activism inside churches, schools, street life, and the media must become increasingly skilled and sensitive. As we proceed, some of us may present the themes of a world of becoming to larger audiences, challenging thereby the complementary notions of a providential world and secular mastery that now infuse too many role performances, market practices, and state priorities in capitalist life. For existential dispositions do infuse the role priorities of late capitalism. Today it is both difficult for people to perform the same roles with the same old innocence and difficult to challenge those performances amid our own implication in them. Drives by evangelists, the media, neoconservatives, and the neoliberal right to draw a veil of innocence across the priorities of contemporary life make the situation much worse.

5) The emergence of a neofascist or mafia-type capitalism slinks as a dangerous possibility on the horizon, partly because of the expansion and intensification of capital, partly because of the real fragility of things, partly because the identity needs of many facing these pressures encourage them to cling more intensely to a neoliberal imaginary as its bankruptcy becomes increasingly apparent, partly because so many in America insist upon retaining the special world entitlements the country achieved after World

War II in a world decreasingly favorable to them, partly because of the crisis tendencies inherent in neoliberal capitalism, and partly because so many resist living evidence around and in them that challenges a couple of secular and theistic images of the cosmos now folded into the institutional life of capitalism. Indeed the danger is that those constituencies now most disinclined to give close attention to public issues could oscillate between attraction to the mythic promises of neoliberal automaticity and attraction to a neofascist movement when the next crisis unfolds. It has happened before. I am not saying that neoliberalism is itself a form of fascism, but that the failures and meltdowns it periodically promotes could once again foment fascist or neofascist responses, as happened in several countries after the onset of the Great Depression.[23]

6) The democratic state, while it certainly cannot alone tame capital or reconstitute the ethos and infrastructure of consumption, must play a significant role in reconstituting our lived relations to climate, weather, resource use, ocean currents, bee survival, tectonic instability, glacier flows, species diversity, work, local life, consumption, and investment, as it also responds favorably to the public pressures we must generate to forge a new ethos. A new, new left will thus experimentally enact new intersections between role performance and political activity, outgrow its old disgust with the very idea of the state, and remain alert to the dangers states can pose. It will do so because, as already suggested, the fragile ecology of late capital requires state interventions of several sorts. *A refusal to participate in the state today cedes too much hegemony to neoliberal markets,* either explicitly or by implication. Drives to fascism, remember, rose the last time in capitalist states after a total market meltdown. Most of those movements failed. But a couple became consolidated through a series of resonances (vibrations) back and forth between industrialists, the state, and vigilante groups in neighborhoods, clubs, churches, the police, the media, and pubs. You do not fight the danger of a new kind of neofascism by withdrawing from either micropolitics or state politics. You do so through a multisited politics designed to infuse a new ethos into the fabric of everyday life. Changes in ethos can in turn open doors to new possibilities of state and interstate action, so that an advance in one domain seeds that in the other. And vice versa. A positive dynamic of mutual amplification might be generated here. Could a series of significant shifts in the routines of state and global capitalism even press the fractured system to a point where it hovers on the edge of capitalism itself? We don't know. That is one reason it is important to focus on *interim goals*. Another is that in a world of becoming, replete with periodic and surprising shifts in the course of events, you cannot project far beyond an interim period. Another yet is that activism needs to project concrete, interim possibilities to gain support and propel itself forward. That being said, it does seem unlikely to me, at least, that a positive interim future includes either socialist productivism or the world projected by proponents of deep ecology.[24]

7) To advance such an agenda it is also imperative to negotiate new connections between nontheistic constituencies who care about the future of the Earth and numerous devotees of diverse religious traditions who fold positive spiritualities into their creedal practices. The new, multifaceted movement needed today, if it emerges, will take the shape of a vibrant pluralist assemblage acting at multiple sites within and across states, rather than either a centered movement with a series of fellow travelers attached to it or a mere electoral constellation. Electoral victories are important, but they work best when they touch priorities already embedded in churches, universities, film, music, consumption practices, media reporting, investment priorities, and the like. A related thing to keep in mind is that the capitalist modes of acceleration, expansion, and intensification that heighten the fragility of things today also generate pressures to *minoritize* the world along multiple dimensions at a more rapid pace than heretofore. A new pluralist constellation will build upon the latter developments as it works to reduce the former effects.

I am sure that the forgoing comments will appear to some as "optimistic" or "utopian." But optimism and pessimism are both primarily spectatorial views. Neither seems sufficient to the contemporary condition. Indeed pessimism, if you dwell on it long, easily slides into cynicism, and cynicism often plays into the hands of a right wing that applies it exclusively to any set of state activities not designed to protect or coddle the corporate estate. That is one reason that "dysfunctional politics" redounds so readily to the advantage of cynics on the right who work to promote it. *They want to promote cynicism with respect to the state and innocence with respect to the market.* Pure critique, as already suggested, does not suffice either. Pure critique too readily carries critics and their followers to the edge of cynicism.

It is also true that the above critique concentrates on neoliberal capitalism, not capitalism writ large. That is because it seems to me that we need to specify the terms of critique as closely as possible and think first of all about interim responses. If we lived under, say, Keynesian capitalism, a somewhat different set of issues would be defined and other strategies identified.[25] Capitalism writ large—while it sets a general context that neoliberalism inflects in specific ways—sets too large and generic a target. It can assume multiple forms, as the differences between Swedish and American capitalism suggest; the times demand a set of interim agendas targeting the hegemonic form of today, pursued with heightened militancy at several sites. The point today is not to wait for a revolution that overthrows the whole system. The "system," as we shall see further, is replete with too many loose ends, uneven edges, dicey intersections with nonhuman forces, and uncertain trajectories to make such a wholesale project plausible. Besides, things are too urgent and too many people on the ground are suffering too much now.

The need now is to activate the most promising political strategies to the contemporary condition out of a bad set. On top of assessing *probabilities* and predicting them with secret relish or despair—activities I myself pursue during the election season—we must define the urgent *needs* of the day in relation to a set of *interim possibilities* worthy of pursuit on several fronts, even if the apparent political odds are stacked against them. We then test ourselves and those possibilities by trying to enact this or that aspect of them at diverse sites, turning back to reconsider their efficacy and side effects as circumstances shift and results accrue. In so doing we may experience more vibrantly how apparently closed and ossified structures are typically punctuated by jagged edges, seams, and fractures best pried open with a mix of public contestation of established interpretations, experimental shifts in multiple role performances, micropolitics in churches, universities, unions, the media, and corporations, state actions, and large-scale, cross-state citizen actions.

first interlude :: *melancholia* and us

The film *Melancholia*, directed by Lars von Trier, presents an attractive, affluent young couple driving down a narrow, twisting, country pathway in a white stretch limousine. Sunlight bathes a muddy roadway tightly lined by bushes. The trip down the drive seems interminable to the viewer, who remains uncertain at first as to its destination. One obstacle after another is encountered: that curve is too sharp, this zone is too muddy, those bushes are overgrown. The scene is also idyllic. Frustration and joy mingle in it, as one oscillates between soaking in the vibrant beauty of that young couple in a delicious setting and wondering when that stretch limo will surmount its last obstacle. We smell trouble on the horizon.

Melancholia tracks beauty and ugliness, intentions and frustrations, glowing surfaces and opaque depths, regular rituals and uncanny events, entanglements and denials. You soon sense why. The couple turns out to be two hours late for their own wedding celebration at a sumptuous, well-appointed mansion. Could they not have least chosen a smaller vehicle for that long driveway? She is received with impatient frustration by friends and relatives, as if her lateness and casualness about it are par for the course. The young woman is afflicted with melancholia. Each intention the beautiful thing forms is countered by an opposing tendency. She cannot act in the world. Or at least planned actions are countered by enervation, and the impulsive actions she does take often hurt those around her. Impulsive sex with another man taken by surprise soon enters the scene. The groom flees the wedding reception. How preemptory was the decision to get married anyway? Where is *he* going?

Two melancholias circle around each other in this film. There is the affliction of Justine and the planet called Melancholia, previously hidden by the sun; the latter is circling ominously around the planet Earth. It gets closer with each orbit. These two melancholias constantly break into each other in ways that disrupt the sense of a smooth narrative carrying a story forward. Maybe that is why the film is divided into two parts, with part 1 focusing on the incapacities and impulsiveness of Justine in relation to her capable, responsible sister and part 2 focusing on how the sister falls apart as Justine rises to embrace the occasion. So Justine's affliction first limits her and later renders her sensitive to what is happening. Her very vulnerability is perhaps linked to her sensitivity, even if it also makes her a trial to those around her.

In one uncanny scene, after the wedding reception has unraveled, two moons of disparate size glow in the night sky, presenting the viewer with two eerie vanishing points rather than one. The result is disturbing. It created a notable stir in the audience when I saw the film at the Charles Theater in Baltimore in the fall of 2011.[1] We are accustomed to one vanishing point. The image of a world with one vanishing point over the horizon fits well with several monotheistic theologies and with the Kantian "necessary" postulate, to be explored later, of indefinite human progress toward a future that is now faintly visible on the horizon. An image with two vanishing points calls such assumptions into question. It disrupts operative conceptions of time and space. Up to this point the people at that rich estate may have reacted to the event to come with delay, denial, and periods of forgetfulness, as our couple had done by stretching out that drive down the winding path. Even the horses are spooked when they are walking in the moonlight, only to return to a degree of quiescence when in the stable. These two bright moons now bathe the sweetness of the evening world in a broken context, as they also bring the abstract prospect of a devastating collision down to earth. This happens both to viewers and, I think, to Justine. Her sister Claire and Claire's husband continue the denial for a while longer. Until he commits suicide. How do you prepare for the end of the world? What do you tell children running around the house who have begun to form ties, skills, ambitions, and hopes? A therapist, a priest, or a philosopher might stutter over such questions. Even Pangloss might hesitate.

Yes, death is a terrible thing. Your mother's death, for instance, filled you with grief. A life lived in work, commitment, and turmoil, drawn to a close. Gradually you may also come to terms with how a set of connections to the world, wired deeply into your memory, have now lost some solidity or sense of reliability with her death. You and she shared, say, a secret that your childhood comedy acts, getting you into trouble with teachers, were subtended by a personality too feminine and sensitive to be acknowledged in the rough and tough of a boy's life. No one shares *that* secret anymore. You may have known, without ever discussing it, how the young woman adjusted painfully when her husband suffered from brain damage after an accident, cutting her love life short. Unspoken connections, lodged in viscerally shared memories, now closed into the vault of your being. Do they still matter? What other events surrounded them? Have they acquired more latent force even as they lose a degree of social reality?

Talking to others about these things may be insufficient. They are busy too, getting on with life. Any presentation is apt to be too abstract, too disconnected from the currents of daily life. Suppose too that something wonderful now happens to you. You are eager to share it, before you recall again that it can't be shared with her. The losses created by the death of a loved one keep returning. Everyone knows this. It short-circuits joy, and it does something to memory. Death teaches how layered memory is and how fragile its depths are. As the deaths of loved ones accumulate, some old people talk endlessly about the past, perhaps to ward off the solipsism they feel closing in. Others write little vignettes.

A massacre, a holocaust, a massive bombing. These are even more devastating and implacable than the death of a loved one. They shatter the bond of trust in the world that had tacitly bound you to humanity and the world. These shocks and losses are so horrifying that some survivors never heal. Healing may be felt as disloyalty to a breach of trust in humanity or

God or nature, or all three, that has now entered the world. Unremitting depression or revenge can settle into the life of survivors. How could the world encompass such acts of mindless violence?

Melancholia has yet different fish to fry. Not simply death. Not even a holocaust. But an impersonal collision between two planets, at least one of which houses adult human beings, ants, children, hippos, crocodiles, rain forests, films, the Internet, TV melodramas, wedding parties, semi-sovereign states, steamy love affairs, rich intellectual traditions, academic quarrels, military adventures, holocausts, an ocean conveyor belt, Picasso, species' evolution, volatile weather systems, multiple gods, and basketball. No more games. No new loves, trips, long slow runs, sunny days, intellectual traditions. No artistic contribution to human sensitivity, promising to enrich future feeling and perception. It challenges every Panglossian conception, and others as well. There will be no memories for anyone after this collision. How do you respond to that?

Some devotees of monotheism, though certainly not all, conclude that an omnipotent, benevolent God makes such an event impossible. It is sinful to think about such a possibility. Think about this life now and your relation to God. Others push the envelope ominously close to the theme of *Melancholia* before veering off radically. They visualize Armageddon, in which a few are lifted to heaven and billions of nonbelievers are punished with the infinite hell of sulfur and fire. Is there, circulating somewhere inside that vengeful story, a certain sense of the fragility of being for the human estate? And a sense of identification with humanity as such? Perhaps there is. Otherwise the reasons given to punish so totally so many would not need to be attached to such a severe conception of a vengeful God. When I read the Book of Revelation, as I do every year when I teach it to undergrads, I sense in it an initial identification with the human estate that is then overridden by a desire to take revenge against a large slice of humanity for features of the human condition beyond human control. We die, we suffer, we get sick, we witness tough events. The brilliance of *Melancholia* is that it temporarily peels away the issues of responsibility and existential revenge to allow the experience of attachment to the world to soak into our pores.

Across important lines of difference between the version of exclusive humanism that is nontheistic and the variant tied to Armageddon there may be a strange, partial complementarity. Only we matter on the face of the Earth, both seem to say; everything else is merely instrumental to us or a condition of our being. It is that partial complementarity that needs to be reworked within humanism, paying much more attention to the ways other dimensions of being are infused into us and help to constitute what we are, extending the radius of care from the human estate narrowly defined to encompass a large variety of entities and processes with which it is entangled.

Some others, who project neither a providential nor a punitive God into being, may act as if the issue of our attachment to larger processes carries little spiritual weight of importance. They may indeed *equate* belief and spirituality, so that their denial of divinity releases them from the need to explore the issue of spiritual tone. That, at least, is what Richard Dennett announced to me during our panel together at a conference at the New School on secularism in 2008, when I asked him whether it was important to probe and develop a nontheistic spirituality after he (and I) had announced that we are not committed to a monotheistic creed. He said no. There is a cadre of "the new atheists" who seem very confident about our ability to know nature definitively by experimental means and to control it for our purposes. They also do not solicit mutual relations of agonistic respect with those who fold different existential faiths into public discourse. Sophocles would detect a strong strain of hubris here.

Others yet, however—with numerous theists and nontheists among them—focus on our deep attachments to the human estate as such. Such a sense often hums in the background of everyday life, amplified periodically by scientific discoveries, dramatic events, artistic work, and existential threats. *Melancholia* dramatizes a sense, already woven tacitly into life, that humanity matters to us immensely. It matters in part because of connections we have to each other across real differences and in part because of how our bodily processes and modes of cultural organization forge complex affinities, connections, and disjunctions with nonhuman beings and processes of an indefinitely large variety. We do not face the probable prospect of a collision between planets in which the smaller one we inhabit is pulverized, though the possibility of a major asteroid shower or a huge volcanic eruption that darkens the sky for a decade or a massive earthquake is nothing to sneeze at. We do face a variety of ecological and military dangers that, if enacted, could radically transform the character of human life. We both sense such possibilities and feel considerable pressure to divert attention from them.

Much of life is organized around daily routines and struggles that draw attention from the attachment to humanity and the world typically woven into the undercurrents of living. That is understandable. Such routines are not to be denigrated; they form part of the fabric of being. Even denial and deferral have a degree of rationality attached to them, since *total* immersion in the dangers of the future and the contemporary condition can lead you to neglect daily duties and needs. Such a denigration is not simply "irrational," then. But it can also be reinforced too much by a general desire to avoid thinking about dangers that no individual, family, locality, or state can resolve alone. The cultural world can even be filled with ideologies that ridicule folding a sense of the fragility of the human estate today into parochial interests, identifications, and a sense of responsibility. Those are the ideologies to challenge.

It may even be the case that the sensitivities wired into the affliction of melancholia as an individual condition sometimes helps one suffering it to come to terms with those attachments, as part 2 of *Melancholia* seems to suggest. Justine, the sister with that affliction who can be callous with other people, eventually comes to terms with the implacable event more sympathetically than Claire, who up to that point has been the efficient, responsible one in the family. She builds a teepee-like frame, without canopy, to face the event with Claire's young son, eventually inviting Claire to join them. The film encourages us to ponder the ambiguous, uncertain relations between vulnerability, attachment to the world, and sensitivity to others.

As is already clear, I am wary of what might be called, in honor of Charles Taylor, "exclusive humanism." To him that is the dangerous idea that humanity is sufficient to itself, without a God. As I rework that theme, exclusive humanism expresses the tacit or articulated idea of human uniqueness, *either* in itself *or* as the only being created in the image of God. The idea can easily slide into the view that only we matter because only we embody reason, or language, or consciousness, or reflexivity, or God, or a long time horizon. You can detect such images in the human sciences, among those who act as if you can grasp the most fundamental character of human culture in this or that historical setting through studies anchored in an idea of *cultural internalism*. On these readings a given culture may be extremely complex, and each culture may be closely entangled with others. But the multivalent connections of each to nonhuman processes tend either to be shuffled to the side, or treated only symbolically, or defined only instrumentally. Such proponents *merely* ask, "What does the planet Melancholia symbolize to us?" not "What will happen if it hits?" I don't think the first question is illegitimate or trivial, but it is *insufficient* to action-oriented perspectives in a cosmos composed of multiple, interacting force fields.

We are not unique; we are merely distinctive. Most things we pride ourselves on are either profoundly contestable (e.g., the debate between ideas of God and several versions of a naturalistic universe) or shared *to some degree* with a diverse set of other beings and things. Bacteria too have simple desires and pursue ends, though ours are much more complex and can become more reflexive if we avoid those bouts of denial that easily afflict us. Moreover we could not *be* without the roles numerous nonhuman entities and processes play within and outside the complex assemblage of the human body, including bacteria and viruses. Microbes not only work on us; many become infused into our neurons and viscera to help *constitute* our very moods and performances. Everywhere you turn connections and infusions between human and nonhuman things of multiple sorts proliferate. To be attached to humanity is also, then, to be attached to varying degrees to a variety of lively things and processes to which it is connected. My tacit attachment to the moon is at first unhinged and then dramatized by that uncanny image in which two moons appear.

Exclusive humanism now bites the dust. It is a conceit. It promotes the hubris and danger of cultural internalism. The call to stretch our modes and sites of awareness, sensitivity, and attachment by artistic means now becomes acute. That is why transcendental arguments that purport to set strict limits on human understanding and sensibility once and for all must be resisted, as I will try to do in a later chapter. Our attachment to humanity exudes a call to *stretch and revise* the species provincialism in which the Euro-American world has been stuck for so long. Not to settle into a set of transcendental limits that stifle exploratory engagements.

There is, however, an uncertain and indeterminate *priority* attached to the human estate that almost always comes with being human when we tap into our own memories and attachments. We cannot now define its boundaries with certainty. It would be a mistake to try, since it is often important to stretch it as we encounter newly identified entanglements with elements within us and with external forces that are not themselves human. To be human, again, is also to be organized by a host of nonhuman processes and to be entangled with others. Nonetheless to act as if there is no species identification flowing into our pores through the vicissitudes of life is to falsify much of experience; it also draws attention away from how sinking into artistic explorations, sciences such as neuroscience, climatology, and geology, role experimentations, and politics can both *deepen* those attachments and *broaden* our appreciations of affinity to other things and processes in which we stand in various relations of connection, debt, dependence, and symbiosis. *Melancholia* provides one example in which both the connections and a cautious sense of human attachment are dramatized, at least for me. That is why the terms *antihumanism*, *posthumanism*, and the like do not draw me much either. While such perspectives do challenge the excesses of both theistic and nontheistic variants of exclusive humanism — a good thing — they too readily leave the impression of not exuding care for humanity at all and thus of not exploring further our ethical *connections* to that which is unlike us or a strange part of us, or more encompassing than us. In the political world, first impressions do make a difference. An ant does not count as much as a human to me, though it is not worthless. We eat other living beings. *E. coli* is a dangerous bacteria to treat when it infects us, being cautious about the secondary effects that may be set into motion by this or that treatment. Climate change is a process to curtail by radical action, if possible, because of its probable effects on the future of humanity and the multifarious forces and beings with which we are entangled. I am pleased that the people of Lisbon constructed more earthquake-resistant structures after that horrific quake destroyed the city. The focus is on our entanglements with heterogeneous entities and processes in a world in which humanity matters immensely.[2]

The point is not to articulate a formula through which to resolve all the issues in advance that might arise when you assess the relative priority of the human species. I doubt that such a formula is available. It is to keep the issue in front of us as we pursue a perspective irreducible to exclusive humanism or to the strongest modes of antihumanism. It may be that watching Werner Herzog's *The Cave of Forgotten Dreams* again shortly after seeing *Melancholia* can have salutary effects. How could that cave art, drawn thirty-two thousand years ago in the France of today, exhibit such delicate sensibilities? Note how finely tuned those artists were to the contours and movements of animals with which they were intimately entangled through mirroring, dependence, and conflict. We carry an earthy legacy larger than us.

Is it necessary to be commanded, inspired, or touched by a God to give flexible priority to the human estate? Can that sort of inspiration, if unchallenged by other perspectives, too often lead to a sense of uniqueness that is itself dangerous and questionable? Is it enough, then, to live and ponder the relational character of life in a world without divinity? Is either indeed sufficient, as articulated and practiced so far in history?

Well, perhaps none of these sources of attachment has proven so far to be sufficient in the short history of the human estate, within and beyond Europe. If these sources were so powerful, so much self-destructiveness, mindless violence, and everyday denial about the fragility of things would not erupt so often in life. Yes, our connectedness across multiple lines of cultural differences must be emphasized, dramatized, and cultivated more sensitively today, as we seek creative ways to forge relations of agonistic respect between different lived creeds, theologies, and cosmologies. I know that I need to extend further my knowledge of non-European orientations to existence. Perhaps the goal is to diminish sharply—though not to eliminate altogether—the priorities humans ordinarily give to the short over the long term and to closer over broader identifications. It is unwise to *eliminate* the former tendencies because a parent must give *some* priority to his child, a teacher to her student, a country to its citizens, a time to its needs.

It is simply that too many forces combine today to render the short-term and close identifications of too many people too exclusive. Our intercoded routines of family life, education, investment, work, prayer, consumption, and voting are saturated by concern for the short term. And dominant ideologies of the day, led by neoliberalism, amplify rather than dampen those tendencies. They pretend that acting alone for one's own limited purposes will balance out to the relative advantage of everyone when each party in investment, labor, and consumption does so; they pretend the market is rational and efficient in regulating these disparate actions. What a joke. To possess self-organizing capacity does not ensure impersonal rationality, not in a world in which innumerable interacting systems possess differential degrees of self-organizing power. That is one reason to be hard on the conceits of neoliberalism in the current world context.

CHAPTER 2 :: hayek, neoliberalism, freedom

Radical and Moderate Neoliberalism

Let's call Milton Friedman and those to the right of him radical neoliberals. Similarly we can call Friedrich Hayek and those to the left of him moderate neoliberals. The compass of neoliberalism itself includes all those who celebrate the self-organizing powers and impersonal rationality of markets while "limiting" state and other political involvements to shoring up market processes; its borders stop at approximately those points where Keynesians, Marxists, and Social Democrats diversely contest its presumptions. The task in this chapter is to appraise the shape and life of moderate neoliberal theory. To define the terms of contrast between its radical and moderate versions, we need only summarize briefly an article published in 1993 by Friedman. He embraces the rationality of self-regulating markets with very limited "interference" by the state. At least, the role of the state seems minimal until you see how elastic are the criteria he asserts for state action.

Then you see how it can expand indefinitely, if only in certain directions. The state is "to defend the nation against foreign enemies, to prevent coercion by some individuals by others, to provide a means of deciding upon our rules and to adjudicate disputes."[1] The underlying assumption is that the impersonal rationality of the market will take care of things if the state, as the contrasting institution of "command," provides minimal regulations. And so Friedman campaigns to resolve the issues of crime, prison organization, homelessness, family values, postal service, school, medical care, and travel congestion by market principles.

When you analyze the criteria he invokes, however, things become interesting. The state, he says, "defends the nation." Here Friedman tacitly adopts an ideal of the nation as a centered culture of regular individuals who have incorporated market principles into work, investment, family life, corporate life, and military priorities, and they may have a variety of minorities ranged around them. The regular individuals have internalized the norms of private ownership, contractual work, and market autonomy. But if the centrifugal pressures become intense enough to produce and expand minorities of multiple sorts, with some of these pressures generated by the very mobilization and expansion of global capital he supports, then the modes of organization and coercion needed to sustain the center against encroachments from minorities will grow too. This is the connection that shows how the idea of the regular individual and the nation can be fit together. It is also the connection that launches that murky relationship between neoliberalism, biopolitics, and the intense pursuit of a nation of regular individuals who have internalized market norms. It helps to explain why neoliberals can support draconian state policies with respect to recalcitrant minorities.

Next, consider "foreign enemies." What if the expansion of state or market practices creates new enemies, of both state and nonstate types? Once again, the state's role now expands significantly according to the criterion invoked, enlarging the military power of the state as state and nonstate adversaries grow. Or consider "coercion of individuals by others." The concept of coercion is narrowly defined here, with the focus on individuals rather than institutions, creating a bias from the start. But if individual leaders are held responsible for the corruptions within and the effects of the institutions over which they preside, this criterion too can become highly elastic, adjusted to support whatever police and military action it takes to support neoliberalism.

Finally, consider "some means" to decide common rules and adjudicate disputes. Friedman avoids the word *democracy* in this essay—with its idea that the state is accountable to citizens through public elections and social movements—all the better to maintain the keystone distinction between self-organizing markets and states as units of command. But if unexpected injuries and surprises occur and the system is democratic, then this criterion too becomes elastic.

Friedman thus promotes formal limits to state action, but his market ideology promotes such an appearance because of the brevity of statements he makes about the rules of state intervention. This allows a Friedmanite to both demand extensive state support for the system he admires and to pretend that it could flourish by reducing the scope of the state, if only the state introduced market principles into more and more aspects of life. That duplicity creates a nice political formula for electoral campaigns, as it shields from view the draconian disciplines needed to adjust behavior to market imperatives.

Radical neoliberals often welcome, and sometimes generate, crisis as a way to enact neoliberal legislation that a democratic majority would otherwise reject.[2] This strategy crystallized during Friedman's cooperation with shock tactics in Chile to introduce neoliberal economic reforms through the state upon the assassination of Allende and the violent advent of the Pinochet regime. It has continued through the willingness of radical right-wing legislators in the United States to threaten national credit default by refusing to pass a debt ceiling bill until their demands for budget cuts and no tax increases for the rich were met in the summer of 2011. Such a recurrent tactic reveals that radical neoliberalism is political in an extreme sense of that word. It often pursues radical state initiatives to produce the institutional arrangements it supports; its goal in these circumstances is often to force a majority to adopt state policies it would otherwise resist.

Moderate Neoliberalism and Market Creativity

Hayek presents a somewhat different case. While embracing the outlines of the Friedman system in advance, he is more alert to the elasticity and potential ambiguity of the principles he advances. He also emphasizes the role of spontaneity and creativity in impersonal market processes, making him dubious about the predictive science Friedman pursues.

To gain our bearings with Hayek we need to gain a preliminary sense of how he comes to celebrate the self-organizing and regulating powers of the market. Consider, then, a large group of people arriving serially for a meeting in a rather small living room. A couple of early arrivals locate themselves on chairs with a decent view of the speaker. As others arrive, they range themselves by individual adjustments in relation to the speaker, paying heed to the locations of those already there. As the room fills, with some sitting on chairs and others on the floor, this undirected process of "mutual adjustment," as Charles Lindblom calls it, becomes increasingly active.[3] The participants, without central coordination or command, creatively adjust to each other so that everyone has a decent view of the speaker and is within earshot. Some younger people have offered their chairs to older people. A few of the elders have politely demurred. As the meeting begins, most participants would agree that the collective result is better for all than would have been the case if the host had assigned everyone chairs and floor positions from a central, authoritative perspective.

Mutual adjustment promotes an unplanned collective rationality in this setting, partly by the adjustments of people to one another and the emergent situation and partly because extant norms of politeness are brought into play as the adjustments unfold. This works better than a single authority telling some people to vacate their seats and others to take them. You dislike it when someone instructs you to do what you were about to do anyway, because of the unnecessary show of authority and the suggestion that you would not have otherwise obeyed the norm of politeness. We have all been there. A market process of self-organized seating works out rather well in this setting.

Such an example, while pertinent, does not conform closely to an economic market. The participants in our example have a common aim; they are not in radically different subject positions; their desires for advantage are strongly hedged by norms of politeness and potential feelings of shame; and the situation is face-to-face. But the example does provide a starting point from which to grasp Hayek's celebration of impersonal, self-regulating markets, in which no one has complete knowledge of the whole, while many have partial knowledge of pertinent aspects that others lack. His idea is that the best probable result, in a situation where no one has an adequate synoptic vision, emerges from impersonal market self-regulation.

Perhaps the impersonal evolution of a language or a species moves us closer to the situation of markets than our face-to-face example. Such examples are illuminating. But they also draw us toward a long list of processes, both human and nonhuman, that both interact and display differential degrees of self-organizational power. The problem is that the more such processes you add to Hayek's list, the more the uniqueness and self-stabilizing power of economic markets become qualified by their relations to these very forces. And the more the ideology is widened to include these other processes, the more the equation between self-organizing markets and market rationality is called into question. This conundrum may explain why Hayek briefly invokes such examples but shies away from exploring their relations to economic markets.

With these preliminaries behind us, let us listen to a few of the statements in which Hayek celebrates the powers of spontaneity in general and the impersonal, self-regulative powers of economic markets in particular:

> The grown order [by contrast to the made order] which we have referred to as a self-generating or endogenous order, is in English most conveniently described as a *spontaneous order*. . . . It would be no exaggeration to say that social theory begins with . . . the discovery that there exist orderly structures which are the product of the action of many men but are not the result of human design.[4]

> Spontaneous orders are not necessarily complex, but unlike deliberate human arrangements they may achieve any degree of complexity.[5]

> Spontaneous orders . . . will often consist of a system of abstract relations between elements which are also only defined by abstract properties. The . . . abstract character of such orders rests on the fact that they may persist while all the particular elements they comprise and even the number of such elements change.[6]

> We shall see that it is impossible, not only to replace the spontaneous order by organization [the other main type of order, needed to some degree] and at the same time to utilize as much of the dispersed knowledge of all its members as possible; but also to improve or correct this order by interfering in it by direct commands.[7]

> So long as property is divided among many owners, none of them acting independently has exclusive power to determine the income and

position of particular people. . . . What our generation has forgotten is that the system of private property is the best guaranty of freedom, not only for those who own property but scarcely less for those who do not.[8]

The successful use of competition as the principle of social organization precludes certain types of interference with economic life, but it admits of others which sometimes may very considerably assist it and even requires certain types of government action. . . . It is necessary in the first instance that the parties in the market should be free to sell and buy at any price at which they can find a partner . . . and that anybody should be free to produce, sell and buy anything that may be produced or sold at all. And it is essential that entry into the different trades should be open to all on equal terms. . . . [Also] any attempt to control prices or quantities of particular goods deprives competition of its power of bringing about an effective coordination of particular efforts.[9]

Hayek thus identifies four virtues of economic markets organized around dispersed private property. First, it allows numerous firms and individuals to adjust spontaneously to each other in a way that promotes an impersonal rationality not grasped or designed by any central authority in advance. Second, it allows spontaneous inventions in products and firms to emerge and be tested by the impersonal market. Third, it generates self-organizing processes to regulate firms, workers, consumers, and modes of organization so that things turn out better for all than they otherwise would through any other mode of organization, particularly a planned one. Fourth, self-balancing market processes, while inevitably accompanied by considerable inequality, uncertainty, and luck, enable participants to face less coercion from other individuals than they otherwise would. These, then, represent the miracles of impersonal market rationality.

One of Hayek's main concerns is to show how central state planning cannot attain these results. If pursued relentlessly, it eventually leads to a totalitarian state. He shows no hesitancy in contending that a heavy dose of state planning will drive a regime toward Nazism or state communism, even when its intentions are benign.[10] And he regularly invokes the putative miracle of impersonal market rationality as the only pertinent contrast model to the drift toward "serfdom."

But Hayek also contends that the market virtues he admires cannot be sustained by the market alone; they must be subtended by a variety of public attitudes and state practices that allow them to flourish. For example, while language development, species evolution, the self-organization capacities of simple organisms, and hurricanes require no reflectively articulated "ideology" to sustain them, a neoliberal economy cannot sustain itself unless it is supported by a self-conscious ideology internalized by most participants that celebrates the virtues of market individualism, market autonomy, and a minimal state. Here is what Hayek says:

> If I am not mistaken, this fashionable contempt for "ideology" or for all general principles or "isms," is a characteristic attitude of disillusioned socialists, which, because they have been forced by the inherent contradictions of their own ideology to discard it, have concluded that all ideologies must be erroneous and that in order to be rational one must do without one. But to be guided only . . . by explicit particular purposes which one consciously accepts, and to reject all general values whose conduciveness to particular desirable results cannot be demonstrated . . . is an impossibility. [An ideology] may well be something whose widespread acceptance is the indispensable condition for most of the particular things we strive for.[11]

This quotation is loaded. Let us state the condition more bluntly than Hayek does, helped by the recent conduct of neoliberalism in actuality. A successful market economy, unlike other self-regulating systems, requires *the incorporation of neoliberal ideology into the behavior of entrepreneurs, courts, bankers, workers, families, schools, citizens, the media, and state officials*. One of the main reasons for this emerges in *The Road to Serfdom*. There Hayek worries that too many people will rebel against "obeying" the dictates of the market when unemployment is high or another disruption occurs. They will act democratically to overturn market principles. The pursuit of short-term interest and the practices of citizenship must both be filled with neoliberal ideology if the regime is to flourish. Otherwise short-term suffering will promote long-term irrationality. Here is what Hayek says late in that book, after noting that the question of obedience to neoliberal ideology has now become paramount with the decline, first, of religious incentives for obedience and, second and later, of unconscious belief in the rationality of the market (all the italics are mine):

It was men's *submission* to the impersonal forces of the market that in the past has made possible the growth of a civilization without which this could not have happened: it is by thus *submitting* that we are every day helping to build something that is greater than any of us can fully comprehend. It does not matter whether men in the past did submit from beliefs of humility. . . . The crucial point is that it is infinitely more difficult to comprehend the necessity of submitting to forces whose operation we cannot follow in detail than to do so out of the humble awe which religion, or even the respect for the doctrines of economics did inspire.[12]

With the growth of market individualism comes a corollary desire to look for collective, democratic responses when major dislocations of financial collapse, unemployment, heightened inequality, runaway inflation, and the like occur. The more such dislocations occur, the more powerful and internalized, Hayek insists, neoliberal ideology must become; it must become embedded in the media, in economic talking heads, in law and the jurisprudence of the courts, in government policy, and in the souls of participants. Neoliberal ideology must become a machine or engine that infuses economic life as well as a camera that provides a snapshot of it.[13] That means, in turn, that the impersonal processes of regulation work best if courts, churches, schools, the media, music, localities, electoral politics, legislatures, monetary authorities, and corporate organizations internalize and publicize these norms. It also means that active state policies are needed to produce this result. It is this imperative of neoliberalism that has helped to create culture wars in each country where it has gained a major presence. That combination of elements also helps one to grasp what I mean when I say that neoliberalism is a form of biopolitics that seeks to produce a nation of regular individuals, even as its proponents often act as if they are merely describing processes that are automatic and individual behavior that is free. Neoliberalism must become an ideological machine embedded deeply in life in order to produce the submission and self-constraints its putative success demands; it is not merely a camera that takes a snapshot of processes humming along without it.

As Hayek acknowledges to a degree, he sometimes teeters on the very tight wire he must continue to walk: he must marshal enough state support to make impersonal markets flourish amid the suffering, inequality, chanciness, and disparate experiences of luck it produces, without introducing so many state interventions and involvements that he too would begin to march it down "the road to serfdom." He identifies democratic enthusiasm as one of the dangers to temper. For, as he says often, some of the largest steps down the road to serfdom are taken by constituencies and leaders who have good intentions but either use bad methods to attain them or fail to acknowledge that they are unrealizable. That Hayek slogan has been translated into a sound bite we now hear every day in the media: leave economic growth and creativity to the free market; treat the democratic state as primarily an agent of coercion.

Defining the magic of the market as an indispensable starting point, Hayek hesitantly now explores multiple ways it must be supplemented, supported, or regulated by the state. The key is to make the state the servant of markets and not to allow markets to become the servant of the state.

The Ideal Hayekian State

Hayek often leaves the impression in his summaries of market processes and virtues that such mechanisms are timeless. These are "abstract" processes, so that a description of market operations at one time and setting will be similar to that at any other. On the other hand, and as we have already glimpsed through our exploration of the role of ideology, the market displays considerable fragility; it cannot simply sustain its own preconditions of being in a spontaneous and timeless way. It needs the state, an institution definitely situated in time. Unlike Friedman, with whom he otherwise shares much, Hayek does not strive to formulate iron criteria to limit or exclude state involvement. Nor does this refugee from fascism express enthusiasm in advance for what later became the "shock doctrine" of radical neoliberalism. Rather he articulates several rules of thumb, governed in descending order, first, by a presumptive desire to leave market processes alone when possible, second, the demands of the specific circumstance at hand, third, a reluctant willingness to supplement market processes in some cases, and, fourth, a readiness to promote state policies that support market processes if and when the self-balancing process itself is insufficient to itself. He is thus both wary of the state and dependent upon it. He supports democracy in a narrow sense of the term. And he constantly struggles with when, where, and how the state—or government, as he prefers to call it—should maintain the preconditions of market vitality.

Following are a few of his recommendations about how the state can help the market to preserve and protect itself, developed in *The Constitution of Liberty* in 1960. Some of them may seem rusty today in a setting where people, money, investments, labor, product innovations, and the media move faster and further than heretofore. But they do give a sense of his dominant tendencies. A democratic government needs to find some way to reduce the level and degree of poverty, preferably by introducing government-supported market mechanisms to do so. The goal is to "provide a uniform minimum for all instances of proved need, so that no member of the community need be in want of food or shelter." The state cannot reduce inequality significantly and should never try to do so, on pain of undermining the delicacy of the impersonal market system. It needs a compulsory education system, because ignorance and dogmatism are adversaries of an effective market system. But, except for an early period in America alone when immigration was rampant and there was a need to forge a "nation" out of a "melting pot," Hayek resists a state-run educational system. He favors something like a charter system of schools, supported by vouchers, assuming, I imagine, that such a system would internalize the virtues of a minimally regulated market economy and inculcate them into the educational process. The best defense of neoliberalism, remember, is a set of institutions that inculcate its ideology; that makes a charter school system ideal from his point of view.

Continuing down the trail Hayek charts, labor should have the right to organize. But in order to curtail union "coercion" of workers there must be no union shops. Hayek worries about monopolies in unions much more than in corporations. The state should run the defense or military system. Medical care should never be nationalized, partly because it transforms doctors, now both imbued with market principles and governed by the market system, into "paid servants of the state."[14]

Monetary policy, however, provides a "loose joint in the otherwise self-steering mechanisms of the market."[15] There is no automatic way to govern it, and political determinations of it are not that trustworthy. So it should be handled by an independent commission, separated to some degree from both market pressures and state accountability. There must also be some general laws regarding "smoke emissions" and the like, since the market does not price well widely distributed emissions, much of whose cost is distributed to future generations. So Hayek opens the door to active state ecological policies even though he evinced the most minimal awareness of ecological issues.

When Hayek delineates the scope and types of state intervention the background is set by his default sense of the normal market operation. It is not that markets are natural: they require a significant supporting infrastructure through ideological hegemony, state action, neoliberal jurisprudence, schools, and the internalized market virtues of participants. When markets are in operation and bolstered by the state in the right ways they exude a rationality, a tendency to stability, and resilience that cannot be found in any other human organization of life.

Multiple Sites of Spontaneity

There are some points of contact between Hayek's theory and the perspective I support. Above all, we both emphasize the periodic significance of spontaneity, uncertainty, creativity, self-organization, and self-balancing powers in the world, and we both think that such processes often exceed our powers to control them. Such points of initial contact may encourage a few fools—who themselves have a too limited arsenal of conceptual alternatives to consider—to assimilate the two theories. But that would be a mistake. My critical engagement with Hayek, rather than denying these initial points of contact, builds upon them. Indeed it expands them well beyond the zone in which Hayek is ready to apply them. And such an expansion changes everything. I list some of the expansions, augmentations, and critiques below, suggesting how several feed into each other. We start with the most obvious and go from there.

The Market-State Doubling System

In a formal democracy, with a large corporate and finance system and an ideology that puts a narrow image of self-interest first, firms can first *enact* initiatives on their own in the market and then use funds, lobbying power, campaign contributions, collusion, and bribery to *consolidate* those advantages through the state. This is part of the process by which oligopolies are forged. It involves the double whammy of *initiating* power in the market and *veto* power to protect those initiatives through local government, legislatures, courts, and the executive branch. That is why a legislature under the sway of neoliberal ideology is always so active.

Hayek does not really come to terms with this combination. To do so would be to impose too many limits, in his view, on the ability of corporations to lobby and influence governing bodies. He does not, for instance, limit corporate spending on political campaigns, confine advertising to product information, or seek to curtail lobbying power. The cumulative effect of the combination he tacitly enables is severe in the domains of product priority, deregulation pressures, income inequality, and wealth distribution. Such a combination already blurs or fudges the neat separation between markets and governance that Hayek seeks to delineate through simple formulae; the formulae both express and obscure the actual tendencies to close interinvolvement. As the advantages accumulate, self-amplifying processes readily grow out of them. Such tendencies are easily exacerbated in a media age when private corporations have by far the greatest capacity to advertise their ideas in the media and the Supreme Court treats money as speech. In the United States today, for instance, you regularly see and hear the ideology of neoliberalism on news and business reports, but the perspectives of labor, the poor, the unemployed, the sick, racial and ethnic minorities, and retirees are seldom voiced. From Hayek's point of view, these are typically the constituencies that have not yet adequately internalized neoliberal ideology.

It is unlikely that Hayek would support, say, laws to limit the use of corporate funds in electoral campaigns, lobbying, and ideational advertising. But some such limit would provide a minimal start in regulating the very doubling system his formulae tend to conceal. When I say "advantage" in this context, I do not mean that the result necessarily protects the initiators from meltdowns that affect all of us. The spiraling processes introduced by the market initiatives of firms and their veto power over state action can indeed foment collective meltdowns. I mean only that the doubling process protects the market initiatives enacted and sets the stage for more of the same.

Workers and Work

Hayek significantly overstates the dangers of unions and union shops during an era of neoliberal hegemony, though that hegemony had not yet arrived when he wrote. When individual workers are discussed in relation to labor unions, he construes them to be free actors who decide to enter into labor contracts and who primarily face the risk of *collective coercion* from unions. This already belies his formal tendency to act as if coercion is something that some individuals do to others. Indeed it shows that such a formula mostly finds expression in his account of employer-employee relations rather than member-union relations, probably because he thinks that the latter relation is already mediated by the self-organizing power of the market. But can't unions be treated as participants in markets, as firms with internal lines of authority are?

Hayek comes close to treating workers as merely abstract factors of production comparable to other factors such as capital, equipment, interest rates, "resources," shipping costs, and the like. Indeed this is one of the concealments that occurs when you insist, as Hayek does, upon treating each unit of society as an "abstraction" so you can get a bird's-eye view of how it works. But labor is not reducible to other "commodities." Workers are both "factors" from the vantage point of the firm and living beings to themselves and their families. They are also citizens. Even a plow horse is more than merely a factor of production. Workers get tired when they work; they suffer; they get sick; and they aspire to grow further as their involvements proceed. They experience joy and pursue life plans. They raise families. They are citizens who seek to participate in the larger life of the society.

Consider the effects of the current neoliberal regime upon workers. Today low- and middle-level workers in offices, factories, fast-food restaurants, airports, movie theaters, agricultural production, insurance offices, advertising agencies, and the like are subjected to severe disciplines. They are often alienated both from the work process and from effective participation in its organization. They face high job insecurity as well as few health and retirement supports. They receive low incomes that often impede active participation in the larger cultural life once they have met the education needs of their children, insurance costs, mortgage or rental costs, food needs, travel requirements, and medical care. Hayek's relative lack of concern about the internal rules governing collectively organized firms combined with his paranoia about the "coercive power" of labor unions that are at least formally accountable to their membership is very revealing. It would be laughable today, if the consequences were not so severe. His abstract attitude reflects the limited experience of one who either never held a low-level job or who always thought he was entitled to much more if and when he did so. Labor unions need to be regulated, but we urgently need laws that support union shops and mandate the robust involvement of unions in firm management. Many neoliberal economists today support deregulation of business and close regulation of labor. Hayek runs with the crowd in these respects.

Market Consumption Binds
Unregulated markets both exhibit powers of self-organization and produce internal binds on their own. There is no better place to illustrate this combination than in consumption markets. As the market theorist Fred Hirsch has shown in considerable detail, when consumers in a market system are guided by the immediate effect a new product will have upon each individual separate from collective awareness of what its quality and value will be like if and when it is generalized, a whole series of consumer binds and congealments form.[16] A good such as a suburban house, an SUV, a private education, a house security system, or a private neighborhood security force exudes one appearance when taken alone and limited to a few consumers during its initial period of introduction. That advertisement showing a person driving an SUV in the outback alone is lovely. But such a fuel-eating, air-polluting, accident-prone, view-obscuring, space-hogging product looks different when it becomes widely distributed as a vehicle of daily use. The collective costs of maintaining it through state expenditures increase; the value to the users decreases; the congestion effects grow; the need for new defensive goods (such as heavier cars, higher insurance costs, more air-conditioning, and vehicles high enough to see under extant road conditions) to compensate for its effects grow; and the cumulative pressures on household budgets are magnified as gasoline and other costs rise. As such goods accumulate in several sectors of consumption, people in the middle class find it increasingly difficult to make ends meet even as their incomes grow. And they often seek to reduce their taxes to resist paying for the collective deterioration of the cities, public modes of education, urban housing projects, and congested highways that the proliferation of these products has inadvertently helped to produce.

Some of the insights Hayek has introduced, indeed, could also help us to see how the irrational effects of initially rational consumption choices accumulate, if only the theorist would step down a bit from his abstract perch. These processes recoil as higher costs faced by families trying to participate in modes of consumption made available to them by the market initiating and state veto power of corporations.

There are ways to reconstitute the collective infrastructure of individual, family, and collective consumption so that the possibilities of travel, housing, medical care, and energy use available reduce individual costs, support the collective environment, and curtail the violence and huge military expenses of protecting oil supplies. They would start as we noted in chapter 1, with reconstitution by the state of its current subsidies for the established infrastructure of consumption in the domains of travel, health care, retirement, and energy production joined to cultural drives to reform the compensatory, self-defeating ethos of consumption now in force.

Spontaneous Social Movements

Sometimes you get the impression that "entrepreneurs" are the sole paradigms of creativity in the Hayekian world, though he does give a nod or two to science. Such a bias expresses Hayek's desire to contain democratic politics in order to let the market run. But the impersonal market is not the only human system that displays moments of creative spontaneity and differential degrees of self-organizing power. Social movements, for instance, do so too. Hayek was so concerned about limiting the efficacy of nonmarket processes, particularly the democratic state, that he failed to take the measure of spontaneous social movements.

When a new right or identity surges into being from a place of suffering below the current register of social acceptance, it often does so by a combination of creative initiatives by activists who seek to place it on the pluralist register of legitimacy, eventual acceptance of these claims by other constituencies, internalization of them by corporate and labor organizations, and state actions that support and protect these achievements. This is the creative politics of *pluralization* by which emerging constituencies expand the scope of established pluralism. Once such a spontaneous movement gets off the ground, spontaneous, self-generated tendencies by other groups can arise to adjust their conduct and to create room for the new entry to be.[17]

The whole process of creative negotiation now involves a degree of agonizing self-reconstitution by several constituencies, including both initiators and respondents. Spontaneous innovation and self-organization, then, greatly exceed the narrow comfort zone in which Hayek tends to enclose them. To appreciate this *is to include politics within the domain of creative spontaneity and to include a pluralist culture as among the processes through which creative self-organization occurs.* Additionally, once you come to terms with how the globalization of capital propels powerful pressures to create minorities of multiple types within numerous territorial states, you also see how contemporary drives to the pluralization of public culture are not mere luxuries. They speak to real conditions of being and pressures in a world that is being minoritized along more dimensions and at a faster rate than heretofore.

In such a setting Hayekians are under internal pressure either to condone draconian disciplines to confine cultural diversity or to construct a generous ethos of engagement within the territorial state. Either/or. The first response, recently exemplified by George W. Bush and David Cameron, blows the benign lid off neoliberalism through its support of expanded disciplinary and exclusionary policies. The second breaks the boundaries of neoliberal ideology so that it no longer assumes the provincial character of market purity, traditionally defined. My sense is that today those in the Friedman camp press eagerly in the first direction, while the responses of those lingering in Hayekian tradition may remain in doubt.

Capital-Nonhuman Imbrications

Spontaneity and self-organizing tendencies are not merely operative in multiple human systems. As we noted in chapter 1, they also find differential degrees of expression in a variety of nonhuman force fields that are entangled with advanced capitalism. It was possible for Hayek to see this, but he nonetheless shied away from engaging the issue. A hurricane displays some tendencies of self-maintenance once it forms spontaneously in a combination of warm water, updrafts, and specific wind currents. Species evolution has spontaneous elements in it. A climate pattern has tendencies toward self-maintenance replete with tipping points. The ocean conveyor belt, which carries many implications for climate, weather, and capitalist performance, also expresses delicate tendencies of self-maintenance. Species' self-maintenance depends to some degree on automatic processes of self-equilibration internal to it. And so on endlessly. Today, as capitalism becomes more global, intensive, and fast-moving, its imbrications with nonhuman force fields of multiple types increase. The internal connection between capital, carbon emissions, and the acceleration of climate change represents merely one example. As systems of heterogeneous types collide and collude, increasingly the need grows for creative citizen movements, enlarged state action, interstate agreements, and global citizen actions. It is through the multiplicity of interacting systems with differential powers of self-organization that the Hayek attempt to anaesthetize politics, curtail the state, and let corporate markets rip faces its most severe limit. Now that we have seen how an internalized ideology of neoliberalism is essential to the performance of the Hayekian economy, we can also discern why so many neoliberals today are tempted either to deny the long-term effects of climate change on the entire world or to pretend the world market will eventually internalize the needed response on its own. When?

The Evangelical-Neoliberal Resonance Machine

During the period in which Hayek wrote, between 1930 and the 1970s, neoliberalism migrated from a minority paradigm to one that became increasingly integrated into the ideological self-understandings and role performances of many states. But it did not initially establish a close association with religious movements. Hayek, a skeptic himself, counseled respect for a few religious traditions, but he did not tie neoliberal ideology to any particular religious constellation. The creative emergence of the evangelical-neoliberal resonance machine in America, starting in the late 1970s and continuing today, would thus have taken him by surprise. It surprised most radicals and liberal secularists too. That machine now consists of parties who hold overlapping political-economic theories bolstered and intensified by some affinities of existential spirituality. They share the dogma that together they should have full hegemony. Both resist or defer regulatory action to respond to climate change, reconstitute prevailing traditions of energy use, curtail market tendencies to create meltdowns, reduce inequality, or challenge the internal authority structures of firms. Neoliberalism does so because of its theory of rationality, evangelicalism because it joins that theory to an image of a God who would not allow human beings to affect the climate. The result is destructive for the country and the world. One ironic contribution the evangelical movement makes to neoliberalism is in displaying just how important the quality of an embedded cultural ethos is to economic performance and the state. Hayek understood this, too, through his focus on the need to internalize neoliberal ideology. The problem is only that all these parties embrace the wrong ethos.

The new neo-evangelical formation amplifies the sites and modes of inculcation through which a neoliberal economy sustains itself, particularly as it faces more and more limits to its expansion. The appearance of this new formation, again, teaches us by negative example about the internal connection between an embedded ethos and politico-economic performance. There are signs in Hayek's work that he could come to terms with how shifts in the culture make a difference to economic performance, since he was worried about how theories of planning in the 1930s and 1940s were taking us down "a road to serfdom." But he stopped writing before it was possible to gauge the dangers of this new turn in the spirituality of politico-economic life.

Globalization and Regional Asymmetries

The first countries to adopt capitalist organization accumulate advantages over later entries. Control over currency, banking, international organizations, and the like merely begins to tap this differential.[18] Soon enough, they depend upon other regions for "inputs" of resources, labor, and investment as well as outlets for their products. Though it is a long story to tell, these and other pressures create extreme regional imbalances in the distribution of wealth, income, health, and security that define global capitalism. These imbalances, in turn, help to create cross-regional resentments, with corresponding pressures inside the metropole to support imperial controls and sustain large military establishments.

Global Climate Change

Hayek's belated attention to "smoke" and other "externalities" belies the most profound worldwide challenge of all to the market system he celebrates. A few theorists did attend to this challenge when he was writing. For example, Habermas sounded the alarm in 1970.[19] But Hayek did not. The now well-documented probability of a significant increase in worldwide temperature, extreme weather events, droughts, and a corresponding rise in ocean levels poses a dramatic challenge to the assumptions around which moderate neoliberalism is organized. The question is whether Hayek would today join the chorus of neoliberal deniers or ratchet up awareness of the need for new social movements, significant shifts in production and consumption, new levels of state intervention, and binding interstate agreements to come to terms with this emerging condition. I sometimes suspect that he would, after considerable agonizing, adopt the second route. But I cannot prove that.

Each of these processes, and all in their relations of internal connection and external impingement, disclose how capitalism, partly *because* of its self-regulating tendencies and bumpy relations with other subsystems, periodically secretes volatilities, instabilities, and meltdowns. It is, you might say, an assemblage of disparate and interacting systems.

Hayek's descendants say regularly in the media that the failures of the past are due to too much Keynesianism, or too much central planning, or external events that temporarily disrupt markets, or labor unions and consumer movements that disrupt its beauty, or some combination of these forces. They advance a utopia of stable market innovation and self-regulation that has never been realized anywhere because, they say, severe obstacles to its potential have so far always been in place. The past is messy and cumbersome, while the potential future is clean and pure, as long as workers, citizens, leaders, states, the poor, and the unemployed can be pressed to exercise patience, to let natural market process unfold, and to curtail inflated demands for full employment, economic equality, social security, state medical care, environmental regulation, and job stability that sow the seeds of instability.

But the list of potential sources of creativity, privileged alliances, self-regulation, and instability drawn up here explodes the Hayek image of neoliberalism from the inside. It appreciates Hayek's identifications of spontaneity, creativity, and degrees of unpredictability, but it also multiplies the sites from which they emerge. We do indeed carry the burdens, wisdom, and prejudices of the past into the mystery of the future, and periodically we must respond creatively to new blockages in ways that break some of those prejudices. This means that we must grasp how new changes disrupt, infect, and unsettle from within the abstract system peddled by neoliberals. For example, if citizen movements, dominant states, and interstate organizations today converged to formulate a set of stringent requirements to reduce carbon emissions within the next ten years, focusing first and foremost on the hegemonic states that have created most of the problem, such a decision would free the creativity of scientists, engineers, inventors, and banks to transfer their technological virtuosity from a focus on oil production, cars, highways, planes, airports, and the like to multiple technologies of renewable energy, fast transit, hybrid cars, innovative bicycle paths, green housing, and urban green spaces.[20] Is one of the things—besides the short-term self-interest of privileged elites—that inhibits many people from exploring such possibilities more robustly the lock neoliberal ideology holds for so many on the very idea of freedom?

Creativity and Freedom

We can consolidate one upshot of these eight intercoded critiques of neoliberal ideology and practice in the following way. Hayek is right in saying that a neoliberal political economy requires the cultural infusion of neoliberal ideology to sustain itself. But he is dead wrong about what kind of internalized ethos is in fact needed today. Today we need an economic ethos—negotiated by interacting constituencies with affinities of spirituality across differences in their final creeds—that acknowledges a critical role for the state as a site of legitimate collective action, infuses a generous sensibility into the jurisprudence and constitutional interpretation adopted by courts, supports a progressive tax system and reforms in the state-supported infrastructure of consumption to reduce inequality so that every citizen can participate in the cultural practices made available, embraces the need of citizens to have one eye on the collective fragility of things and another on their interests when they make consumption and investment choices, presses the state to carry out its responsibilities to the present and collective future, supports the regulation of economic markets, appreciates the powers of metamorphosis of several nonhuman systems with which the economy interacts, and infuses each of these practices with due attention to the fragility of things.

We have now reached a bifurcation point at which the exploration could move in any of several directions. We could examine more closely the most fundamental elements of a capitalist system, starting with Hayek's appreciation of spontaneity, to carry an account of labor, class, and exploitation well beyond the scope of his formal account. (That task will be pursued in the Second Interlude.) We could seek to ascertain how significant shifts in the scope and speed of market processes today pull the image Hayek projects too far out of touch with the world. We could examine more closely the role that a neoliberal ideological ethos of market, corporate, union, university, media, state, and church life plays in cultural life. (We started such pursuits in chapter 1.) All of these explorations are pertinent, and so are the intersections between them.[21]

Here, however, I want to focus on the image of freedom Hayek advances, using it as a way to show how much tension there is between Hayek's optimistic concept of the impersonal market and his fascinating ideas of spontaneity and freedom. That tension was already suggested in the previous discussion of the severe role of ideology in Hayek's image of neoliberalism.

Hayek never, to my knowledge, accepted that crude image of market freedom and instrumental choice by which egoistic individuals and firms pursue only their own private advantage, narrowly construed, as they produce through unconscious modes of coordination a collective result that is better for everyone than any other system could promote. He was not a "rational choice theorist." He expresses *tendencies* in this direction, to be sure, when he celebrates entrepreneurs almost exclusively and relentlessly demeans labor unions as coercive because they impede the ability of self-interested individuals to choose from among the employment possibilities and modes of discipline that hierarchical, disciplinary firms make available. But he has a more expansive vision of dispositions to action than that; he also acknowledges that "information" is often not equally distributed and transparent; he even conveys a sense sometimes that the mood or temper within which information is collected and assimilated may make a difference too. But above all, he is too impressed with spontaneous modes of action and creative interjections to support an image of a predictive science anchored in the aggregation of narrow self-interested actions through an impersonal market. In a world where creative explorations unfold, even what counts as self-interest can easily become an object of experimental exploration. Part of the attraction of neoliberal ideology to many today is how its contribution to the binds of workers, the unemployed, and the down-and-out is always said to be temporary. Follow these rules, its proponents say endlessly, and the down-and-out of today will become the up-and-coming of tomorrow. A rising tide lifts all boats, they say, ignoring the strictures by Hirsch reviewed earlier in this chapter. Another attraction for many is how it tethers a bright image of future individual freedom to a utopian vision of the market. This image even pulls on people whose interests are damaged by its practices. An urgent need today is to articulate and publicize an image of freedom that challenges neoliberal orthodoxy as it carries one strain in Hayek to places he could not himself go.

The classic debate over freedom, we hear, is between the negative and positive images of it.[22] The first image asserts that a person is free—constituencies and larger collectivities are generally ignored because of the methodological individualism in which the theory is set—to the extent an individual can pursue his or her wants or purposes without coercive pressure from others. In such a theory the source of the agent's wants are not themselves explored, partly because many versions take them to be narrow from the start, partly because such an exploration would open the door to examine the internal, disciplinary practices of firms that the theorists of neoliberalism want to avoid, and partly because the internal link between neoliberal practice and the internalization of neoliberal ideology would be exposed for critical review. It is further assumed that such a practice of freedom fits only a market society because, on the purest claims of such a model, such a system both provides the impersonal organization that leaves room for individuals to act upon their preferences and sets a practice that inhibits the ability of some individuals to intentionally coerce others.

Other, more holistic and positive images of freedom focus on collective modes of behavior. They pursue freedom in a "positive sense" by opening governing institutions to self-conscious scrutiny whereby participants reconsider reflexively desires and common ends already implanted in them by habit and ideology. The agents involved can thereby act to reconstitute preliminary dispositions already in play if needed and then realize the reconstituted ends by institutional means. Many positive images of freedom embrace a dialectical process by which participants increasingly uncover and enact modes of self-realization that are already "implicit" in their practices and assumptions. So, negative and positive freedom.

It is impossible to defend a sophisticated image of freedom without folding some positive elements into it, even if you do not support coercive means to reform people's operational desires. But the tradition of positive freedom, once its proponents have exposed the limits, cruelties, and crudities inside images of negative freedom, tends to make it too easy on itself by assuming the reflexive process works in a productive direction within a holistic system that becomes more rational and whole as freedom expands. Its critics, including Hayek, jump on the story of communal rationality. The good intentions of those who pursue the path of positive freedom, they say, are all too likely to undermine market rationality as they inadvertently magnify coercion. Hayek's claim that extensive state intervention leads almost inexorably to "serfdom," to the envelopment of individuals within large, oppressive, bureaucratic institutions, represents the paradigm of such claims. There is certainly something to his worry, even though Hayek fails to distinguish closely enough fascist states with dictatorial power, mobilized populations, one-party systems, internal and external scapegoats, and militarism from, say, Keynesian states with two- or multiparty systems, an active citizenry, considerable room for citizen action within and beyond the state, and a media that periodically challenges corporate and state priorities. He also fails to explore how his vision of spontaneity joined to self-organizing processes edges his theory closer to an image of protean connections between multiple, protean actants than to *either* an individualistic or holistic image of freedom.[23]

Hayek, then, is not entirely a philosopher of negative freedom, if by that you mean only the ability to act upon desires or "preferences" already there. There is too much appreciation of creativity, spontaneity, and uncertainty in his thinking to fit such an image neatly. I build upon his embryonic appreciation of spontaneity, creativity, and uncertainty inside freedom and extend it to practices and institutions that Hayek omits or depreciates.

As individual and collective agents of multiple types, we exercise one dimension of freedom when we pursue existing desires and another when we reflexively reconsider them and seek outlets to act upon revised desires. But those desires are not merely given in the first instance, and the reflexive process in the second does not always render explicit what was already "implicit" in operative assumptions and desires. *There is often more pluripotentiality in the rush of desire forward to consolidation in action than is captured by the lazy idea of the implicit.* There is also pluripotentiality during those fecund moments when an entire constituency coalesces under new circumstances, with the change in "circumstances" often shaped by rapid shifts in nonhuman force fields with which they are involved. In such circumstances the creative element of freedom comes into play. To put the point briefly, neither the tradition of negative freedom nor that of positive freedom comes to terms sufficiently with the role of creativity in freedom.

Creativity here means, as a first cut, action by the present upon ambiguities arising from the past oriented toward the future in a way that is not entirely reducible to the past as either implicit in the present or an aggregation of blind causes that produce the future. It might involve an exploratory movement back and forth between different parties in a cloudy situation that issues in a new result none intended at the start. These initiatives may then be consolidated by disciplinary processes and tactics that help to sediment them into the soft tissues of cultural life.

Reflexivity, you might say, begins to do its work *after* the uncanny, creative element in freedom has begun to unfold, for good or ill. Creative processes flow through and over us, and reflexivity doubles the creative adventure. Actions are thus not entirely controlled by preexisting intentions; rather the creative dimension helps to compose and refine intentions as they become consolidated in action. To articulate the creative dimension of freedom, then, is to insert a fundamental qualification or hesitation into the ideas of both the masterful agent and agency as the activation of intentions already there. The creative element is located somewhere *between* active and passive agency. When creative freedom is under way in an unsettled context we may find ourselves *allowing* or *encouraging* a new thought, desire, or strategy to crystallize out of the confusion and nest of proto-thoughts that precede it. An agent, individual or collective, can help to open the portals of creativity, but it cannot will that which is creative to come into being by intending the result before it arrives. Real creativity is thus tinged with uncertainty and mystery.

The creative dimension of freedom discloses an ambiguity that haunts extant ideas of intention, desire, agency, and reflexivity. It exposes the ambiguity of agency in the practice of freedom. This ambiguity may find expression, say, in a basketball game as an accomplished player under intense defensive pressure spontaneously fires up the first jump shot ever attempted amid the flow of action. The shot, initially lacking a name, surprises the shooter and mystifies defenders. It was not implicit in the athlete's repertoire; it emerged in the pressure of action. After being repeated, named, and perfected through relentless training, it may spread like wildfire across the basketball landscape, as that type of shot did in the 1950s in the United States. Everything else in the game now shifts to some degree too. Other players, coaches, and referees now adopt creative responses to it, generating changes in the game through a mélange of partisan mutual adjustments that no individual or organization intended at the outset. Or take a young point guard who spontaneously completes a fast break with a blind, behind-the-back pass and then finds himself negotiating with his coach to decide just when such passes can be allowed in the future.

Such modes of creative, mutual adjustment, neither simply assignable to one player or coach, nor fitting neatly into extant notions of preformed intention, nor reducible to a reflexive dialectic, occur all the time in multiple domains. They form part of the essence of freedom.

Spontaneous creativity is accompanied by an element of real uncertainty; it occurs in that liminal moment when the limits of an activity have been experienced and before a definitive response to that limit has emerged. It thus occupies a fecund zone of indiscernibility. The result can be checked after the fact to see whether the results are positive or negative. A behind-the-back *shot*, for instance, might arise spontaneously in the flow of a game, startling the defense the first time it is enacted. It is apt, however, to turn out to be too hard to perfect and too easy to defend once other teams adjust to the initial surprise.

The example of the first jump shot, however, does not adequately take into account how the very context of action may sometimes change through an even more rapid shift in circumstances. To fill that bill you would need to have a setting in which a significant shift in the rules governing the game had been made, or, better, the players now find themselves in a new situation in which the opponent has a roster with only seven-foot players. Creative freedom, then, is spontaneous activity within a shifting setting with constraints in which an element of real uncertainty circulates through the setting. The spontaneity now flows *through the agents and the open-ended rules of the practice*, for good or ill. It operates within limits, even though those limits cannot all be stated in advance. It is unlikely, for instance, that a point guard will spontaneously flap his arms to fly from the backcourt to the basket in order to dunk the ball, no matter how intense the defense is. Human arms lack the needed preadaptations to negotiate such a maneuver, even though a few players do start a dunk at the free-throw line.

If creativity finds expression in the human estate, it will sometimes do so at surprising moments during a disruption in a practice, opening the door to a scientific invention, a new concept, a political initiative, a new social movement, an artistic innovation, market spontaneity, a language change, a cooking invention, teaching improvisation, a new type of film scene, a musical production, the use of new media, or the invention of a new product. And so on endlessly. Our identification with life—our tacit sense of belonging to a human predicament worthy of embrace—is partly rooted in the identities, faiths, and surroundings that already inspire us; it is partly rooted in negative freedom; it is partly rooted in reflexive reconsideration of established desires and ends. But it is grounded too in those uncanny experiences of creativity by means of which something new enters the world. This may be one of the reasons people cleave to the sweetness of life. It ties the sweetness of life to a *vitality* of being, even more than to a preordained end, purpose, or "fullness" with which it is officially invested. The intimate relation between freedom and creativity is why freedom is never *sufficiently* grasped by the idea of a lack to be fulfilled, successful action upon preset desires, or the drive to render the implicit explicit. The experience of uncertainty or incompleteness is sometimes an occasion of fecundity.

The creative element of freedom is episodic rather than constant, and it is tinged with mystery. That is one reason why those drawn to a nontheistic philosophy of speculative realism (to be explored in chapter 4 in relation to a theistic version of it) will be wise not to allow devotees of monotheism to monopolize the theme of mystery. We are beings flopping around in one corner of a cosmos that exceeds our capacities for knowledge, self-awareness, and mastery. An element of mystery is woven into the uncanny operation of creativity.

The basketball example already suggests that creativity and spontaneity are not confined to economic markets. So consider politics. Take that moment in feudal Ireland in which peasants exploited by a landlord named Thomas Boycott creatively organized an entire community to stop using his products, fomenting an innovative strategy of protest that also produced a creative innovation in language. We call such now well-honed strategies boycotts today. It is unlikely that any of those who joined the meetings to resist Thomas Boycott intended to invent a boycott before participating in that collective process of gestation. Or consider the dispersed, illegal minority that organized and sustained an underground railroad to provide those striving to escape plantation slavery a route marked by periodic tunnels, river crossings, overground trails, and safe houses. Or follow the life of Frederick Douglass as he assembled creative strategies to learn how to read in a state when it was illegal to acquire such a skill. Or those who "invented" and participated in the first teach-in in America at the University of Michigan to protest the Vietnam War and to educate ill-informed citizens about its effects. Or that governor in Michigan who ordered the National Guard not to crush the 1937 sit-down strike, itself creatively organized by workers in Flint, but to protect the workers who had introduced the innovation. Or those protesters in Egypt who creatively used Twitter, cell phones, and Facebook to organize themselves and outwit the police. Or the gays at Stonewall who organized a series of protests after yet another violent police raid. Or Mahatma Gandhi, who roused a whole country to nonviolent resistance to free India from English imperialism. Or those students, professors, and investors in several countries who organized investment boycotts to oppose apartheid. Or multiple minorities within territorial states who have gradually found themselves shifting from seeking tolerance in a state organized around a hegemonic center to demanding a more decentered mode of pluralism that forges an ethos of agonistic respect between and among minorities of several types.

And consider the shifts in language occasioned by such creative innovations, through which a new term or phrase is introduced into a web of discourse that had heretofore seemed complete to many. Terms such as *boycott, underground railroad, safe house, teach-in, sit-down strike, sit-in, Twitter, Stonewall, agonistic respect*, and *nonviolent resistance* consolidate such innovations, rendering them ready-made possibilities to consider in the future. To the extent such innovative terms stick, they augment the supply of future actions and set a stage for new alternatives yet to riff upon them. The array of strategies becomes augmented, even as authorities prepare to respond in new ways to their most recent iterations.

There are certainly negative innovations too, such as becoming a scab, inventing fracking, inventing the Guantánamo Gulag, or organizing a neoliberal Tea Party to protest a new regime right after the last regime has presided over an economic meltdown. But noble innovations must also be listed from time to time, particularly as you engage a philosophy of neoliberalism that both celebrates spontaneity and limits its application so severely. Good night, Professor Friedman. Good morning, Mr. Hayek.

Creative acts are *conditioned* by the past, but they are not entirely explicable by either causal antecedents or dialectical processes through which the past unfolds into the future. There is in creative freedom a gap or incompleteness filled by a spontaneous, searching act. A gap in things is sensed before the creative intervention, but it is more dramatically exposed retrospectively, as it were, after the creative innovation has been consolidated. This involves the present acting upon a past pressing toward it rather than merely obeying its pressure. In one study of creativity by jazz musicians, neuroscientists at Johns Hopkins found that the dorsolateral prefrontal cortex, the part of the brain involved in inhibition, slowed down when improvisation was under way, while activity in the medial prefrontal cortex became more intense. This latter area is linked to improvisational activity. The door was thus open for improvisation to flow through the performer into the collective performance, being neither a product of pre-formed agency nor a simple effect of prior determinants. You shut your eyes and let it become, as we do too when we relax to allow a new thought, tactic, or concept to emerge after a period of intense engagement with a problem at hand. The researcher at Hopkins is both a neuroscientist and a jazz musi-cian.[24] When we participate in a creative initiative and when we respond to a creative initiative from elsewhere that jostles received assumptions, *we both change the world and become otherwise than ourselves to a large or small degree.* That is the creative potential lodged between the open logic of identity and the evolution of circumstances with which it is entangled. A creative act, even though it may backfire, is an uncanny power that helps to bind us to the vitality of existence itself. It ties together vitality and the sweetness of existence, amid the risks that accompany the former and the deadness that would accompany the loss of the latter. Freedom: to be and to become otherwise than we are.

I suspect that the traditions of negative freedom, positive freedom, individualism, collectivism, holism, communitarianism, neoliberalism, Keynesianism, and Marxism are all pressed to shift to varying degrees to the extent that they come to terms *robustly* with the bumpy interdepen-dence between vitality and those bouts of real creativity distributed across venues of existence. The gift and risk of freedom as conditioned creativity.

Attention to the gift and risk of freedom may also involve attributing dif-ferential degrees of conditioned creativity to some nonhuman forces with which we are entangled, including bacteria and hormones acting within us and larger forces acting upon us. Attention to the uncanny element of cre-ativity in freedom is part of the process by which we transport kernels of insight in Hayek's theory into several domains from which he tried to ex-punge or marginalize them. It is important to do so: to support the expan-sion of freedom into domains beyond the comfort zone of Hayek and to develop a more robust sense of the sporadic element of spontaneity in free-dom. Perhaps we must also work upon ourselves today by creative means to cultivate a positive austerity of material desire. Hayek would not love that combination, but the rocky trajectory of economic history between 1970 and today suggests that he would be under immense pressure to come to terms with it.

The danger of "serfdom" today, you might say, is the emergence of a regime in which a few corporate overlords monopolize creativity to sustain a bankrupt way of life; in which military, prison, and security budgets are increased significantly to cling to American hegemony in a world unfavorable to it; in which the element of creativity is squeezed out of work life for many citizens; in which the ideology of freedom is winnowed to a set of consumer choices between preset options; and in which compensatory drives to extremism in secular dogmatism and religious faith intensify.

Moderate neoliberalism cannot sustain itself under these circumstances. Its erstwhile proponents are today pressed either to allow a new priority to course through them or to give themselves to an extremism many have heretofore hesitated to accept.

But is there not also a tension in the positive account pursued here? Yes. If you embrace both an ethos of responsibility encoded into multiple interacting practices and the creative element in freedom, you have introduced a tension between these two values. Any theory that acknowledges a plurality of values will embody some such tension. And any that acknowledges only one value, as radical neoliberals tend to do in one way and holists in another, is not worth its salt. The question is how to negotiate the tension.

Perhaps the best hope is to keep one eye on each of these values. We keep the door open to creativity in the practices of art, citizen movements, entrepreneurial innovations, court interpretations, sports activity, scientific experiments, religious movements, consumption choices, state modes of regulation, and the like as we also commit ourselves to debate the quality of these innovations situationally with one eye on their probable effects upon the interim future. That is one reason the elements of care for the world and reflexivity are so important to a culture that prizes the element of creativity. There is no guarantee we will always get the balance right, particularly in a world that is periodically jolted by surprises. But at least we will have committed ourselves to pay due attention to the several elements in play, keeping in mind that both the element of creativity and participating with dignity in a larger system help to make life worth living.

second interlude :: modes of self-organization

One theme of this book is that the planet, and indeed the cosmos, is replete with self-organizing, spatiotemporal systems flowing at different speeds, levels of sophistication, and degrees of self-sustaining power. These impersonal systems are open to some degree and never in perfect equilibrium; they interact, with each having a degree of entanglement with several others. They interact in two senses of the word: each impinges upon others, and some may become partially infused into others, as when a virus becomes absorbed into a human genetic pattern or free DNA enters a nonnucleated bacterium and the response of the latter creates a nucleated bacterium. That process is called *symbiogenesis* and very early it helped to set the stage for species evolution. The biosphere itself is an open, thermodynamic system, driving heat into space and contributing to the conditions of life on Earth. Such a perspective does not deny self-organizing power to economic markets. It does, however, suggest that these systems are much more fragile, interdependent, and volatile than their fervent supporters imagine, partly because they are closely involved with other self-organizing systems operating at various scales and tempos.

But what is a self-organizing system? Hurricanes, organisms, the Earth's biosphere, species evolution, and economic markets have all been construed as modes of self-organization. Let's start with a simple example.

The Millennium Bridge, crossing the Thames River in London near the Tate Modern Museum, is designed for walkers alone. It was built to be flexible and flow with the wind, reducing the typical rigidity of bridges so the walkers could sensitively respond to the elements. I walked across it a few times before it was redesigned, and I enjoyed the experience. But a problem arose, from the vantage point of the human designers and users. The bridge would rock comfortably back and forth in a pleasant rhythm on days when the wind was mild. The walkers would then unconsciously adjust their rhythm to the swaying of the bridge. Not only that, but each walker would also unconsciously adjust his or her rhythm to that of other walkers. Over a short time, a process of self-amplification would set in, with the bridge and walkers responding to each other until the swaying became intense and dangerous, threatening to make the bridge collapse. The bridge was thus closed for repairs a few years ago, and its capacity to sway was dampened considerably. We can now walk across it again, but it no longer captures something of the experience that walking across a rope bridge over a cavern in Peru may provide.[1]

This is a simple self-organizing system. No individual commands the bridge or the walkers to amplify its vibrations. There is no collective decision to do so either. The result emerges from the interplay between two self-organizing systems: the emergent system of walkers unconsciously adjusting to each other and the amplification of the swaying capacity built into the bridge. Note that the humans involved do not consciously plan to adjust their rhythms to one another and to the bridge. But there is an element of what I will call *teleodynamism* in their responses, as they tacitly and reciprocally adjust and readjust their gaits *in order to* reduce impediments to walking in a relatively smooth, unconstrained way. One of the things that makes this self-organizing system simple is that the constraints—the construction of the bridge and its intended uses—are built into it from the outside. There are other examples in which the constraints themselves are self-organized to a considerable degree. One thing that makes the example pertinent to markets as self-organizing systems is that the dampening of the destructive elements in that latter dynamic also requires self-reflective intervention by the human users of the system. You can call the latter a self-conscious regulation of the system needed when its self-organization creates dangerous or exploitive results.

:: :: ::

Hurricanes are self-organizing systems that construct their own boundaries and constraints to a considerable degree. They become highly self-amplifying and yet do not sustain themselves for long. How do they work? Roughly, at least as I understand it, in an ocean with high temperature the warm, moist air is drawn upward. The warm air reaches lower temperatures in the upper atmosphere, creating a temperature gradient. "Air sucked into the hurricane at the sea surface seeks a free vent at its top. . . . Expansion, heat from condensation, cooling by influence of cold water and space, evaporation and even the weight of the air in the rising air columns conspire to control the fate of the hurricane. And these systems are self-reinforcing." Now "moving air particles, once independent, coalesce in the organized storm. . . . The hurricane, now a system—not just a set of molecules in equilibrium—tends to homogenize surrounding temperatures and pressures."[2]

A hurricane, once its boundaries self-organize, resists the tendency to entropy for a while, eventually to collapse into a state in which the order of the molecules is more random. The ocean conveyor system, which issues in the Gulf Stream warming Europe and the eastern seaboard of North America, also seems to be self-organizing in this sense. There is evidence that it is now slowing down, as the warming water near Greenland decreases the rate at which cold water plunges to the bottom of the sea to allow the upper water to flow in one direction and the lower water to flow in the other in a way that sustains the world circuit. All hell will break loose if this trend continues. Much more could be said about hurricanes and the ocean conveyor system. But the point I want to underline is that both are thermodynamic, self-organizing systems. They lack, or at most exhibit to a bare minimum, teleodynamic capacities.

:: :: ::

As Kant sensed (see chapter 3) and complexity theorists in biology such as Stuart Kauffman and Terrence Deacon now support with experimental evidence, even a simple organism, in its sensitive exchanges with its environment, is a more complex self-organizing system than a hurricane. If there are powerful tendencies in the universe for organized systems to devolve into states of entropy, as a hurricane does after its moment of glory, an organism defers and resists these tendencies actively. And the process of species evolution does so for innumerable centuries.

A simple organism, say a bacterium in imperfect equilibrium, depends upon thermodynamic processes that would in themselves falter rather soon. But it converts some of those energies into "work" by which it draws selective sustenance from the world it helps to define and metabolizes that sustenance into a durable system with boundary and function maintaining capacities. As it contributes to the construction and maintenance of its own boundaries, it acquires simple capacities to *pursue* goals. A tick, for example, has simple powers to perceive heat and movement. It can sense heat and butyric acid, too. When a warm animal emanating that acid walks beneath its perch in a tree after it has remained motionless for up to eighteen years, the tick perceives the movement and heat and drops down upon the animal, which now serves as its host. It does not aim to maintain itself, but it does *respond* to its perception of the acid, and the aim it pursues plays into the processes of self-maintenance that mark it. And, of course, its simple perceptual and ambient skills could foster disaster. Its limited perceptual capacity could make it ignore poison that has been rubbed onto the skin of a mammal. A mishap for the tick.[3]

An organism consists in part of an intercoded set of simple perceptual and intentional systems, with some components having the capacity to pursue an end, change direction, and respond energetically to shifts in the environment. A paramecium, for instance, can head toward glucose and shift direction to do so if needed. And a variety of microbes and hormones in the human body both contribute to the shape of its being and play a role in its evolution. For example, during a moment of excitement in sporting, gambling, sexual, or investment activity, there may be a surge of testosterone in men, and adrenaline and cortisol may increase just enough to accelerate the flow of dopamine. The excitement increases the tendency to take risks. If, however, the increase of adrenaline and cortisol is too great, stress will result. All of these are what Jane Bennett and Bruno Latour would call "actants," microforces with variations and powers that flow into the brain's higher decision-making areas to help accelerate, decelerate, intensify, or dampen complex decisions.[4]

Bonnie Bassler has shown how bacteria in the human body wait until they have accumulated enough numbers to launch a collective attack on this or that part of the body. The process of intercommunication is called "quorum sensing."[5] And according to Dorion Sagan, viral proteins "have been hijacked and integrated into mammal reproductive tissues, immune systems and brains." As he says, "Human gut *microbiota* are not simply hangers-on but influence the timing of maturation of our intestinal cells, our internal nutrient supplies and distribution, our blood vessel growth, our immune systems, and the levels of cholesterol and other lipids in our blood. They also influence human mood."[6] There is evidence that *Toxoplasma gondii*, often entering the human body through contact with cats, both infects large numbers of humans and influences their moods by altering levels of dopamine. Our sexual drives change through interventions from these entries with simple end-seeking powers. These are active microagents, irreducible to simple processes of efficient causality. That is, there are multiple, simple end-pursuing activities within organisms—including the inhuman within the human—as well as the global ends an organism pursues as a collective assemblage. It seems reasonable to say that an organism's end-pursuing capacities often help to preserve it, but they also exceed those functions. The relative simplicity of an organism's searching mechanisms can mean that unexpected shifts in the environment periodically open it, when it does not collapse, to evolutionary development it does not itself intend.

While an increasing number of scientists now focus on *thermodynamic* processes in "far from equilibrium systems," the biologist and neuroscientist Terrence Deacon, perhaps impressed with the kind of evidence noted above, also talks about *teleodynamic* processes in both human life and, to varying degrees, nonhuman organisms. We humans engage in such activity all the time. "Teleodynamic work is what we must engage in when trying to make sense of an unclear explanation. . . . And it characterizes what is difficult about creative thought processes."[7] If you and I, say, are searching for a new settlement in a setting that is conflictual and cloudy, the exchanges between us may take the shape of a teleodynamic search. The result of that search is not always implicit in the beginning; it often involves a creative element that emerges from these movements back and forth in a way that is not entirely reducible to such precedents. A similar process is often at work *within* the self as a constellation of teleo-drives below conscious awareness adjust to one another in a changed setting, allowing a new idea, thought, tactic, or awareness to bubble up into action or to set the stage for further reflection.

According to Deacon, such processes are at work, though to an unsophisticated degree, in biological evolution: "Organisms are spontaneously emergent systems that can be said to act on their own behalf (although acting and selfhood must be understood in a minimal and generic sense)." What's more, "organisms are both components and products of the evolutionary dynamic."[8] Persistently incomplete in themselves, and periodically facing shifting internal and external environments, they unconsciously search and strive beyond the scope of their current organization without having a precise end initially in sight.[9] Indeed "autogens," situated somewhere between life and nonlife and between teleodynamic and thermodynamic processes, seem to have set preconditions for the emergence of life.

When a genetic mutation occurs—sometimes generated by the effects of cosmic rays on the gene pool—much of it is received as noise by the organism. But a simple self-searching process may occur within this or that aspect of the embryo as it unfolds, eventually enabling it to respond to aspects of the mutation as a new "signal." This is approximately what Deleuze means, I think, by the "involutionary" aspect of evolution. It means that organic evolution typically involves the following: mutation, teleosearches that selectively convert the noise of mutation into signs, further self-organization of these signs into new dimensions of the organism, and natural selection, very broadly defined, of some of the new formations. Deacon emphasizes the difference between his identification of teleosearches within organisms that contribute to evolution and his corollary assumption of the absence of an overall *telos* within the long evolutionary process itself: "So, although the evolutionary process can further the pragmatic convergence between interpreted content and extrinsic reference, information is not in any sense available *to* evolution, only to the organisms that are its products. Evolution generates the capacity to interpret something as information. This capacity is intrinsic to a self-perpetuating, far from equilibrium system, which depends on its environment and does work to modify that environment in a way that reinforces its persistence."[10]

A mutation, then, is only part of what is involved in organic evolution, and even it can proceed through, say, cosmic rays, viral infections of genetic tissue, or sexual exchange. Another component is the *teleodynamic element* that engenders a creative process of self-organization in response to a mutation that has introduced a new element of instability into the system. That teleodynamic process may promote a dead end or contribute, inadvertently, as it were, to the evolution of the organism. So species evolution, on Deacon's reading, is neither pulled by a final purpose nor reducible mostly to chance, nor simply explicable as a mechanistic process. Successful evolution involves mutation, teleodynamic activity that translates some aspects of the mutation into received signs, and creative self-organization by which the unfolding organism adapts to the sign. Only now does the issue of the organism's adaptability to a changing external environment come into play. And that adaptation is not entirely reducible to the issue of survival.

Deacon's theory of evolution is designed to fill a gap in the reductionist, genocentric readings of neo-Darwinism rather than to summarize an account that is already confirmed. But that situation holds true for neo-Darwinism too, since it has difficulty explaining *how* mutations become converted into new organic developments before selection sets in. And because, too, it tends to limit the process of selection to the issue of survival. If you find plausible Deacon's account of teleodynamics and the modes of self-organization it makes possible, as I do, a set of questions still remains: How did the transition from nonlife to life occur? That is, how did the transition from the simplest processes of thermodynamic self-organization unfold into the teleodynamic and more intensive self-organizing powers of the complex living systems we call organisms? Does it make sense to speak of vague searches within organisms without reference to consciousness, as this biological theory does? To what extent is the history of species evolution bound up with intersections between shifts in the environment, drives to persistence, and learning processes growing out of organic searching mechanisms amid incompleteness? Do other systems besides organisms, the biosphere, and ecosystems exhibit self-organizing capacities with enough power to defer the tendency to entropy apparently folded into the universe?

To Deacon, "information" involves a dicey exchange between (sometimes new) cloudy signs and (sometimes emerging) capacities of an organism to receive and absorb part of that noise as a sign. He thus rejects a notion of information that reduces it to a code resulting in a passive mode of replication. Evan Thompson goes further and rejects the metaphor of "information" altogether because of the crude images of code and replication it conveys: "The causal chain between DNA sequences and phenotypic characteristics is too indirect, complex, and multifaceted for there to be any robust, one to one relationship between them."[11] And Alicia Juarrero suggests that once you take seriously the idea of a creative element within the evolutionary process, you also need to appreciate how the simple demands of experimental replication in classical science need to be modified. It now becomes more dicey both to identify the initial conditions in two different experiments as the same and to ascertain whether (what Deacon calls) the uncertain element of the teleosearch will issue in the same outcome twice.[12]

Perhaps one more statement by Deacon will focus our attention on the role of self-organization within organic evolution:

> Because information generating processes emerge in systems constituted by a pragmatic selection history, the ground of the correspondence between information and context is determined negatively, so to speak. . . . No specific correspondence is embodied with full precision. . . . With functional correspondence underdetermined, novel functions can arise de novo in unprecedented contexts, and incidental properties of the sign or signal may come serendipitously to serve emergent functions. . . . This is the basis for the evolution of a new function, but it is also why information is always potentially fallible.[13]

:: :: ::

If simple organisms display teleodynamic, self-organizing capacities, some of which maintain an organism, some of which promote evolution, and others of which create dead ends, we might expect that such processes would be at least as complex in human cultural life. We do not now discuss the question of what difference it makes to the character of human culture that a variety of nonhuman systems with which humanity interacts also possess some degree of self-organizational and evolutionary power; that issue was posed in chapter 1. We also bypass the important topic of how self-organizing capital markets now turn various organisms into pure commodities, as happens with chickens, pigs, and cows in the current market. Let us focus now on a teleodynamic market process during one tipping point in the American political economy, one that intensifies a dimension of the class system already there. The example shows how you can sustain the idea of self-organization in markets without embracing the neoliberal drive to treat them as regularly and uniquely rational.

Participants in a stratified financial market system pursue ends, though they vary significantly in the intensity with which those ends are pursued and the extent to which one set of ends is qualified or overridden by others. The owners in the system seek profits as they read and assess general market tendencies. The system of assessment provides feedback to them in the form of prices, endowing the financial market with some degree of self-organizing power. And sometimes a new disruption sets a teleosearch into motion. There are therefore periods of stability, bubble, and bust, as buyers and sellers anticipate trends, respond to shifts in the pricing system, and make gambles based upon projections into the cloudiness of the future.

A series of "preadaptations" enables such a market to organize and amplify itself, without, however, determining in advance exactly how it will do so. What is a preadaptation in one sense is a constraint in another: it enables and limits current modes of action, and it provides a platform from which unexpected shifts might promote the evolution of the system under shifting circumstances, as the nose in Pangloss's image of the best of all possible worlds provided a preadaptation to the use of glasses unknown to nosy humans for innumerable centuries before glasses were invented.[14] The human nose, given its inability to smell carcinogens or to detect cancer at an early stage, also poses a severe constraint on human life during the late modern era. Dogs exceed us in this respect.

In this example the constraints and preadaptations in play include a capitalist economy of private ownership, contractual labor, the priority of the commodity form, a state focused on military and punitive assignments, a preset history of racial, gender, and ethnic discriminations, and temptations among white working-class males to protect a fragile sense of identity by distinguishing themselves more sharply from other such constituencies. There is racial division and inequality in the preadaptations, but neoliberalism itself is neither yet a dominant ideology nor embedded deeply in institutional practice. Moreover inequality is not as sharp as it later becomes, when a large constituency defined as "middle class" shrinks in size and the distance between the top and bottom rungs inclines more steeply.

The concern here is to identify some self-organizing shifts in financial institutions, the state, the media, and ideological practices that coalesce to pull these preliminary conditions in a specific direction. Under these conditions, self-organizing tendencies can emerge to exacerbate inequality and to encourage consolidation of a neoliberal public philosophy, though none of these actual outcomes is *determined* by the system as a billiard ball is determined to drop into the hole when hit at the correct angle and speed by a cue ball in a bounded system with fixed constraints. We are not, of course, charting the entire class system but the intensification of some class dimensions *within* a subclass of participants who display at least some capacity to save and/or invest in capital markets, even though these processes do carry ramifications for the larger class system too.

Here are a few pertinent differences within the investment and savings class, broadly defined, that turn out retrospectively to have functioned as preadaptations for the series of ugly changes we are charting: some participants base their income primarily on low-taxed investment returns and others on higher taxed labor; some are closely involved with the financial market on a daily basis, while others are so more sporadically or through the medium of retirement funds; some investors use high-speed methods to make investments, while others are limited to slower processes; some have access to staffs and inside information, while others lack both; some can draw upon disproportionate gains they have made to lobby the state to minimize regulation of financial markets, while others have fewer gains and less access; some can lobby the state to internalize retirement and medical care systems into the market, while others depend upon the stability of those very systems; some have regular access to the media to help shape public interpretations of how markets work, while others do not; some can fund think tanks to propel a favorable vision of the world, while others cannot; some have impressive buffers in the shape of savings and favorable bankruptcy laws to ride out market downturns, while others do not.

There are also a few countervailing pressures at work. There are some retirement funds, financial advising teams, union organizations, activist social movements, and media watchdogs that resist these trends, as long as they do not become sucked into the ongoing dynamic. It turns out, for instance, that a disproportionate number of whistleblowers in financial firms have been women. But to the extent those counterpressures become neutralized, the general drift of the microprocesses is to fold advantages in each of the above zones into the others. The more such differences accumulate, the more the financial market system becomes a self-organizing system that extends the preliminary system of class difference. Intensely involved, high-speed, insider-lobbying, ideologically active, media-savvy, high-capital types increasingly cluster at the top of a progressively rarefied wealth and income hierarchy. At the same time participation in the savings and financial system becomes more indispensable to those at the middle and lower middle levels of that hierarchy, as, for instance, more private employee retirement pensions are translated into retirement investment funds and middle- and lower-wage incomes stagnate. Those on the lower levels find themselves more pressed to participate in the unfolding system as they increasingly set the financial base for speculation by a high-roller, investment class.

As the system evolves, many at the top of the financial hierarchy acquire access to even higher speed computers. These computers can be programmed to make an apparent bid in a millisecond, check the market response to that bid automatically, and then withdraw it and buy at a more favorable price than otherwise. This connects them to an emerging hedge market system, introduced by high-speed investors to play against the trend of the market. The situation is also volatile. High-speed investors, for instance, are required to make rapid judgments about the probable stability of this or that regime, without access to close, situational judgment. If the situation breaks the wrong way, the whole thing could blow up.

Situational judgment is often fraught with uncertainty, in two senses of that word. Sometimes there are stable factors in play that escape the gaze of investors, as when tectonic plates rubbing together offshore were missed by the parishioners in Lisbon or ignored by investors in Japanese nuclear power. Sometimes there are vague murmurings in this or that section of a populace under the control of a harsh regime, hardly noticed by insiders or outsiders. This *noise* could erupt into a new social movement that changes expectations radically. The murmurings often express an *incipience* that could actually break in more than one way rather than merely an *implicit* process that either finds expression or is suppressed. When incipience is in play, a teleodynamic process is underway.

The difference between the first and second instance of situational judgment is roughly that between one that is *epistemic—in which the participants* are screened from aspects of the process by conceptual, observational, or experimental limitations—and another that is *ontological*, rooted in a world replete with moments of real uncertainty and conditioned creativity. Both can come into play. Let us call the latter a situation containing *noise* that is worked upon teleodynamically. It rises to significance periodically, as when teleodynamic microbe shifts unconsciously seed the transduction of a flu virus from birds to humans, or when a cloudy process of thinking and experimentation issues in a new invention that opens up energy sources not anticipated before, or when a new financial instrument emerges out of the mist of uncertainty, or when a new social movement arises out of a series of disruptions, experiments, and charismatic leadership. The noise and teleodynamism that Deacon attends to in biological evolution has numerous and more complex counterparts in and around financial markets. High-speed investing amplifies noise.

We are beginning to delineate how self-organization in markets can periodically be both real and destructive. In our example, the initial differences within the financial market have now become exacerbated. While you—say, a low-level, slow-moving individual or institutional investor—follow the general investment trend, the top stratum often bets against it at high speeds you cannot match, making it now even more in their interest for that trend to break. Moreover, since they make a lot of money from countercyclical trading and because they have buffers available, they become more intensely inclined, first, to press the state to reduce the deposit amounts it requires when banks make investment loans to them; second, to eliminate the distinction between investment banks and commercial banks; third, to reduce regulation of investment markets; and fourth, to support elimination of restriction amounts on political campaign contributions.

As this process unfolds, replete as it is with coalescing microsearches between intersecting parties, a variety of participants become more susceptible to neoliberal theory. Sure, such an ideology preceded the self-organization dynamic outlined schematically above. But it was initially confined to a small minority of economists and participants. Now more constituencies become *intensely* attracted to it, some because it redeems the idea of a positive connection between their actual role performances and the apparent welfare of the system, others because they aspire to reach higher levels of the income system, others because the evangelical faith in which they participate is now drawn to the idea that Divine Providence is uniquely operative in unregulated markets, others because of their daily access to TV financial news saturated with such an ideology, others because they have a generic need to be optimistic about the collective future and the consolidation of that ideology speaks to that need, and many for several of these reasons. Upper-, middle-, and working-class white males with macho tendencies are particularly attracted to such an ideology, at least as long as a major crisis is avoided. If such a crisis does emerge they might then teeter between an attraction to collectivist, egalitarian solutions or to fascism.

This array of attractions, again, is not entirely reducible to judgments of self-interest, which itself, recall, involves teleosearching activity to varying degrees in shifting situations. More profoundly, the attractions involve uncertain judgments of short-term self-interest in some cases and a hopeful mode of aspirational politics in others, joined to generic faith in the future supported by a stubborn desire to avoid thinking about potential storm clouds on the horizon. These teleoprobic tendencies, often invested with a bellicose spirituality, now become sublimated into a neoliberal ideology of the public good. The latter justifies an emerging set of role performances, limits posed by specific institutional intersections, defined interests, and existential aspirations. That SUV, you see, is *needed* to express masculinity in a market world in which masculinity is indispensable; those bank foreclosures *clear* markets for a more efficient economy; this derivatives system automatically *stabilizes* financial markets without invoking a cumbersome state; those wondrous powers of creativity are *concentrated* in entrepreneurial activities within impersonal markets; these deregulated banks *improve* the rationality of the impersonal market; the increase in inequality *allows* job creators to produce more jobs; and Fox News *discloses* the bankruptcy of liberal and socialist professors, climate change proponents, cumbersome government regulations, and "entitlement" programs for the poor and middle class.

It was not inevitable that proponents of the right edge of evangelicalism and neoliberalism would search out each other in this system over a short period of time, with each party eventually settling on a set of priorities and tactical silences that allowed it to consolidate connections to the other.[15] Now that such a reciprocal microsearch has crossed a tipping point, however, some elements of neoliberalism penetrate the right edge of the evangelical movement, and the ugliest aspects of evangelical spirituality (though not always its creed) slip into neoliberalism. For example, the previous intense evangelical opposition to gambling now recedes as it treats financial modes of gambling to be rational. And neoliberals, internalizing bellicosity on the right edge of evangelicalism, often become even more aggressive than before.

The teleodynamic ideology formation in play here does exceed the nonhuman organic processes of self-organization charted earlier, showing once again how *affinities* between processes in different domains do not amount to *identities*. The neoliberal ideology provides several functions: it reassures supporters that they are promoting the public good, blindly, as it were; it cuts off efforts to alter the hierarchy in which they participate; it plays to many working-class white males seeking to protect fragile conceptions of masculinity in a pluralizing world and an economy increasingly inhospitable to them; and it recruits a political class to take governmental action to extend the self-organizing class system now underway. It folds those functions into the teleopursuits of political activists, promoting feedback mechanisms that amplify the whole system. This is my way of saying what Hayek acknowledges, as we saw in chapter 2: a neoliberal economy requires the hegemony of a neoliberal ideology embedded in a variety of practices.

The self-organizing market has now evolved into a more extreme financial class system embedded in a set of teleo–role performances redeemed by a reflexive ideology that increasingly penetrates a variety of social practices. Those on its activist edge now become unhappy if people talk about a "class system," labeling that very phrase an expression of "class envy." "Job creators" talk in the media about their unhappiness in this respect. To them, the interplay between role performance and the way neoliberal ideology redeems the roles they play translates the appearance of a class system into a functional hierarchy that promises to lift all boats as it supports a high level of inequality and efficient growth.

:: :: ::

Whenever you chart a self-amplification process that has become consolidated there is a temptation to overlook or minimize potential forks and countervailing interventions that might have been pursued but were not. This is what makes retroactive explanation—the kind actually the most common in the human sciences—appear more closed than it can be in a world of multiple, open-ended, interacting systems, with several expressing teleodynamic capacities. For example, at an early moment in the above process, some creative advocates of new pluralizing movements might have displayed more *sensitivity* to emerging anxieties and hostilities apparent in sections of the white working and middle class. Creative interventions at the right moment might have pulled together the concerns of pluralization, job and retirement security, and a reduction of income equality. It might have drawn the new pluralizing movements, white workers, and labor unions closer together, as they had been before the explosion of those pluralizing movements in the 1960s and 1970s.[16] Similarly, Protestant, Catholic, and Jewish activists might have supported minority campaigns inside the evangelical tent against the consolidation of racial coding and neoliberal ties, amplifying in this way counterpossibilities already in play that would otherwise be overwhelmed. Such interventions might have cut off at the pass the surprising, creative link forged between neoliberalism and evangelicalism through the celebration of market self-regulated rationality by one party and the other's new faith in God's providential investment in markets. In a political economy in which processes of self-organization stimulate and dramatize some pluripotential strains simmering in the present and dampen others, the specific actuality that unfolds is not necessarily what it must have been. To imply otherwise is both to take real politics out of the equation and to fall prey to the academic hubris of "narratocracy," "explanatocracy," or both. Two ugly words for two ugly temptations in the academy to act as if change can be explained without reference to real, creative moments that exceed the conceits of closed explanation.[17] The creative alliance between neoliberalism and evangelicalism constitutes one of those simmering moments.

Once the amplification process reviewed here does become consolidated, it becomes a more difficult system to oppose politically. Its self-organizing and reflexive tendencies now form self-amplifying loops. It can be opposed, but opposition requires close public attention to the dangerous trajectory underway, to the role of the media in energizing the machine, to hidden ambiguities in the role performances of some constituencies on the edge of the movement, and to a growing self-awareness among young participants of the collective dangers the complex promotes.

While keeping its injuries in mind, let's also turn to some dangerous tendencies that arise from the evolving market, class system. This is how the insensitivity of financial ideologues to both *noise* within the financial system and the *self-organizing powers* of other systems with which markets are entangled becomes important. These latter processes can include untoward events such as a tsunami, a radical shift in the ocean conveyor system, rapid climate change, a military class that takes unilateral action; an economic breakdown by a major trading partner, a concerted military attack, nonstate terrorist action, a cross-country general strike to support a systemic response to climate change, an extreme religious movement, a crisis in energy supply, an internal political explosion in another state holding a high portion of the national debt of the state you inhabit, or an internal amplification process that threatens to blow the whole complex apart.

To redeem the numerous role performances entwined within it neoliberal ideology minimizes the potential impact of these other systems in its ideological presentations. Such blindness is not merely an "ideology" that people believe explicitly—though that is operative too. The ideology becomes embedded in institutional priorities of the state-economy machine, finding tacit expression in technologies of investment, computer programs of data collection and processing, the bundling of investment options, ingrained habits of consumption, an infrastructure of consumption that organizes consumption options, traditions of state involvement and inhibition, the market presumptions built into the jurisprudence of the Gang of Five on the Supreme Court, and the like. These practices, in turn, press neoliberalism to become identified with a large military, punitive, disciplinary state. Its most fervent advocates ignore, tolerate, or support an economy and foreign policy that depends upon oil in unstable countries, sensing that to head in a different direction would turn state regulation of the economy in directions they find objectionable. They resist thinking about the relation between neoliberalism, climate change, and new barriers to performance because that too would call for extensive shifts in state and market practices. They support or tolerate huge military expenditures that strain and distort the economy. If they encounter an increase in crime and tendencies by youths on the lower rungs of the class-race system to resist or disrupt the ongoing system, they are moved to support increases in state expenditures for crime control and intensive modes of corporate and state discipline of racially coded, urban constituencies. Thus as they become reflexive about how to protect their winnings, they both make others suffer more and set the stage for an urban upheaval that could be set off by a minor trigger.

Such an intersecting set of systems is apt to exacerbate dangerous possibilities unless and until other pressures emerge to challenge and redirect it. And yet its most active ideologues now pretend that the incorporation of everybody more fully into the practices of a neoliberal system through, for example, the marketization of pensions and Medicare, will reduce the collective risks to nil. That, for instance, was what Alan Greenspan thought before the 2008 crisis. And then, after a short period of self-criticism, he seems to have returned to such a view.[18]

This is a self-organizing, ideologically amplifying, class-extending market system that is more a collective emergent than a planned outcome, at least during its early stage of transition. Many increasingly become committed to it because of their positions in its system of roles and their attractions to divine, market, and racial creeds that *redeem* those roles. Others become resigned to it because any other ideology seems too far removed from the role dictates in which they are enclosed, a process that underlines the element of self-organization woven into the interplay between ideology and role performance. The new complex, however, is also vulnerable to collapse because of intersections between its internal fragility and other self-organizing force fields with which it is closely imbricated.

:: :: ::

This planet, arguably, would not have generated a rich biosphere, life, the evolution of complex organisms, or the emergence of humanity without an evolving cosmos composed of a plethora of interacting, self-organizing systems with differential powers of persistence and metamorphosis. But the tendency of American neoliberalism, first, to pretend that markets are the only important systems in the world with self-organizing power, second, to equate self-organization in markets with impersonal rationality, third, to read the extension of class inequality and discipline as the artifact of a rational market system, and fourth, to remain blind or inured to the sources of suffering, unevenly distributed vulnerabilities, and fragility in the system celebrated, sets a potentially tragic dynamic into motion. Would it take a late modern Sophocles to dramatize such a multiplicitous dynamic and the dangers it spawns? He, at any rate, was exceptionally sensitive to periodic, volatile intersections between nonhuman systems, mythic screens, the hubris of rulers, the volatility of friendly critics, untimely events, fecund moments when a possible turn was not taken, and disastrous results. Indeed today we need late modern political economists with Sophoclean insights and sensibilities, not to read the economy through the rubric of a preordained fate but to dramatize fragilities and positive potentialities folded into the teleodynamics of the current regime.

CHAPTER 3 :: shock therapy, dramatization,
and practical wisdom

Understanding, hypothetical or instrumental reason, speculative reason,
practical reason, aesthetic judgment, teleological reason. The Kantian list is
familiar. Its divisions and priorities are culturally entrenched, even among
many who do not confess Kantianism. Each office is supported and sustained by the others and by arguments that specify it once the divisions
have been delineated. What if you seek to crack that frame in order to create space for an alternative? Why would one want to do that? How would
you proceed? The *why* question is difficult to answer in advance, since it
consists of suspicions and hopes that must be redeemed through positive
alternatives as well as critique. Suffice it to say that I suspect that Kantian
and neo-Kantian impulses function to inhibit creative experiments in
thought and practice, to squeeze explanatory projects into too narrow a

compass, to define instrumental reason too sharply, to obscure a needed dimension of ethical life, to cover conditional elements in aesthetic judgment, to deflate the independent powers and nonprovidential character of nonhuman systems, to express an existential anxiety that needs to be challenged, to demand an unrealistic image of time, to underplay the extent to which the cosmos in which we are set is filled with volatile tendencies that threaten the welfare of the human estate, and to make it more difficult than otherwise to pull presumptive care for the diversity of life and the fecundity of earth to the forefront of practice. I also admire the system because of the positive openings its rigorous approach creates before squeezing too many down, the issues it helps to define, and the discernible care for this world that circulates through it. My goal is not to *defeat* either Kantianism or neo-Kantianism; it is to enhance the appreciation in each of its own *contestability* amid the deep plurality of life; it is also to stretch its appreciation of the *fragility of things* today for the human estate.

How to proceed? My strategy is to move on two fronts. On one front you compress the arguments in support of Kantian entrenchments, doing so to identify flashpoints at which key existential investments enter the complex, sometimes unconsciously and sometimes as a juncture treated by the theorist as an undeniable starting point of everyday experience. On the other front you engage in shock therapy to *dramatize* those same flashpoints differently, doing so at first through an encounter with a very different cultural setting in which experience and experiment are organized. The idea is not to embrace everything in those little shocks but to allow them to open a door to creative thinking. This twofold movement is approximately what I mean by a genealogy of reason. The focus in this chapter is on practical reason, the mode that Kant takes both to govern morality and to provide the lynchpin of reason itself in the larger sense. The idea is to confront the intercoded Kantian system of morality with an alternative ethicopolitical vision that is apt to be misunderstood and misrepresented until more people face and interrogate the little Kant that already circulates within them. It is a powerful system on its own terms, and even more so when compared only to its own representations of alternative traditions. We begin with a light dose of shock therapy.

Daughters of Zeus, I greet you: add passion to my song, and tell of the sacred race of gods who are forever, descended from Earth and starry Sky, from dark Night and from salty Sea. . . . Tell how in the beginning the gods and the earth came into being, as the rivers, the limitless sea with its raging surges, the shining stars, and broad sky above. . . .

The great Cronus, the cunning trickster, took courage and answered his good mother . . . : "Mother I am willing to undertake . . . your plan." . . . Then from his ambush his son reached out with his left hand and with his right took the huge sickle . . . and quickly sheared the organs from his own father and threw them away, backward over his shoulder.

Rhea submitted to the embraces of Cronus and bore him children with a glorious destiny: Hestia, Demeter . . . , Hera, Hades . . . and Zeus the lord of wisdom . . . , whose thunder makes the earth tremble.

She [Earth] took him [Zeus, the youngest son of Cronus] and hid him in an inaccessible cave, deep in the bowels of the holy earth. Then she wrapped a huge stone in baby blankets and handed it to the royal son of Sky [Cronus] who was king of the gods. He took the stone and swallowed it into his belly. He did not know that a stone had replaced his son.

When the Olympian gods had brought their struggle to an end and had vindicated their rights against the Titans, Mother Earth advised them to invite Zeus . . . to be king and lord over the gods. . . . Zeus' first consort was Metis [Wisdom]. . . . But when she was about to give birth to bright eyed Athena, he deceived her with specious work . . . and trapped her and kept her in his belly . . . so that the kingship would not pass from Zeus to another of the gods.

Lastly Zeus took Hera [his sister] as his wife to bear him children. . . . Likewise Semele, Cadmus' daughter, lay with him in love and became the mother of a son with a glorious destiny—Dionysus the giver of joy. She was mortal when she bore her immortal son; now they are both immortal.[1]

What a world! Several points differentiate it from the mythic and spiritual determinations that infiltrate Kantian and neo-Kantian philosophies. First, the gods may live forever, but they defeat each other periodically;

they also fornicate with humans rather often. Second, the idea of cause in that world is not reducible to efficient causality. Sex, love, sensuality, and deceit provide better metaphors with which to think causality than that of human-designed mechanisms from which the idea of efficient cause is drawn, or even that of a classic idea of an organism in which each of the parts is determined by the whole in which it is set. Absorbing, swallowing, intermingling, digesting, and strengthening are all modes in which defeat, transformation, and transfiguration occur in this Greek world. Third, the gods are multiple and not entirely subsumed under a single cosmic principle or historical trajectory, either through direct knowledge or through "postulates" they cannot avoid making. Fourth, the modes of interplay between gods or forces and humans are also multiple, with some humans becoming gods. And—as the tragic playwrights who later work creatively upon the *Theogony* emphasize—such forces both enter into human passions and operate upon events from the outside to support a sweet victory or tragic result. Fifth, the late introduction of Dionysus into the divine mix both points to an element of wildness in nature-culture imbrications and appreciates the sweetness of life in such a world. This does not mean that everything is always in flux but that the element of wildness *periodically* disrupts this or that pattern of regularity. Dionysus, himself the result of an illicit crossing between a human and a god, speaks to a Greek readiness to join together the element of wildness and that of joy in the human condition.

If you combine these five points you can see that the cosmos to which Hesiod is profoundly attached is neither deeply providential nor receptive to consummate human knowledge and mastery, even if it does become a bit more tidy with the Olympians. It thus did not take all that much for Sophocles to transfigure this myth into a tragic vision, as Athens confronted its own conflicts between old and new gods. Conflicts, surprising turns, and unexpected events periodically punctuate the regularities of civil life, steady tradition, and ethical precept, creating new issues for decision and judgment. The result is not "chaos," as some devotees of a straitjacket image of order love to say whenever they encounter a vision identifying a whiff of volatility in the very essence of order; rather the world consists of durable periods of relative order punctuated by periods of disruption and significant change in this or that zone, due in part to conjunctions between conflicting human agencies and between them and nonhuman forces.

I said "gods or forces." As Jeanne Pierre Vernant has shown, Ionian philosophers such as Anaximander and Democritus did not have to work that hard to translate these intermingling and contending gods into multiple forces. Hesiod may have already opened that window a crack with his notions of primordial Earth, Sky, Cronus, and so on. "The fundamental concepts that the construction of Ionian philosophy is based on—the separation from a primordial unity, the constant struggle and union of opposites, and an eternal cycle of change—reveal the ground of mythical thought in which Ionian cosmology is rooted. The philosophers did not have to invent a system to explain the world; they found one ready made."[2] These latter ideas may also surface as minor themes in Sophocles, as when Jocasta explains to Oedipus about the active role chance plays in life and the cosmos, before he, the chorus, and (most of?) the audience interpret their tragic fate as anchored in the hostility of the gods.

What would practical reason, as the rules and dispositions appropriate to moral life, look like if our world had evolved from this one rather than taking a detour through two thousand years of Christianity? What about instrumental reason? There is no reliable answer to these questions, so such a counterfactual will seem badly posed to some. Nonetheless I pursue it. A genealogy of the present pursues such counterfactuals to expose and disturb unconscious presumptions, feelings, and insistences that infuse contemporary argument and judgment.

With that caveat we can suggest, first, that the Kantian idea of the necessary character of human understanding would be disrupted, since the idea of blind, efficient cause is too simple and schematic to grasp the interplay, infusions, and transfigurations that constitute relations between gods, humans, and nature in the *Theogony*. As Michel Serres has shown in his attempt to "modernize" early Greek notions of science developed after the *Theogony*, the ideas of fluids and flows were central to them, while those of solids and mechanics have been given much more priority by moderns, at least until recently.[3]

Second, the idea of practical reason, which can be protected only by embracing a corollary set of postulates about freedom, a salvational God, and the necessary, subjective sense of a design of being that must remain mysterious to us, would now devolve into a quest to inculcate *wisdom* into everyday affairs in an interconnected world neither intrinsically designed for human benefit nor susceptible to consummate mastery, nor replete with apodictic starting points of experience from which the benign Kantian postulates of reason are generated.

Cultivation of the right kind of character also becomes a matter of prime importance, partly because there is no characterless moral subject available in this world that issues universal moral laws and partly because, on such a cosmological account, *the larger world is not postulated to be highly predisposed to humanity in the last instance.* Here I concur with Bernard Williams in his review of similarities between the classic Greek tragic vision and ideas operative in some circles of modern life that are obscured by dominant philosophical accounts of morality, though I do think he downplays the importance of appreciating the sweetness of life in the Greek world.[4] The upshot of these reflections for the cultivation of character has a corollary for the negotiation of a generous cultural ethos. For this orientation sees individuality as emerging out of a larger intersubjective culture rather than the other way around. That too would now emerge as crucial to the quality of public life.

Instrumental reason would be touched too. In the most stark version of the Kantian tradition, a version, as we shall see, that Kant himself qualified and refined in the Third Critique, instrumental reason is demarcated in sharp contrast to the purity of practical reason and the disinterestedness of aesthetic judgment. It is calculative action guided by a set of "sensuous" interests not contained by supersensible moral considerations. But if character is critical to practical wisdom in the worlds of Hesiod and Sophocles, it would also make an internal difference to definitions and pursuits of self-interest as you pursue power, income, sexual liaisons, reputation, and self-security. The infusion of practical reason with elements of sensuous character and our close attention to the fragility of things in a nonprovidential world would thus combine to suggest a reformulation of Kantian, Habermasian, and neoliberal notions of *instrumental* reason as well. In this world, character, instrumentality, and ethos are interwoven. When you calculate your interest and the means to it, elements of habit, character, and tradition invested in you slide into the calculus, tacitly drawing it along some tracks rather than others. And some of the elements of character that now enter practical reason also infuse instrumental reason, blurring the sharp boundaries between them adumbrated in Kantian philosophy. Kant himself skates rather close to such a perspective, when he begins to talk about how important it is to practice gymnastics of the self to prime the bodily sensibility to receive the dictates of the moral law. But what he may see less clearly is how this very qualification, once acknowledged, touches instrumental reason as well as practical reason.

What I will press in this chapter is how this admission opens a door he does not walk through. First, it allows us to appreciate the potentiality of an ethic of cultivation to challenge a morality of subjectively constituted law in ways that Kant himself would not accept. Second, it enables us to sense how Kant, *in contrast to Hesiod*, projects more or less providential metaphysical assumptions into the world even before those projections are given the official standing of "postulates" necessarily projected to sustain and protect the logic of practical reason.

To bump these considerations into a late modern register you could say that the culturally infused, memory-saturated "somatic markers," that the neuroscientist Antonio Damasio identifies as nonconscious, culturally saturated dispositions of character that prime and narrow the range of options before conscious reflection enters the picture, play a constitutive role inside "instrumental reason," narrowing in advance the acceptable range of options within which instrumental judgment is made.[5] Even more, those "mirror neurons" with which humans seem to be equipped from birth infuse infants with preliminary cultural experiences, feelings, and tendencies to interaction that become embodied as "passive syntheses" operating below self-consciousness. These culture-body exchanges start before the emergence of language and continue through adulthood.[6] They show us how interpretations that start with a sense of individual interests or inclinations and then ask how to override or inform them with universal moral obligations oversimplify the affective, emotional, and relational connections folded into character, morality, instrumental judgment and social relations from the start. They *begin* to call into question both rational choice theory and Kantianism before either gets off the ground.

To focus on variable, embedded, and preconscious cultural tendencies does not mean, however, that an ethos of community must replace a morality of obligation. Such a drive would anchor thought in an ontopolitical perspective quite different from the post-Hesiodic view to be elaborated here. Rather, in a world of intense social coding, replete periodically with conflictual situations between humans *and* between them and a variety of nonhuman force fields, both the individualistic and communitarian orientations emerge as too one-dimensional.

Suppose you belong to a political science department. A colleague first campaigns militantly against a candidate and then, upon losing that round, campaigns just as militantly to put the candidate up for tenure immediately, against the advice of her supporters. Kill the candidacy this way or that. Is that an instance of "pure" instrumental reason? Not really. Even ignoring the long-term effect of such transparency, a character trait of ruthlessness has entered the calculus, turning the judgment differently than if, say, a trait of gentleness or generosity had infused the calculus before decision. If, then, character is ubiquitous to ethical judgment, there is no such thing as pure instrumental reason either. There is no instrumental judgment fully separate from the character structure that expresses in part those passive syntheses that have become wired into us. Yes, some of those components can become more self-conscious. But the contours of this indispensable component do vary from person to person, culture to culture, and time to time.

But what about aesthetic judgment? My engagement with Kant will focus on *The Critique of Practical Reason* and *Religion within the Limits of Reason Alone* because it is there that some of the themes resistant to the ontopolitical perspective I am developing are adumbrated most sharply. But in part 1 of *A Critique of Judgment* Kant ventilates his system in a way that, if both amplified considerably and imported vigorously into these other texts, could pull him closer to themes advanced here. There he speaks of aesthetic judgment as preconceptual and governed by an implicit concord of the faculties. He also focuses on the *receptivity* of the subject to the world in a way that speaks in advance to those mirror neurons and passive syntheses that help to compose us culturally as relational selves from an early age. Authors such as Whitehead and Deleuze have worked on Kant at these exact points, seeking to bathe the earlier texts in an expanded version of the later themes. Here is the way a recent author, Steven Shaviro, responds to those attempts:

> I have been dwelling on Whitehead's self-proclaimed inversion of Kant because I want to suggest that Kant himself already performs something like this inversion or self-correction in the Third Critique. For there

Kant proposes a subject that neither comprehends nor legislates, but only feels and responds . . . ; this subject is itself informed by the world outside, a world that (in the words of Wallace Stevens) "fills the being before the mind can think."[7]

Such a project is admirable and full of promise, though it must work upon Kant as much as it draws sustenance from him. Shaviro may concur, since he himself later speaks about how the openings that Kant creates at specific junctures are later taken back or severely confined.

Let's look briefly at one flashpoint in the *Critique of Judgment* that speaks to some of the themes in this study about self-organization. In part 2, "The Critique of Teleological Judgment," Kant states that the distinction between a mechanical understanding of nature and our grasp of humans as free agents leaves out other entities that fit neatly into neither slot. An organism is neither reducible to mechanical or efficient causation nor invested with the pure autonomy of rational beings. Here are a couple of things Kant says in a prescient way:

I would say, provisionally, that a thing exists as a natural purpose if it is both cause and effect of itself.

[The tree] is both cause and effect, both generating itself and being generated by itself ceaselessly, thus preserving itself as a species.

Only if a product meets that condition . . . will it be both an *organized* and a *self-organizing* being, which therefore can be called a natural purpose.[8]

These impressive formulations speak both to Hesiod and to very recent developments in complexity theory, though in different ways. As we noted in the Second Interlude, some versions of complexity theory focus on teleodynamic searching processes that emerge when an organism goes through a phase transition. The latter do not alone determine the result, since it may well exceed these processes, but they do contribute to it. Kant, however, does not pursue this issue further, probably because the conceptual and experimental resources to do so were not available. So, given the Kantian deduction of a necessary concept of efficient causality that we must pursue in our explanations of nonliving nature, he concludes that we are obligated to construe these special qualities of living organisms as *signs* of a supernatural Intelligence that exceeds our powers of understanding. We certainly can't, in his view, grasp anything further about organisms by developing the idea of self-organization as a mode of explanation. We must subjectively, as it were, *postulate* a historical teleology and a mysterious God who is the agent of it. These two postulates now underpin a complexity that cannot be otherwise understood. That being said, Kant does move from a Cartesian, dualistic rendering of nature and man toward a trifecta image of inanimate nature, organisms, and humanity. Only the latter have a human will and a capacity for autonomy. Here Kant opens a critical door of experimental thinking and inquiry that others explore later.

I am impressed with the way Kant exempted organisms from the explanatory power of "the understanding" in part 2 of the Third Critique. The point is to walk through the door he opened, to proceed further, and to allow these modified themes to ventilate other Kantian texts. Once you do so, you create possible connections between the Kantian assessment of organic processes and the contemporary turn to complexity theory in biology. For, as we saw in the second interlude, the latter also treat organisms as entities that cannot be reduced to a set of simple elements because they participate in complex processes of self-organization.

Back to Hesiod. What about Hesiod and time? My sense is that there are pregnant connections between a world of becoming accepted by some moderns such as Nietzsche, Whitehead, and James and the orientations to time in Hesiod and Sophocles, even though there is no identity. Both perspectives play up the possibility of sudden shifts and turns in human temporal experience, even though the modern version I pursue links those shifts to an interplay between different temporal systems at strategic moments while the Greek tradition tends to focus on the volatile interplay between gods and humans, with the gods often not predisposed to the interests of the humans. Each perspective hesitates to project steady historical progress toward an identifiable good as it appreciates the character of tragic possibility in human affairs. Here is the way Jacqueline de Romilly makes these points with respect to Sophocles:

> Sophocles, of course, knew about divine justice, and about suffering caused by ancient fault. Yet he seldom insisted on the idea. He does not say that the event which comes and destroys man arises from a just or unjust power: he says that it was God's will. And the consequence is that

the long delays in divine justice are less dwelt upon than the sudden intrusion of God's will in human life. Even when punishment is mentioned, we find, instead of an impending threat, quickness and contrast.[9]

Still, I am running ahead of myself. I have not yet addressed closely the *arguments* Kant presents to sustain the unity of reason, the complex relations between its offices, and the subjective necessity of what I will call, polemically, several providential postulates. I call these postulates providential, recall, by comparison to a set of post-Hesiodic assumptions that Kant himself did not entertain as alternatives to explore. Nor have I yet noted how a neo-Kantian like Habermas, after taking a linguistic turn, modifies the letter of Kantian reason while preserving much of its spirit. It is time, then, to let Kant speak. Is it also timely, since we have noted how the *Theogony* may speak through the likes of Democritus and Sophocles, to probe what sort of preliminary cosmological demands might speak *through* Kant? That is, to ask what non-Hesiodic cosmic premonitions *in-form* the moral and aesthetic background of Kantian thought even before they filter into its foreground as postulates.

Cosmology and Practical Reason

Augustine on God:

> Who are we mere men to presume to set limits to his knowledge, by saying that if temporal things and events are not repeated in periodic cycles, God cannot foreknow all things which he makes. . . . In fact his wisdom is multiple in its simplicity, and multiform in uniformity. It comprehends all incomprehensible things with such incomprehensible comprehension that if he wished always to create new things of every possible kind, each unlike its predecessor, none of them could be for him undesigned and unforeseen. . . . God's wisdom would contain each and all of them in his eternal prescience.[10]

On the divided will after Adam's fall:

> It does not will in its entirety: for this reason it does not give this command in its entirety. For it commands a thing only in so far as it wills it. . . . But the complete will does not give the command.[11]

On Divine Grace:

> Open his eyes then by exhorting him and praying for the salvation he ought to have in Christ, so that he may confess the grace of God the saints are proved to have confessed . . . ; for these things would not have been commanded . . . , nor would they have been asked for, unless for the end that the weakness of our will should have the help of Him who commanded them.[12]

On eternal life:

> This faith maintains and it must be believed: neither the soul nor the human body may suffer complete annihilation, but the impious shall rise again into everlasting punishment, and the just into life everlasting.[13]

What a world! According to Augustinian Christianity, the will simultaneously separates human action from the simple effect of God's creation, protects humans from material determination, contracts the painful rift tragedians found in the character of being itself into a human will profoundly divided against itself after Adam's rebellion, shows the human need for grace because of the divided will, and shows how human beings themselves are alone responsible for the rift in being and the production of evil. Free will helps to protect the omnipotent Creator from responsibility for evil; the result is also supported by the faith that apparent evil contributes eventually to a just final result; it thereby supports a divinity powerful and benevolent enough to fulfill the Christian hope for eternal salvation. According to Augustine, after Adam's first disobedient act of full freedom humans can will bad things by themselves, but divine grace is now required to will the good. The will is thus profoundly entangled in aporias; it needs the entry of divine grace. This need for grace, amid profound existential uncertainty about if and when it is received, flows from the Augustinian faith in original sin, divine omnipotence, historical providence, and an everlasting life of bliss or punishment.

These articles of faith reemerge in revised form within Kantian reason. The *similarities* express how the postulates of God, will, freedom, grace, and salvation he adumbrates bear affinities to those Augustine founded more "dogmatically." The *revisions* are funneled through his system as a series of necessary postulates, hopes, and "as if" assumptions of reason, each receiving a distinct standing of its own. He thus translates Augustinian faith, grounded directly in scripture and experience, into a series of postulates (and other subjective projections) that can be grasped as subjectively necessary only after he has adumbrated authoritatively the basic character of moral experience. The revisions and relocations are needed in part because Kant accepts a Newtonian account of inorganic nature unavailable to Augustine and in part because Kant, drawing upon the advances of his day in hermeneutical research, concludes that the sacred texts upon which Augustine had anchored his faith are filled with problems of translation and "redaction" that compromise their authority.

In thinking about affinities and differences between Augustine and Kant the larger terms of comparison from which I proceed should be remembered. Despite the revisions and relocations, the affinities between Augustine and Kant stand out by comparison to the tone, texture, and vitality of a Hesiodic cosmos.

So what about the postulates and so on of practical reason? Do these operations of faith, conceptualization, edict, and hope already express cultural predispositions that are then folded into practical reason as postulates? Or, as Kant contends, are such iterations secreted only *after* the base line of practical reason has been set in indubitable experience, that is, *in features of human experience itself that are undeniable by anyone once they have been delineated*? Put another way, is the unity of reason a culturally circuitous affair that is veiled from its propagator? Or is it the effect of tight arguments whose necessary starting points flow from indubitable experience?

Comparative attention to the Hesiodic and Augustinian traditions may help us to identify some flashpoints in the Kantian system. By "flashpoint" I mean a mundane experience taken by Kant to set an undeniable or apodictic starting point for a transcendental argument. To accomplish a transcendental deduction you proceed from such an undeniable point to the presuppositions that must be accepted to vindicate it, and then you treat those presuppositions as necessary postulates. The question now becomes: Are these flashpoints actually apodictic starting points for definitive argument? Or are they vague, culturally infused, variable intensities that can in fact be dramatized in more than one way?

Each flashpoint, again, provides Kant himself with a starting point for transcendental arguments in the various offices of reason, arguments whereby you show that once that starting point is acknowledged as undeniable, there are other things that you must presuppose to sustain it. There are several such flashpoints. There is the everyday experience of time as succession that helps to prepare the ground for Kant's deduction of the categories of the understanding. There is the "apodictic" recognition that morality takes the form of law, setting the base line from which categorical imperatives are constructed and the postulates of God and immortality are generated as well as the looser secretions about providence, grace, progress, cosmopolitanism, and an ethical commonwealth. There is the "nonsensuous feeling" that enables respect for moral duty to be *felt* as the humiliation of a wayward inclination while insulating that feeling from a *sensuous domain* that would otherwise contaminate the purity of morality. There is the radical distinction, emphasized late in the day, between nonorganic nature susceptible to categories of the understanding and organisms that exceed those categories, escape efficient causality, and require the postulate of a higher intelligence pulling the world toward its highest end. There is also the spontaneous accord of the faculties below conceptual articulation that enables the experience of beauty and makes it possible to expect that experience to be communicated and universalizable. I focus on the recognition of morality as law.

That morality takes the form of law—rather than, say, expressing preliminary human attachments to the earth and the diversity of life that are then cultivated further and applied situationally—is *not* something to be proven. It is, in the first instance, to be exhibited experientially, as when a man who is ordered by his sovereign to testify falsely against another or face death finds himself embroiled in an internal moral conflict. His conscience and his lower desire, says Kant, point in different directions, showing how we have a phenomenological awareness of conscience. This first test, however, does not suffice. It merely points toward a more fundamental mode of apodictic awareness. There are, for instance, several theories, including those by Spinoza, Freud, and Nietzsche, that acknowledge a role for conscience but treat it is a complex, *secondary* formation passing through the vicissitudes of sensual, cultural life. And Epicurus, whom Kant does engage, could be seen as offering a similar reading—though Kant himself does not quite see it that way. So the wise Kant takes a more fundamental step.

We can't "know" that the supersensuous will, morality, and law are inherently interwoven. Nor can we "experience" it in a sensual way, that is, in a way that passes through the sensorium into the higher intellectual faculties flowing out of it. We can, however, become aware of it immediately through a higher faculty of nonsensuous freedom that becomes undeniable once its status and role are pinpointed. Here is a key statement by Kant:

> For whatever needs to be drawn from the evidence of its reality from experience must depend on the grounds of its possibility on principles of experience; by its very nature, however, pure yet practical reason cannot be held to be dependent in this way. Moreover, the moral law is given as an apodictically certain fact, as it were, of pure reason. . . . Thus the objective reality of the moral law can be proved through no deduction, through no exertion of the theoretical, speculative or empirically supported reason. . . . Nevertheless, it is firmly established of itself.[14]

This perhaps obscure statement is reinforced by saying that the nonsensuous concept of morality, rather than being deduced, "itself serves as a principle of the deduction of an inscrutable faculty which no experience can prove but which speculative reason had at least to assume to be possible."[15] Speculative reason took us to the idea of form and to the idea of law as form. The form of morality as law and free will together now become *expressed* through the very activity of pure practical reason itself.[16] Morality requires a universal law and the freedom to obey or disobey it, a moral law we are both subjected to and participate in legislating through the tests we devise. If this were to be denied, the very freedom we necessarily invoke when we are thinking (or reasoning) would defeat itself as it folded back on itself. And, as Kant says, one cannot consistently deny the element of freedom in reasoning, for if one tried to do so one would inadvertently deny the very activity one is engaged in by treating it as determined inexorably by antecedent forces. These are powerful themes in Kant, and a critic, rather than simply denying them, is under pressure to offer an alternative articulation of such experiences. We turn to this issue in the last section.

These fugitive, indubitable, self-given credentials of free will, law, and morality now provide the base point from which the transcendental deductions of God and immortality are established. These latter two are necessary, subjective postulates in part because they enable the possibility of a progressive history to realize the tenets of the moral law in ways that exceed the capacity of humans by themselves to do so.[17]

Let's tarry a bit longer on Kant and the will. The will (as the higher mode of desire) can consent to abide by the moral law when it conflicts with the sensuous or lower mode of desire, or it can consent to the pressure of such inclinations. But Kant, repeatedly and admirably alert to complexities that emerge in his own system, also proceeds deeper in thinking about moral conflict. Under the duress of the latter pressures upon the will, Kant eventually finds that *the internal structure of the will itself moves rather close to the characterization of a will divided against itself earlier projected by Augustine.* And in the cases of some human beings it closely tracks that structure, becoming a will intrinsically divided against itself. So by the time of *Religion within the Limits of Reason Alone* we find that

> there is in man a natural propensity to evil; and since this very propensity must be sought in a will which is free . . . , it is morally evil. This evil is radical because it corrupts the ground of all maxims; it is moreover, as a natural tendency, inextirpable by human powers, since extirpation could occur only through good maxims, and cannot take place when the ultimate ground of all maxims is postulated as corrupt; yet at the same time it must be possible to overcome it, since it is found in man, a being whose actions are free.[18]

So the will is the faculty that separates acceptance or rejection of moral laws from mere "inclination." But to cope with complexities internal to *it* Kant is also pressed to acknowledge how it can become divided against itself, coming close to installing within the internal structure of the will itself (rather than in the first act by Adam) the Augustinian theme of original sin. The will sometimes falls into a quagmire out of which it cannot pull itself; nonetheless we are obligated to hold those stuck in such a quagmire responsible for their choices.

The meticulous Kant has now reached another flash or bifurcation point: he could either dramatize a tragic element in the very logic of responsibility—whereby the cultural need for responsibility is imperfectly matched by the actual responsibility of willful agents so that the logic of responsibility is then loosened in pursuit of tragic wisdom—or he could hope for a means to close the rift he has almost identified in the very logic of responsibility his morality demands. He heads in the second direction. He thereby introduces a notion with affinities to Augustinian grace into his existential equations. The grace by which God helps one to pull out of the quagmire of the will, for Kant, is not officially derived from Christian faith as such; it is not simply another postulate of practical reason either, though it is close. It becomes an indispensable "hope" that exceeds the limits of reason "itself" *but is nonetheless needed to protect responsibility and the integrity of the will's free relation to practical reason.* It is a necessary supplement to the unity of reason because of morality's need to tie the will closely to responsibility. The audacity of Kantian hope.

To secure the autonomy of agents from material determination we must, Kant reasons, not only embrace a philosophy of the will that breaks the closed logic of causality he finds operative elsewhere in nature (except in organisms to a degree); we must also hope that divine grace will lift us above the *internal division of a will divided against itself if and when it is unable to do so unaided.* Otherwise what morality requires may not be possible. And it is necessary to the very idea of morality itself, he says, that it be possible to promote it progressively through history.

Kant's Market-like Postulates

This growing set of postulates and hopes also crosses into collective life. The Kantian projection of cosmopolitan progress toward an ethical commonwealth is not grounded primarily in empirical evidence of historical progress. These are, in the first instance at least, assumptions *we* must project to protect and secure a pure morality that is itself ubiquitous and ineliminable. So when Kant affirms cosmopolitanism and universal progress he is not simply saying that the evidence of actual history supports these developments. He is, above all, stating an implication of his moral philosophy: he is drawing out a collective implication of the apodictic idea of morality as law and joining it to other postulates and projections already in place to secure that recognition:

> I will thus permit myself to assume that since the human race's natural end is to make a steady cultural progress, its moral end is to be conceived as progressing toward the better. And this progress may be occasionally interrupted, but it will never be broken off. It is not necessary for me to prove this assumption. . . . For I rest my case on my innate duty . . . the duty so to affect posterity that it will become continually better (something that must be assumed to be possible).[19]

"I will thus permit myself to assume . . . ; its moral end is to be conceived. . . ." This means that it is necessary to adopt such a postulate about civilizational progress to secure Kantian morality more than that the actual empirical, historical record supports that assumption, even though Kant does mine the empirical record for supplemental support. (Some theories of Kantian cosmopolitanism seem to slide over the point that it follows from his initial sense of morality more than corresponding to an attempt to give an actual historical account.)

The relation between the innate duty to assume historical progress and the historical evidence of progress, however, acquires yet another complexity. If there were no "signs" in the natural history of the world indicating that it actually approximates the story of progress that it is our innate obligation to impute to it, then confidence in the morality of law might start to unravel. This tension creates a sore point in Kantian universalism, whereby he is pressed by the requirements of morality to project gradual moral progress into history to treat actual, early modern treatments of races, women, and non-Europeans to be progressive and to express the need of each constituency for differing degrees of tutelage from European Christendom. So, for instance, he projects a hierarchy of races with "Caucasians" at the top and "Negroids" at the bottom. Some Kantians treat these views as his participation in mere prejudices of his day, to be separated from the logic of his moral universalism. But it is not merely that some other philosophers and thinkers did not hold those prejudices at that time; those assumptions and expectations are themselves more expressive of his philosophy than that. The "prejudices" *express* the connection his philosophy demands between the duty to project progressive universalism and the receipt of signs in actual history that such "unbroken" progress is actually underway.

The "lower" races need the tutelage of Caucasians. The Kantian hierarchy of races, then, does not merely express a cultural prejudice of the day; it has *some* roots in the relation between history and progressive universalism he must postulate to secure his image of morality. This issue has received further attention elsewhere.[20]

The hope for individual grace acquires a collective and historical face too. The assumption of collective historical progress is necessary to redeem the idea of moral universality. Otherwise an impasse would be reached at which what is required morally is not possible in the world, and that antinomy would begin to unravel obedience to the moral point of view from the outside in. But the progress needed, even when an ethical commonwealth has been established to a considerable degree, exceeds the ability of an ethical commonwealth itself to foresee the long-term effects of its collective actions. So it is now necessary to project an element of divine wisdom and grace into the trajectory of collective history too. Kant says we *must* believe, as a *collective* upshot of the ineliminable idea of morality as law, that "the love (assured to us through reason) of God toward man, so far as man does endeavor with all his strength to do the will of God, will make good in an upright disposition the deficiency of the deed, whatever the deficiency may be."[21] He puts a similar point more dramatically in *The Conflict of the Faculties*: "It has to be made clear that we ourselves must work at developing that moral predisposition, although this predisposition does point to a divine source that reason can never reach (in its theoretical search for causes), so that our possession of it is not meritorious, but rather the work of grace."[22]

This, then, is one of the points at which Kant postulates divinely inspired marketlike processes in nature to close the gap between what humanity can accomplish on its own with an upright morality and what else is needed for those moral projections to be progressively promoted.

The theme that what morality cannot provide directly to support itself must be assumed to be provided by "nature" is continued in a late essay (1795), "Perpetual Peace": "Perpetual peace is *insured* by nothing less than that great artist nature (*natura daedala rerum*)." We cannot know these essential supporting processes cognitively, but we must infer their existence to sustain our confidence that the moral image of life finds progressive approximation on Earth.

What shape does the inference take?

But now nature comes to the aid of that revered but practically impotent general will, which is grounded in reason. Indeed, this aid comes directly from those self-seeking inclinations . . . and [in a world of nations] one inclination is able to check or cancel the destructive tendencies of others. The result for reason is the same as if neither set of opposing inclinations existed, and so man, even though he is not morally good, is forced to be a good citizen.[23]

This statement is loaded. It simultaneously shows how a Kantian postulate of "providence" (one of the words he uses to capture the aspect of "nature" that is not reducible to efficient causality) is needed to protect an unfolding logic of morality that is necessarily insufficient to itself on its own terms, how that protection takes the form of benign market-like balances projected as postulates into both nature and the relations between "nations," and how Kant thereby slides very close to a tragic vision of *possibility* for the human estate just before he rescues his progressive image of morality by market-like postulates. This is where Kant both prefigures some existential demands unconsciously folded into contemporary neoliberalism and reveals how precarious they in fact are. For he makes them *postulates*. Kant was not, of course, a neoliberal before that ideology was consolidated. But, first, there are some affinities to it in the impersonal processes he projects into nature and nations, and second, those affinities may help to reveal how naïve neoliberal conceptions of nonhuman processes are today. For Kant, again, understands how he needs to advance postulates about nature and unconscious national inclinations in order to provide the canopy his moral theory requires, while neoliberals are less conscious about corollary needs their theory generates in the same domains and how credible their own assumptions are. How congenial *is* nature, either through its own tendencies or by divine intervention, to neoliberal practices? Once the inner relation is delineated between Kantian morality and the postulates of history and nature it solicits, it may become a bit less surprising how American neoliberalism has been bolstered today in some quarters by a set of evangelical supplements.

The connection between Kant's image of morality and the postulates of universal progress we need to impute to carry it beyond the reach of human intention into nature and the unconscious drift of relations between nations may help us to augment our account in chapter 1 of the pressures that drive so many today to reinstate a neoliberal ideology a short time after it has fostered a meltdown. The items we listed earlier included the short-term self-interest of some, the politics of upward identification among many white working- and middle-class males, intense American drives to world entitlement under increasingly unfavorable conditions, and the way the daily grind encourages many "moderates" to pretend the world would mostly take care of itself if only politicians caught in gridlock would allow the market to function. Do these pressures also have circulating within them a more elemental drive to ward off the sort of existential anxiety that Kant himself felt? I am uncertain. The interpretive supplement introduced speculatively here points in this direction only if the other factors noted above are already in play.

But during an era when Kantian transcendental arguments have fallen onto hard times, a reversal of sorts already long active below the image of the secular social sciences may be underway in this culture. What to Kant were postulates and hopes needed to sustain performatively an image of morality secured at its base by apodictic recognition and tight arguments has now migrated into a desire to secure a beneficent image of impersonal market processes in their intricate entanglements with the nonhuman world. The contemporary contest between conceptions of secular self-interest in impersonal markets and divinely sanctioned morality may indeed also express a certain complementarity between them, as the emergence of the evangelical-neoliberal resonance machine in the United States suggests. The two orientations *are* at odds in obvious respects. But they also function together to ward off a contemporary anxiety: the *intensity* of cultural desires to invest hope in the images of self-regulating interest within markets and/or divine providence wards off acknowledgment of the fragility of things and acceptance of the burdens it places on democratic politics. Kant provided one way station to quell such existential anxiety in his interlocking portrayals of morality, postulates, nature, and market-like processes between nations. But that doctrine is now frayed around the edges and soft in the middle. These other, more popular images supplant that attempt. The point to remember, however, is that in order to launch the *postulates* Kant had to have already felt the *anxiety*. That speaks to the nobility and wisdom of Kant.

I thus admire from a distance Kant's commendation that, with respect to speculations about the world, the moral point of view commends us "not to brood over what their objects may be in and of themselves and in regard to their nature; instead, we have to think of them with a view to moral principles concerned with the ultimate purpose of all things."[24] The Kantian anxiety and response to it are both on exhibit in that formulation within an essay entitled "The End of All Things." I pursue a relation of agonistic respect in which I respect it as a faith and deny its claim to necessity. In doing so I press in my own voice the view that it is now wise to pursue evidence and speculation well beyond the limits set by the Kantian distinction between speculative and practical reason, and to do so in a different key. And then I seek ethicopolitical alliances across difference with Kantians and neo-Kantians. We may find ourselves sharing affinities of spirituality across our differences in creed. Kant's own exploration of self-organization could even provide a place to start closing the gaps between us in creed.

Back to Kant. The list of necessary postulates, hopes, and upshots continues in Kant's work, all bearing family resemblances to the faith Augustine had rooted in divinely inspired scripture and a more direct experience of God. We may have reviewed enough of them sufficiently, however, to see how the logic of practical reason and cosmopolitan progress is said to grow out of an indubitable seed said to be apodictic.

It may also be pertinent to see how neo-Kantianism, which has often sought to proceed without reference to such apodictic moments, postulates, and hopes, now increasingly acknowledges dependence upon them. For instance, Habermas, who earlier translated Kantian reason into a philosophy of language with unavoidable counterfactual assumptions, now inserts into it an "as if" supplement of Christian evangelicalism reminiscent of Kant. He does so to insulate human motivation from biological explanation and intervention understood by him in reductive terms. He says:

> Because he is both in one, God the Creator and God the Redeemer, this creator does not need, in his actions, to abide by the laws of nature like a technician. . . . From the very beginning, the voice of God calling into life communicates within a morally sensitive universe. . . . Now, one need not believe in theological premises in order to understand what follows from this, namely, that an entirely different kind of dependence, perceived as a causal one, becomes involved if the difference assumed as inherent in the concept of creation were to disappear.[25]

It seems to me that Habermas, in his later work, moves another step closer to Kant, both articulating a reductive notion of scientific understanding too close to his and adopting an "as if" postulate to protect human beings from such reductive explanations and modes of biomanipulation. But complexity theorists in biology, the earth sciences, and neuroscience have gone well beyond the reductive account that sets such an "as if" logic into play. Some (as we saw in chapters 1 and the second interlude and will pursue again in chapter 4) are prepared to say that we participate modestly in modes of real creativity that also exceed us.

My question is this: How do you counter, not the contestable *possibility* of a Kantian logic of postulates and hopes as part of a onto faith but the *necessity of such a logic, that is, (a) the unavoidability of such postulates after (b) the apparently indubitable basis of universal morality has been acknowl-edged*? One way is to bring alternative theories and philosophies of cau-sality, experience, and time to bear on Kantian philosophy. Another is to compare the theocosmological background of Christendom installed in the Euro-American culture in which Kant participated to the countercosmol-ogy of the *Theogeny*. A third is to show through these comparisons how his "apodictic" starting points are more cloudy, inchoate, and filled with pluripotential incipiencies than Kant admits them to be. And a closely re-lated way is to recall how confessions, devotional practices, church ritu-als, juridical assumptions, seminar assignments, school repetitions, paren-tal inductions, media news reports, TV dramas, and institutional modes of responsibility and punishment both become infused into such disposi-tions, however imperfectly, and flow into higher registers of thinking and judgment.

Putting those considerations together, I suggest, may disclose a deeper source of all those "as it were" statements Kant makes at pivotal moments ("given as an apodictically certain fact, as it were, of pure reason"). People in the Christendom of Kant's day (and beyond) often already, as it were, experience the call to be ethical through the rubric of obedience to in-trinsic law; they already, as it were, demarcate a sharp difference between nonhuman events and human action through the respective discourses of efficient cause and a free will above sensibility; they already, as it were, ex-perience competing dispositions to action as conflicts of the will; they often already, as it were, hope for grace when the divisions of the will are sharp and failures of collective action are severe; they often project, as it were, the necessary assumption of historical progress into life on the pain of other-wise falling into tragic despair; and they eagerly project, as it were, a human relation to a nature that is either providentially attuned to our needs or sus-ceptible to our technical mastery. Other appreciations, earthy affections, character development, existential experiments, and calls to courage are cut off at the pass by such a collection of culturally induced modes.

Keeping the *Theogony* in mind, let's return to that pivotal moment of apodictic recognition upon which so much hangs in Kant's practical philosophy. Kant himself was inducted into a quasi-Augustinian tradition, broadly defined by comparison to the world of Hesiod, in his case following the pietist movement of his youth. Moreover young people in Europe, according to him, *need* to be educated into such a tradition too, first, to sharpen the fugitive awareness already there that morality takes the form of law and, second, to prepare sensuous dispositions to become more receptive to the demands of suprasensible reason. This, you might say, is the moment at which character, mirror neurons, and the passive syntheses of cultural induction reveal their importance inside the Kantian corpus. Here are a few of his formulations about the induction process:

> Certainly it cannot be denied that in order to bring either an as yet uneducated or a degraded mind into the path of the morally good, some preparatory guidance is needed to attract it by a view to its own advantage or to frighten it by fear of harm. As soon as . . . these leading strings have had some effect, the pure moral motive must be brought to mind.

> In teaching a man to feel his own worth it gives his mind a power, unexpected even by himself, to pull himself loose from all sensuous attachments (so far as they would fain dominate him).

> The pure thought of virtue, when properly commended to the human heart, is the strongest drive to the good and indeed the only one when it is a question of continuous and meticulous obedience to moral maxims.[26]

Kant seeks to induct young people into that cultural mode of re-cognition, as it were, that enables them to sharpen (or dramatize?) the fugitive acknowledgment of morality as law from which his transcendental arguments proceed. And, as the pages that follow show, casuistry, exemplars, and other tactics of induction are commended to sharpen the experience of morality as law and to render the sensuous dispositions receptive to its dictates. That is, to build a sensuous *character* appropriate to respond obediently to the dictates of Kantian morality.

Perhaps, then, Kantian practical reason does not simply start from indubitable awareness? In a way that contacts obliquely a more receptive image of the subject elaborated in the Third Critique, it may *dramatize* in a particular way a set of fugitive experiences already installed to some degree in the pupils by the culture in which they are embedded. It then enacts additional tactics and disciplines to fix those dramatizations securely in the soft tissues of life. It is this complex of experiences, I want to suggest, from which that apodictic acknowledgment is in fact fashioned. Such an embedded background, its recognition, and the Kantian postulates now enter into spirals of mutual amplification.

Such a background of intercoded beliefs, dispositions, assumptions and hopes differs significantly from those installed in the Greek world of Hesiod. Plato's attempts to dramatize a few precursors to Kantian morality, for instance, required more radical mythic shock therapy than the stage-fright gimmicks Kant applied to wayward students.

My way of putting the point is to say that Kant does not actually render explicit an *implicit* recognition already there; he *dramatizes* in one way a festering, culturally embodied mode of *incipience* that, as it were, could be solicited, amplified, and dramatized in multiple ways. He participates in a spiral of interactions between his law-like concept of morality and embodied cultural starting points of the day, none of which is apodictic. He must obscure the element of *dramatization* in this process to secure the aura of necessity in the transcendental arguments he advances. Doing so to sustain and protect the logic of practical reason. That is why I suspect the numerous "musts" in Kant's presentations carry both a logical and an existential element. The latter element is actually an existential plea: "The world must be the way I take it to be or we would collapse into despair." I do not confine such an existential element to Kant, however, since an existential element of *some* sort or other plays a role in every philosophy and theory. Nor do I disdain dramatization. Both elements are operative in ethicopolitical theories. That is one of the reasons that both argument and conversion play roles of importance in philosophy.

It is pertinent to note that Kant does not root the grasp of morality as law only in apodictic recognition. For example, he also draws an authoritative analogy between the idea of law in Newtonian science and the idea of law in morality. Newton's laws of nature were, as Whitehead discusses, treated as impositional laws. A creator God established them as the eternal imperatives of nature. So Kant can say that Newton's laws of nature, which he pretty much embraces for all nonorganic processes, are impositional in one way and that moral laws are so in another. The latter are also eternal and impositional, but, unlike the impositional laws of nature, they can be accepted or rejected by the will. This combination is what makes the analogy between nature and morality *authoritative* rather than merely suggestive. Is it certain, however, that the laws of nature are impositional? Under the influence of quantum mechanics, Whitehead contests the idea of impositional laws of nature with a concept of "immanent" laws. The latter emerge as the cosmos unfolds, and they are not entirely closed or complete.[27] Indeed the relations between different temporal systems foster variable degrees of creativity in the cosmos. Moreover Whitehead offers a corollary conception of human thinking that retains an element of creativity and freedom without inexorably tying that element to morality as law.

To the extent that Whitehead's "speculative philosophy" makes a plausible case, the analogy that Kant introduces to support the idea of morality as a mode of lawfulness is pulled away as a *necessary* prop. These two critical activities together—redramatization of the Kantian starting points and contesting the impositional reading of Newtonian laws—may help to pull the sense of *necessity* from the Kantian notion of morality. You can still defend such an idea as an existential faith—to be put into conversation and contestation with others—but its apodictic source now becomes too shaky and uncertain to provide an indubitable basis from which transcendental arguments proceed and undeniable analogies are fashioned.

Kantian practical reason can now be subjected to a counterinterpretation as a civilizationally implanted practice culturally represented as a morality of law. Whereas he emphasizes how gymnastics prepare a young student to obey the moral law, it now also becomes credible to argue that the combination of the deeply embedded cultural practices of his day and the gymnastics he commends sustain his contestable take on the will and moral life. The philosopher of universal reason becomes a reluctant culturist under the skin who was already predisposed existentially to the postulates he found to be necessary. And the pivots from which his arguments proceed can be read as embedded cultural experiences rather than apodictic starting points.

I do not seek to return to the Greek world but to draw some sustenance from it to help reorient us to a set of new possibilities in this one. I worry, for instance, about the psychology of obedience installed in Kantian moral philosophy in a world that periodically encounters sharp twists and turns. It emphasizes morality as obedience without insulating its followers enough from transferring that drive to obedience to other authorities. I am not content, either, with the type of moral skepticism that is sometimes projected as the only alternative to pursue if and as the closure of Kantian argument is contested. Since there is never a vacuum on the visceral register of subjectivity and intersubjectivity—the register that includes culturally infused mirror neurons and passive syntheses—we are always already predisposed in some direction or other with respect to metaphysical questions, historical projections and moral priorities.

My agenda, then, is to loosen up Kantian starting points to dramatize another possibility of attachment, thinking, concern about fragility, freedom, ethical nobility, and responsibility here and now. To dramatize that possibility, to tap into cloudy strains in us that can be drawn in that direction, to attract others to it, and to argue on its behalf, while conceding without deep resentment that neither my arguments nor those I contest are apt to be airtight. There are few airtight arguments in a world in which cultural processes of induction and dramatization working on the soft tissues of life persistently play roles of significance. Persuasion in such a situation involves mixing together doses of dramatization, argument, inspiration, and acute sensitivity to periodic shifts in the situations you inhabit. Trying to attract people to your vision by showing them how specific pieces of tradition and seeds of care for this world can both be amplified and brought to bear creatively on the situations we face. If you read between the lines in Kant you will find those modalities in play there too.

Some Maxims of Practical Wisdom

One thing Hesiod, Sophocles, and Kant shared was love of the sweetness of life and care for the way of the world, as each grasped and engaged it. It is amply expressed in the distinctive style of each and, as already suggested, at key moments of receptivity by each. As, for example, when Kant speaks with affection of the starry heavens above and seeks to communicate the experience of beauty. By "care for this world" I mean attention to the larger course of things that marks the era in which you live, infused with positive affect toward the most fundamental terms of human existence and nonhuman entanglements as you grasp them. This care for being can be situationally joined to political militancy, if and when events threaten the integrity of that which you care about the most. And that militancy will also be inflected by the underlying sensibility infusing it. That is a lesson to learn from all three thinkers, even as under the global circumstances of today, it is wise for an enlarged minority of people in a variety of subject positions to cultivate a vision of the world that is neither providentially ordered, teeming with gods, equipped with universal moral laws, well protected from a variety of nonhuman force fields with capacities to morph, susceptible to consummate mastery, nor securely lodged on a trajectory of linear progress. It is a world of becoming composed of many interacting human and nonhuman force fields marked by different periods of slowness and speed and degrees of metamorphosis. The periodic intersections between them can produce both positive and dangerous configurations for the human estate during a period when several aspects of human culture move faster than heretofore and several modes of intervention into nature do too. The practical wisdom I pursue and commend in the first instance emerges out of such background understandings and sensibilities; its carriers seek, in the second instance, to enter into productive relations with others whose assumptions and maxims diverge in this way or that from their own while also affirming without existential resentment what Deleuze calls "this world." We thus draw part of our ethos from Kant, but we do not share his conceptions of practical and instrumental reason.

To pursue practical wisdom is initially to project a set of positive dispositions and preliminary bearings appropriate to the cosmos you embrace. Those projections are then adjusted as you pursue productive relations with others adopting and defending different cosmic projections. The idea is to invite positive political connections across differences of creed and affinities of spirituality. For to the extent a lived philosophy is infused with existential resentment, to that extent it is apt to foster a spirit of punitiveness toward diversity in the present and a refusal to give very much priority to dangers and possibilities of the future over the present. It can be highly intelligent and calculating, but it does not qualify as a variant of wisdom in my book. So, to say it again, I seek positive connections across differences with Kantians and neo-Kantians (and others too) anchored in affinities of spirituality bumping across significant differences in creed and philosophy.

The relations among the elements of practical wisdom embraced in the first instance do not assume the standing of entailments rendered necessary by an ineradicable point of departure. The complex, rather, takes the shape of a problematic. The elements suggest and support each other as moving elements in an interfolded assemblage. The image of the cosmos into which the matrix is set calls into question the will to system in philosophy, whereas the exigencies of life suggest the need to delineate affinities and interinvolvements between the elements. If it becomes advisable to change an element in the problematic, that change will exert pressure upon others too. But the specific shape of those changes will involve experiment and exploration rather than a tracing of entailments from indispensable starting points. Above all, this kind of problematic expresses the preliminary judgment that the quest for a systematic morality is dangerous: it too readily projects crude, blunt responses to complex, shifting situations.

As we proceed—the *we* is always invitational—we situate the preliminary understandings and maxims we adopt between atemporal formulae and immediate contingencies, folding into the maxims an awareness of collective issues to be addressed in the near future. We seek the sort of assumptions and dispositions that might help us to address issues such as global warming, the failures of neoliberal economics, the excesses of the evangelical right, the authoritarianism of the Vatican, the expansion of economic inequality, and the refusal of many constituencies to affirm the veritable minoritization of the world that today tracks the acceleration of pace and the intensification of capital. We also bear in mind how our vision of the human relation to the cosmos remains contestable. It is *how* such contests over these questions are waged that is important.

Here, then, are a few operational assumptions, virtues, and projections expressing a post-Kantian pursuit of practical wisdom,[28] even though I continue to wonder whether *wisdom* is the very best word to express what I am trying to do. To introduce practical wisdom provisionally, it expresses an orientation infused with care for the world that is attuned to the need to make situational judgments in settings that sometimes pass through rapid phase transitions, transitions that unsettle some things in the moral habits, passive judgments, and preliminary assumptions of self-interest already encoded in us. There is never a vacuum on this visceral register of subjectivity and intersubjectivity. If there were, we would not be able to think or judge; because it is always already coded it presents us with both a resource and a problem.

The Will

The will is projected neither as a timeless expression of suprasensible free-dom nor reducible to the blind determinations of efficient causality, nor the carrier of an original taint of sin. It is decriminalized in the first instance as part of a larger effort to overcome a culture of existential resentment that so easily sprouts up within and around the experience. The will is here con-ceived as an *emergent*, biocultural formation that bears many traces and marks of the past from which it evolved. This earthy and rather clunky force nonetheless is not reducible to the history from which it grew. Just as life has evolved from nonlife but is neither reducible to it nor devalued by that connection, the will need not be devalued because it is a partial, sen-sual formation installed in beings who were not predesigned to be agents of free will. I am not saying, either, that we can now resolve entirely the mysteries of the will. I agree with Kant on this point, and I see no need to allow theo-centered faiths to monopolize the appreciation of mystery. They (often) invoke it to call attention to faith in a God whose Being exceeds our grasp. Fair enough. We invoke it to call attention to immanent processes that speak to our faith in an ungoverned cosmos that is not fully assimilable to the limited powers of conceptualization and experimentation available to Earthlings. Our notion of mystery is fungible and moveable, then, but perhaps not eliminable.

It is partly because the will is tinged with mystery that it is possible to entertain an alternative to the Kantian rendition of it, an alternative that makes sense of phenomenological experience and work in contemporary neuroscience and is also anchored in a cosmology at odds with Kantian presumptions, postulates, and hopes.

As an embodied cultural formation the will is simultaneously imperfect in shape, critical to our self-identities, a periodic site of creativity needed culturally, and at risk, as it were, to be criminalized by those who demand *universal* faith in an omnipotent God who bears no responsibility for the rifts in being we experience. It is not faith in the suprasensible character of the will that is the most dangerous—though I do not myself read it as suprasensible; it is the demand by some that it *must* be conceived in this way by everyone that is so. The alternative conception of the will supported here is advanced as a credible set of conjectures (at least for those who al-ready have doubts about the suprasensible rendering). There may well be modes of emergent causality that have creative elements folded into them (as Kant himself started to explore with respect to the self-organization of organisms and as Whitehead will argue in chapter 4). An earthy image of the will can be defended in this changed context, even if it is unlikely that a knock-down argument on its behalf will eliminate all other candidates as contenders.

The will, so conceived, consists of three dimensions: (1) culturally emergent incipient tendencies to action that well up within you as you respond to events, (2) a limited capacity to veto or redirect some of those tendencies reflectively as they rapidly approach the tipping point of action, and (3) a modest reflexive capacity to work tactically upon the embedded tendencies in both (1) and (2) to change them in the light of new findings or concerns. The neuroscientist Benjamin Libet, who has tried to clock the approximately half-second delay between the incipience of body-brain activity and its consolidation in perception and thought-imbued action, suggests that the will is reducible to that nanomoment when you accept or veto a tendency to action already under way.[29] We have all experienced such moments, as when you feel an impulse to shout at someone and stifle it at the last second. So he has a case to make. To me, however, the will consists of all three dimensions in their shifting relations to each other: thought-imbued tendencies to action already in motion, a certain power to veto or redirect a tendency as it reaches the tipping point, and a capacity to rethink embedded tendencies of desire and action in the light of new situations. The will *thus can become divided against itself*, as Augustine said, when one of its tendencies is at odds with another.

But since we do not criminalize the will at its core as primordially divided in sin, it also can be informed and reworked to a degree. The limits of such work cannot be specified until experimentation is actually under way. The projection of divine grace, elaborated in different ways by Augustine and Kant, is here replaced by the capacities of reflexivity and tactical work upon the self by the self. And, of course, by the micropolitics by which we work on others and they upon us. The tactics of the self and the micropolitics of, say, media practices are related, but neither is reducible to the other.

Each dimension of the naturalized will is thus open to a degree of situational self-correction or modification. You adjust incipient tendencies, when reflection or a new shock renders this advisable, by tactics that work upon imbued predispositions to action below the reach of the self's direct intellectual control. That is, in response to an emerging aspirational self you now consciously apply tactics to yourself to help recode some of the preliminary dispositions to action below direct intellectual regulation that are at odds with those aspirations. For example, you may prime your dream work before going to bed at night, or solicit a couple of new friends who express the virtues you now admire, or practice neurotherapy, or experiment with adjusting a few role performances to see what changes occur in your future tendencies to faith, belief, and action after those performances are altered. Or you may seek yet more radical adjustments, depending on the issue.

You can also work on the capacity to exercise veto power (#2) by periodically reengaging the relation between the temporal turn you now face and presumptions of practical action already installed in your memory bank. And, as new issues arise, you can rethink a settled maxim of morality in relation to the felt tension between it, the new situation, and a protean care for this world that already finds expression in your moods and sensibility. Such rethinking may suggest the need to experiment with new tactics to modify some inbuilt desires, hopes, and ethical priorities. The three dimensions are thus embedded in a spiral of interinvolvements.

So the will, thus conceived, is both an expression of a creative element in freedom and periodically fraught with internal conflict. But it is neither linked to primordial guilt nor elevated above organic life. The projection of original sin is not needed because this conception is not tied to the idea of a pure, creationist, omnipotent God who bears no responsibility for any evil that emerges from his creation. The will is a thing of this world in the way that thinking is, and all three of its dimensions are both interwoven with thinking and susceptible to being worked upon tactically to an uncertain degree. This conception of the will ties thinking, situational judgment, experimentation, and creativity together, though which of these elements gains priority depends upon the circumstances.

Finally, it is partly *because* the will is sometimes divided against itself that creativity in thinking, judgment, and action periodically bursts forth. A divided will can promote evil action, as Kant saw, by which I mean the infliction of radical, undeserved suffering upon others. But it also provides a bumpy precondition for creative thinking and ethical reform. The will is thus an essentially ambiguous formation. And conscience is too. Sometimes conscience obligates us to do what we are not inclined to do. Sometimes the pressure it foments turns out, after painful reflection and new attention to others, to have promoted injuries and suffering for others that need to be rethought. You bring a sense of care for this world to those uncanny situations that invite you to think again whether the current constitution of your conscience has become part of the problem. Think about how millions have now reconsidered their conscientious objection against same-sex marriage in this way over the last few decades.

Aha! Does this account not rest, then, upon a sensible notion of "care for this world" that hovers outside it? Do we not experience a command to enact and sharpen such a care? Isn't it true that something akin to apodictic recognition and authoritative command are finally needed?

Ethics

In a world of becoming, in which periods of perdurance in this or that zone are on occasion punctuated by currents of accelerated change, the notion of pure, universal morality and the idea of linear progress attached to it need to be reconfigured. One question now becomes: How do you proceed in an ethically serious way when a sudden, unexpected turn takes place with respect to the trajectory of ethical responsibility you had previously projected forward and to which your judgments of moral principle had been attuned? For, unlike a Kantian, you do not project forward an assumption of "unbroken progress" (with periods of slowing down and speeding up) along a linear trajectory. .

As an unexpected event occurs, it might be important to adjust significantly the encoded logic of extrapolation upon which your recent projections of ethical progress have been based and to work on those reserves of habit and disposition that have grown up like tropical undergrowth in and around your operational principles. Now practices of the self, ethics, micropolitics, and macropolitics can all be drawn into the fray in ways that support each other.

Given a world of becoming, an ethic of cultivation now assumes priority over a morality of universal law. Because such a world is marked by oscillations between periods of embedded tradition and those of more rapid change in this or that domain, you move back and forth between periods of provisional acceptance of established ethical convictions and those when a significant change in them is explored. The underlying drive is to amplify, by whatever means available, those preliminary strains of care for the Earth and presumptive concern for the diversity of life that already circulate to some degree in many people much of the time. The idea is to fold *amplified versions* of those dispositions into operational patterns of desire, faith, will, identity, and self-interest, rather than to rise to an entirely disinterested level entirely above the mundane worlds of desire, instrumentality, and politics. And it is to fend off, from time to time, the transcendental authority of this or that reading of moral principle set in a putative matrix of the timeless. What, for instance, has been tacitly included in "respect for persons" in one period may become shaken in another as you encounter unexpected modes of suffering, political drives, and creative proposals that jostle the undergrowth that has unconsciously accumulated inside that idea. For instance, the very idea of a person may now be seen to harbor an image of human uniqueness in need of reconsideration.

It is not merely that you now render explicit what was implicit; rather you sometimes initiate new claims, or respond to those of others, that burn out sections of the old undergrowth to replace it with new plantings. The very trajectory of what counts as progress may now take a turn. A care for being, an ethic of cultivation, and the sense of periodic turns in a world of becoming thus work upon each other as you engage the fragility of ethical life.

Such entrenched dispositions have both individual and collective dimensions, as their corollaries in Kantian philosophy do too. With respect to constituencies and larger collectivities, the quest is to fold a more positive ethos into the institutions of work, investment, church, schools, consumption, corporate practice, and state policy.[30]

What do you do, however, if you encounter those who are apparently without such contingent strains of care for this world? If that turns out to be really the case you can't order them to find that strain. The problem here is comparable to a corollary one in Kantianism, recalling the points at which he moves either to sharpen the sense of morality through tactics of gymnastics or to enact punishment against those who flout it. The first move within an ethic of cultivation at such a possible juncture is to listen more closely than heretofore to strains in the unfolding aspirations and understandings of others that have heretofore escaped your attention, as you also attend more closely for those chords of attachment in them and you to the vitality of existence; the second is to dramatize more vibrantly this seed of existential attachment so that it may become enlarged; the third is to join forces with others, when necessary, to resist the most ruthless attempts to foreclose diversity or to sacrifice the future of the Earth to the demands of the present. For an ethic of cultivation cannot guarantee that the contingent seeds from which it grows will always grow. That is part of the fragility of things.

The cultivation of sensitivity to those moments when a previous period of stability and a sense of belonging to it is disrupted or shattered by a new event is not *derived*; it is not merely an expression of preexisting *preferences* either. Such a binary conception of possible ethical philosophies is too crude to come to terms with the complexities of life. An ethic of cultivation is, rather, *grounded* in a protean care for this world, a care that may both infuse and exceed the array of defined preferences that have to date prevailed in the life of an individual or collectivity. And that care, again? Where does it come from? Well, it emerges in the first instance, if and when we are lucky, from those caresses, exemplars, teachings, social connections, and shocks poured into the passive syntheses that help to compose us as human beings even before we acquire language. It is a thing of this world, passing through the portals of the sensorium to help compose relational sensibilities. It grows, along with the shocks and interruptions that disturb and spur reorientations of it, until we die or lose the fund of presumptive generosity essential to outreaching life. There is, once again, an element of *luck* folded right into the sources of ethical life; that element of luck may be located at approximately the points at which Kant invokes *grace*. Subtract the element of luck, and you are apt to end up with a morality that squeezes too much creativity from life. An ethical life needs this periodic tension between felt, stable obligations and moments of creativity when some obligations undergo recasting. The ideas of gay rights, doctor-assisted suicide and a deep pluralism that invites torsion between existing diversity and the politics of pluralization were not, for instance, entirely *implicit* in principles previous generations misinterpreted. They involve creative interventions that helped to reconstitute assumptions about persons built into the culture as they also help us to forge and/or acknowledge new identities, faiths, and rights in novel circumstances.

An immanent ethic of cultivation grows out of a soil rather than being constructed upon a rock foundation. Indeed, given the recurrence of volcanoes, earthquakes, mudslides, sinkholes, tsunamis, and floods, the metaphor of solid ground may do less work for foundational philosophy than its proponents have imagined. The soil from which an ethic of cultivation grows, moreover, does not merely emerge as "preference"—as Kantian and Straussian critics sometimes love to charge, perhaps because of the paucity of their own rendering of "the inclinations." A sense of obligation, responsibility and listening are cultivated. But an immanent ethic does express an earthiness, a quality appreciative of the cultural element of luck from which an ethos of courage, receptivity, presumptive generosity, self-responsibility, obligation, situational reflexivity, and agonistic respect can be negotiated. It is an ethic well devised to come to terms with a tragic vision of possibility in cross-cultural relations and human-nonhuman intersections; it is also well devised to come to terms creatively with those strange forking moments during which you sense that an embedded principle you have been following up to now is filled with a tropical undergrowth out of touch with the new situation unfolding. An ethic of cultivation is oriented, for instance, to the possibility of creating new rights in new situations without demanding that they be already "implicit."

The ethical life is not, then, derived in the first instance. But it *is* fragile—and not merely because self-regarding desire often threatens to overrule a categorical imperative. It is fragile in that the earthy, familial, educational, and social practices that sustain it may be insufficient or wither; in that it embodies at its center an essential *tension* between affirmative habits tied to the past and periodic adjustments that need to be forged creatively in the light of new events; in that one aspect of the will may be overcome by another; in that the adjustments needed to respond to new circumstances may not be made in time; and in that festering resentments against affirming responsibility in a world that may not be attuned to us in the last instance can twist and turn an initially noble set of ethical tendencies in destructive directions. An ethic of cultivation set in a world of becoming thus contains an element of tragic possibility within it. This follows from the contingent seeds of care from which it grows and its refusal to generate providential postulates. In a world of becoming, replete with innumerable intersections between heterogeneous force fields and alternating periods of slowness and speed in specific domains, it is wise to fold into the disposition of presumptive care modes of heightened sensitivity to new events on the way.

The noble Kant recognized how difficult it is to be moral in his sense of the word. He also recognized that a moral philosophy worth its salt in his day had to come to terms productively with the Newtonian conception of nature that had thrown earlier teleological moralities into turmoil. Those were admirable and courageous dimensions of his thought. The alternative tradition supported here folds an appreciation of difficulty into itself too, as it seeks to respond to a future that challenges several elements in the Kantian problematic.

Periodic Hesitation

Ethical cultivation, then, is crucial to the practice of practical wisdom. But it does not suffice. It is one element among others needed to come to terms with the ways of a world of becoming. A world of becoming is replete with multiple forces that sometimes intersect to throw something new into the world. So strategic events (including relatively extended periods) periodically arrive when it is pertinent to dwell in an exploratory way in the gap between the disturbance of an emerging situation and those prior investments of habit, passion, faith, identity, progress, and political priority you bring to it. In the Greek tradition those who specialized in similar activities were called seers; in the religions of the Book they are often called mystics or prophets. Those who experience the world as becoming also seek to be seers periodically, in a somewhat different key. We do not listen to gods who exceed our knowledge, limited as it is. We allow multiple pressures and concerns to reverberate through us as new tipping points arise in the hope that a new, untimely idea, theme, or strategy will emerge for further exploration. The emergent idea, if it arises, is untimely in part because it does not yet find close connections to many others that have marked the time prior to that event.

How do you proceed? As Nietzsche said—himself much more an advocate of an ethic of cultivation in a world of becoming than many have acknowledged—during a protracted present of potential metamorphosis, "it is important to ignore no signal from the emotions of whatever kind"; you also seek to absorb "the slightest instigation" as you immerse yourself in a *hypersensuous* situation in which new disturbances are absorbed experimentally and some fixed judgments begin to melt away.[31] To have previously cultivated care for a world in which such moments of accelerated change periodically arise is to prepare for such exercises in dwelling at junctures of real uncertainty. When things are relatively stabilized, presumptive faith in established judgment may often be reasonable enough. Such a judgment, however, is only presumptive because stable contexts can readily obscure or legitimize sources of danger and modes of suffering in need of redress. Things become even more dicey, however, during periods of accelerated change in this or that zone of life. Now the task is to dwell with exquisite sensitivity in an emerging situation, allowing unpursued incipiencies from the past, latent memories, established codes, care for being, existential worries, and emerging pressures to resonate back and forth, almost mindlessly. Out of such a process a new idea, maxim, strategy, directive, or practical imperative may emerge for consideration. The next task is to subject it to experimental action to explore its consequences in the emergent context. Here judgment, creativity, and experimental action fold into each other, each making a difference to what the other can be at its best.

Responsibility

The task here is to readjust the Kantian and neo-Kantian balance between attributions of responsibility to self or others for wrongs committed and the cultivation of *presumptive responsiveness* to beings and processes whose ways are not yet so discernible to you. The prevailing priority, the one to be adjusted, reflects the primacy of the Augustinian-Kantian tradition in the Western world, though some contemporary Augustinians draw upon his theme of love to pull away from the punitive themes of sinfulness and heresy that also mark his work.

In a world of becoming new drives to identity and freedom periodically emerge, and during such a time it may become important for those on the receiving end of such pressures to work on their embedded sense of responsibility and obligation to recraft elements of both creatively. Also, in this tradition it is often not the case that a simple equation can be drawn between an evil that has been experienced and a set of agents held to be singularly responsible for it.

In a world of becoming it is sometimes important to cultivate presumptive responsibility—critical responsiveness—to new constituencies, emergent demands, and calls to engage future dangers as they surge into being. Here you explore the possibility of becoming otherwise than you are, in this or that way. You absorb a degree of self-suffering to come to terms with an unfamiliar call to change what you already are. Both the attributive and responsive dimensions of responsibility are needed, but the current distribution of priority between them requires adjustment today. This is true in part because we inhabit a time when the Euro-American world, and elsewhere too, is now being minoritized along more dimensions at a faster rate than heretofore.

A Timely Militancy

At this historical conjuncture, as it were, neither the élan of total revolution nor liberal reform seems to suffice. The former too often devolves into waiting for the next radical break to arrive on its own or to unwittingly invite a fascist reaction. The latter confines itself too severely to electoral politics and is not nearly attentive enough to how time is out of joint with itself. For those reasons its conceptions of ethics and politics are not open enough to an active politics of experimentation at key junctures.

Perhaps the most radical difference between the view advanced here and that sustained by Kantian postulates and hopes of freedom, God, grace, the market-like self-balances of nature, the progressive self-balancing progress between nations, and an ethical commonwealth is that we view his extrapolations as too human-centered, in the sense of demanding that the cosmos be treated "as if" it were for us in the last instance. But, to take merely one example, the eight-hundred-pound gorilla of climate change running rampant during this era, with its power to defeat the future projected forward by the teleological postulate that protects the Kantian idea of morality, throws such projections into crisis. Life is sweet and so, too, are the starry heavens, but the cosmos in which we are set is not highly predisposed to us in the first or last instance. And it may be unwise to develop postulates that suggest otherwise. Hesiod and Sophocles, on this score, are both more prescient than Kant. Today, under the conditions of neoliberal capitalism and the onslaught of massive climate change, what is needed above all are, first, militant drives to *slow down* and *retune* practices of production, consumption, and demands for material "progress" and, second, resolute strategies to *speed up* shifts in our orientations to self-identity, production and consumption processes, and the shaky place of humanity in the cosmos. The cosmos is neither all that predisposed to us nor that controllable by us, and historic Western assumptions that it is—expressed in various ways within Kantianism, secularism, evangelicalism, neoliberalism, and socialist utopias—contribute to the dystopian possibilities of the future.

The new task is to revisit the role performances that captivate us, to modify several of them, and to use those modifications to open more people to pursuit of a militant politics that transforms cultural relations to nature and the future. It is how these different modalities interact that is crucial. Perhaps the most important task today is to undertake creative action at multiple sites to demand that our states, corporations, universities, churches, and international organizations roll back climate warming before it is too late to make a real difference.

Today one unconscious neoliberal strategy to avoid or defer the issue of climate change—because of how acknowledgment of it would require the transformation of state, production, market, and consumption priorities—may be to render inequality more extreme so that the superrich can pretend that they will be able to take care of their families on their own when the worst effects of climate change hit. But such a fantasy is unlikely to work, in part because of the violent territorial conflicts that are apt to be unleashed as disrupted and displaced populations seek to migrate more rapidly and threatened states respond with an escalation of violence.

As we proceed, and in the place of pursuing a world ethical commonwealth implicitly modeled on the extrapolation of European life, we seek to make something positive out of that veritable *minoritization* of the world that has accelerated under the globalization of capitalism. A new radical, pluralist assemblage, if it emerges, will consist of alliances between minorities of multiple types who join together to reorient the common life. Many of its movers and shakers will be young members within each cohort, those with creative energy to burn whose life chances are severely affected by the dismal future that is now being prepared. Anchored entirely in no single class, gender, ethnic group, creed, or generation, the formation of such a vital pluralist assemblage involves moving back and forth between the micropolitics of media life and local involvements, the internal ventilation of the faith constituencies to which we belong, the confrontation of corporate leaders, active investments in electoral politics, and participation in cross-state citizen movements. Each of these practices can secrete potential energy for the others, though there is, of course, no guarantee that such synergies will occur.

Neither Relativism nor Absolutism

The will as biocultural *emergent* irreducible to the sources from which it evolved, dramatization, an ethic of cultivation, a world of becoming, periodic dwelling, presumptive responsiveness, untimely wagers, a timely militancy. What a world! This problematic is not a species of "relativism." Those of us who think that existential resentment is a dangerous temptation built into the human condition itself and who seek to address it today in ethicopolitical ways are hardly relativists. Those who think the current world condition exacerbates that very danger are not either. It is not relativism, first, because it identifies recurrent forces to overcome in several contexts; second, because it does not automatically accept all the rules and norms currently embedded in this or that place; third, because it solicits a protean care for the Earth and a presumptive care for the fundamental diversity of being across various traditions; and fourth, because today it commends militant engagement with some prevailing forces. It is called relativism only by those who think that you cannot sustain an ethic unless it is anchored either in tight argument or a common faith and those who resist the effort needed today to forge a positive ethos of engagement out of a plethora of minorities of several types. It is called relativism, perhaps, in order to resist coming to terms positively with pressures to minoritize the world that are now apt to be stymied only by violent means.

It is not "absolutism" either, since the call to dwell creatively in new situations may issue in an insight that challenges something in a preexisting interpretation of God, principle, morality, agency, will, rights, causality, nation, science, instrumental reason, providence, mastery, or time. And it is also not absolutism because its advocates seldom contend that they have *proven* the most basic creed they bring to the public world. It is rather a set of maxims of practical wisdom, oriented to a world of becoming in which multiple force fields set on different tiers of chronotime periodically collide or coalesce to foment a new danger, risk, or possibility. Such an assemblage of understandings, projections, and maxims tracks and displaces corollary movements in Kantian instrumental reason, practical reason, a derived morality, cosmopolitanism, the moral duty to assume linear progress, and a world ethical commonwealth. Such a process of critical tracking and replacement expresses its greatest debt to Kant.

The next task, after lifting the veneer of necessity from Kantian reason and from other theologies and philosophies too, is to pursue, where possible, relations of *agonistic respect* with Kantians, neo-Kantians, Buddhists, Hindus, and supporters of the three monotheisms who either come to acknowledge without deep resentment the relational contestability of their own theo- or atheophilosophies or do a hell of a lot better than any has done heretofore in demonstrating their necessity. In pursuing such engagements we seek to identify overlapping dimensions of understanding and sensibility that open potential lines of connection across multiple differences. We seek to contribute to a positive ethos of pluralist engagement.

The final axiom of practical wisdom advanced here, then, is the idea of *self-reflexivity*, as you work to acknowledge without existential resentment the comparative contestability, incompleteness, and tensions of the problematic in which you are deeply invested. We advance our own perspective with a mixture of shock therapy, argument, evidence, dramatization, and tactics to augment attachment to this world. We invite others to pursue complementary tasks and assignments. And then we periodically recoil back upon the potential contestability of our operational assumptions and maxims, including our image of a cosmos of becoming. That is the reflexive dimension invested in such a set of maxims, a dimension already discernible in minor figures such as Jocasta, Haemon, Ismene, Eurydice, and the Messenger in the plays of Sophocles, even if it is less visible in the major figures. Haemon, for instance, calls upon his father to relent and compromise his principles of statecraft at a critical moment in *Antigone* when time is running out. And the Messenger poses a severe doubt as to whether there is any "horoscope" available to humanity that allows either clear obedience to the gods or consummate mastery to occur. By the time Oedipus reaches Colonus, even he may present a dying challenge to the above generalization about the major figures.[32] Does the old man finally embody something of the practical wisdom of the mature Sophocles? At any rate, it is a modern conceit to pretend that an awareness of the reflexive element in agency does not arise in Europe until the emergence of Christianity. The debates between these traditions are metaphysical and cosmological much more than they are manifestations of differences in the historical capacity to reflect upon a self's or culture's own preliminary assumptions. To overcome the conceit built into the "necessary" postulate of progressive history helps us to perceive this.

third interlude :: fullness and vitality

In a rich and compelling book entitled *A Secular Age*, Charles Taylor explores how Christian faith has become increasingly "optional" in the countries of Christendom over the past couple of centuries. In comparing the options available to constituencies he identifies some overarching pursuits within which this diversity occurs. A key one is the idea that we all pursue "fullness," though we differ on what it is and how to approach it. Here are a couple of formulations:

> Somewhere, in some activity, or condition, lies a fullness, a richness; that is, in that place (activity or condition), life is fuller, richer, deeper, more worth while, more admirable, more what it should be. This perhaps is a place of power: we often experience this as deeply moving, as inspiring. Perhaps this sense of fullness is something we just catch glimpses of

from afar off; we have the powerful intuition of what fullness would be like if we were in that condition.

The sense of orientation also has a negative slope, where we experience above all a distance, an absence, and exile, a seemingly irremediable incapacity ever to reach this place; an absence of power; a confusion, or worse, the conditions often described in the tradition as melancholy.[1]

As Taylor says, his description does seem to "tilt toward the believer," leaning toward the idea that fullness is approached in life if and when divine grace becomes infused into it. But he then assures us that in a pluralist society "unbelievers" too can and do pursue such a condition. "The unbeliever wants to be the kind of person for whom this life is fully satisfying." Too bad, as he suggests in a light, sardonic spirit, they find themselves visiting therapists as they follow this pursuit without an "outside source for the reception of power."[2] Indeed he thinks many in all faiths pursue multiple, contending strategies to compensate for the lack of fullness, as the traditions of romanticism, humanism, post-Nietzscheanism, secularism, and a couple of versions of postmodernism reveal. Quite a category, then, "fullness."

It may be pertinent to note that those who are "unbelievers" from his vantage point often adopt an alternative set of positive ontobeliefs. A few of us, for instance, believe in a cosmos of becoming set on multiple tiers of chronotime, as we identify an outside to every specific human and nonhuman force field, an outside that periodically helps to set the stage for the creative evolution of a climate, an ocean conveyor system, a glacier flow, a species change, a civilization, a human life. The outside is multiple, active, and real; it is merely not, to us, divine. We also construe transcendence as that which is *coming* into being rather than a Being beyond being. Taylor would probably acknowledge these oversights built into the loaded term *unbelievers* in a generous spirit. But it points to a related issue. Within such a minority perspective, and perhaps within several others too, the general definition of fullness as the goal of all traditions is worrisome. We resist both the universality of its *affirmative* expressions and its double in some versions of critical theory that treat fullness as a necessary and paradoxical goal. To many carriers of a negative dialectic, transcendence must always be pursued and must always fail. We worry, then, about both versions of the pursuit of fullness, not as traditions to debate and contest, but as traditions that set that pursuit as the authoritative framework within which dialogue occurs. Put another way, the "fullness" to be valorized here is a vitality in which incompleteness is sometimes the sign of a lack of vitality but is often the sign of a positive searching element essential to a world of becoming.

What is the version of transcendence Taylor favors most? It does not seem to be Augustinianism, in which an omnipotent, omniscient God monopolizes all creative power in the universe, denying any portion of positive agency to either humans or nonhuman force fields. (Thus you can will evil alone but cannot will the good without the grace of God.) It is not lodged in the nominalist tradition of the late Middle Ages either, which stripped believers from all insight into any purpose God served while intensifying the pursuit of devotion. Or Calvinism. It certainly does not correspond to the right edge of evangelicalism, a movement much more active in the United States than in Canada.

I am uncertain, but my sense is that Taylor's faith has evolved rather far. He seems to invoke a benevolent, somewhat limited God who does not punish humans with devastating natural events, who calls upon us to draw closer to his love, and who provides a gratifying court of appeal and sustenance whenever the worst happens. "Many who are relatively innocent are swept up in this suffering, and some of the worst offenders get off lightly. The proper response to this is not retrospective book-keeping, but making ourselves capable of responding to God's initiative."[3]

This is surely an insufficient rendering of Taylor's faith. What is noble within it, even as so far summarized, is Taylor's recognition that its living expression is too often entwined with stringent, punitive Christian traditions that are hard to disentangle definitively from it. In this respect, Taylor is an admirable warrior against dangerous tendencies in the tradition he imbibes. Doing so, he also sets a noble example for those who imbibe other traditions.

:: :: ::

The theme I support to attenuate the pursuit of fullness is advanced by a set of thinkers who cut across theistic and nontheistic traditions. William James, Bergson, Whitehead, Nietzsche, and Deleuze, while differing from each other on the issue of God, converge in projecting an open cosmos of becoming that exceeds and includes the human estate. They also inflect Taylor's pursuit of fullness into an appreciation of vitality. More sharply, they treat the vitality of being as both a crucial precondition of the good life and a potential source of danger. Both. Today most would probably emphasize the fragility of things for the human estate in its intra- and inter-civilizational relations and its imbrications with a host of nonhuman force fields with differential powers of metamorphosis. I refer, again, on the latter register to climate patterns, ocean currents, glacier flows, bacteria and viral evolution, and so on.

To Whitehead, for instance, the vitality of life is crucial to our modest participation in the creative aspect of the universe as it unfolds. Vitality and creativity are interlinked.

But how? It is through the periodic acceleration of "vibrations" within and between actual entities that novel formations emerge. As Whitehead says, "Newton would have been surprised at the modern quantum theory and at the dissolution of quanta into vibrations."[4] Human vitality, then, expresses our distinctive and modest participation in larger processes that slide back and forth between periods of accelerated and those of decelerated vibrations. Indeed for him, human vitality and a sense of belonging to the cosmos are bonded together.

How does human vitality find expression? It may be dimly experienced as the excess of life over a specific course of action actually taken; or as a stutter that bursts forth as you search for the appropriate word to express an unfolding thought not yet clear to you or in the lexicon; or dwelling in an uncanny experience of duration in which incipient pressures from a past potential, which never became consolidated into actuality because another potential in that cluster was consolidated, now enters into subliminal exchanges with a set of established habits in a new setting; or as a jazz musician or point guard improvises in the middle of the action; or as participants in a burgeoning social movement allow a new strategy and/or relational conception of themselves to emerge as if from nowhere from their negotiations.

The experience of vitality involves oscillations between moments of accentuated imbalance and the temporary recovery of precarious balance, with the latter sometimes set on a new plateau. That plateau may be a new thought, strategy, tactic, concept, or inspiration. Such oscillations sometimes cover a short compass, as when you start a sentence and find it being adjusted and refined as you proceed. In many cases, the end of that sentence was not simply implicit in its beginning. The implicit is attached to the pursuit of fullness; the incipient is tied to the practice of vitality. Spontaneous humor too expresses the sudden condensation of a mode of pluripotential incipience on the way. That's why Nietzsche prized laughter and dance so much, even though I have never heard that he was a good ballroom dancer.

How such oscillations work in everyday life may be brought out by considering a person who has lost the fragile equipoise between a train of thought on the way and periodic triggers that nudge it in new directions. In *Time Regained*, the aging hero, Marcel, encounters Charlus, the arrogant intellectual he had known as a young man. The proud Charlus, who now has aphasia, finds that the uncanny mode of oscillation I call vitality has become compromised. In the conversation between them that ensues, two Charluses struggle against each other:

> Of the two, one, the intellectual one, passed his time in complaining that he suffered from progressive aphasia, that he constantly pronounced one word or letter by mistake for another. But as soon as he actually made such a mistake, the other M. de Charlus, the subconscious one, who was as desirous of admiration as the first was of pity and out of vanity did things that the first would have despised, immediately, like a conductor whose orchestra had blundered, checked the phrase which he had started and with infinite ingenuity made the end of his sentence follow coherently from the word which had in fact been uttered by mistake . . . ; his vanity impelled him, not without the fatigue of the most laborious concentration, to drag forth this or that ancient recollection . . . which would demonstrate to me that he had preserved . . . all his lucidity of mind.[5]

The second sentence consists of phrases that enact in their form the struggle within Charlus. The lost equipoise between two interdependent and dissonant elements also discloses something about the rhythm of reciprocal elements in play when you do maintain poise. As Proust knows, perhaps better than others, the unconscious triggers from an incipient process in the past that never became realized because another possibility was actually taken can sometimes help to jolt a new train of thought into being under new circumstances. Poise amid vitality is the difference between allowing creativity to be folded into thought and being the victim of odd triggers that disorient thought and action.

Such is the fragility of human vitality. Stutter and stammer as a new meaning or phrase begins to surface from a subliminal trigger in touch with a new situation, but not too much or too often. An excess of disruption overwhelms the element of creativity; its absence freezes it.

Vitality, then, exceeds fullness. It is closer to the overfullness or abundance of life over identity that Nietzsche explores in "The Gift Giving Virtue," when you become sensitized to an unfamiliar inflow of experience, absorb it, and allow the energies and trajectory that emerge as it digests itself to find positive expression in your relations with others. The gift-giving virtue involves an unfamiliar inflow, uncanny self-organization of that which is unconsciously absorbed in relation to that which is already there, and bouts of creative thinking and generosity in your relations with other beings and forces.[6] Whitehead, Proust, Bergson, Nietzsche, James, and Deleuze all advance distinctive characterizations of vitality. James's positive valorization of "litter" in the world, I think, points to uncanny moments of creativity during which something incompletely formed within or between us plays a new role in an unfolding situation. It takes at least two to perform the dance of vitality, either two within or two between. Often it takes more.

:: :: ::

A theory that links agency to vitality, and in which intrusions from the outside periodically become catalyzing events, is one in which the active, masterful idea of the "agent" enacting a preformed set of intentions gives considerable ground to opaque processes of self-organization that unfold within and between us as a new intention or relation crystallizes within a self or through negotiations between constituencies. In these circumstances we ascertain a new goal as it unfolds rather than intending it before it is enacted. Now it becomes timely to decide what to do with it.

Strong theories of intentionality kill creativity. Vitality, agency, creativity, and freedom are interdefined terms in the perspective supported here; none dissolves entirely the element of mystery circulating through these connections. How could it, if vitality is bound to real creativity, for good or ill? That is why the received traditions of both negative and positive freedom in Anglo-American political thought may both need to be worked upon reflectively, as we began to do in chapter 2. The gift and the risk of vitality.

I am not confident that vitality can be absorbed smoothly within an overarching category of fullness without changing the latter. There are affinities between them, however. When you suffer grief, or a terrible illness, or depression, or an overwhelming loss, or a devastating defeat, vitality is drained from life. During such times, a lack of being is felt. It takes time for the vital juices to arise again, if they do. Also, when you engage in everyday, action-oriented perception the vital dimension is necessarily less intense, active, or vivid. It becomes subjugated to the need to reduce the complexity of perception in order to carry out a preset intention. This must be so, if we are to walk across the street, recognize a friend walking toward us, or engage precinct monitors on election day. There are, of course, variations of degree here. But vitality comes into its own during odd moments of hesitation, dwelling, suspension, stuttering, laughter, collective negotiation, collective experimentation, and uncertainty. It has both individual and collective manifestations.

To say that vitality *inflects* fullness, then, is not to say that it eliminates it. It, rather, compromises and turns it. Yes, a semblance of fullness arises when a love is consummated, a faith is deepened, a demonized sexual orientation finally receives social acknowledgment, a struggle to enact a mode of sustainable energy succeeds. At these moments the clamor of reverberations becomes hushed in the zone under review and a sense of attunement is attained. But destabilization will soon occur in other zones or in some of the same ones again, and the play of vitality will again be accentuated. If a creative result unfolds in this or that case, the very *process* of its emergence may carry its own gratifications, and the result may engender a shift or turn in that vague horizon of possible progress to which fulfillment had heretofore been attached.

There is another issue here too. Suppose you seek a pluralist society with periodic movements back and forth between (a) consolidating an ethos of diversity that is already in play and (b) a politics of pluralization by which new movements surge from below the threshold of acknowledgment and legitimacy onto that register. An ethos of agonistic respect is needed to enable the negotiation of common settlements between constituencies, but a periodic politics of pluralization is needed to extend plurality in new directions. To adopt such a bicameral cultural ideal is thus to support periodic oscillation in which the fullness of diversity at one moment is punctuated by a new drive to diversification at another with corollary adjustments in the political ethos of engagement. Paradoxically, "fullness" would now involve periodic oscillations, oscillations that lift vitality into the very life blood of ethico-political processes. A society that froze such modes of oscillation would be one lacking one of the constitutive conditions of the good life. I think it is misleading to call such a complex the pursuit of fullness, partly because once the latter term is stretched to make a formal concession to the punctuated character of the pluralism-pluralization combination the term itself encourages people to slide back to a more singular reading of a settled horizon of pursuit. Vitality and pluralism condition each other.

Similar arguments can be made with respect to the issue of justice. You pursue justice on a now visible horizon (which means there is a lack of full justice), but then some elements in the trajectory of that very pursuit may shift as a new creative movement places new claims on the cultural register. Such a change was not always implicit in an ongoing horizon; it sometimes involves the admission of a new claim into an altered setting. All of this carries us back to the ethic of cultivation and a positive ethos of negotiation discussed in chapter 3. It also sets the agenda, which I have pursued elsewhere, to probe the limits of tolerance a pluralist and pluralizing culture can sanction.[7]

If we are minor participants in a larger cosmos composed of multiple, interacting force fields that periodically morph, *part* of our experience of attachment to the world may be tied to the experience of vitality and to those small and large moments of real creativity to which it is connected. The idea is to cultivate subliminal experiences of vitality further, even as we work to diminish the risks that accompany acting recklessly upon its fruits. In this way we resist the embrace either of an ideal of fullness through the transcendence of a divine Being already fully formed or a negative dialectic in which "failed transcendence" inevitably accompanies the unavoidable pursuit of fullness. We find it difficult to believe in the first creed, and we worry about tendencies to existential resentment that can be set into motion by the second mood. As we seek to enter into relations of agonistic respect with these two orientations, we bear in mind that there are both theistic and nontheistic visions of vitality as well as theistic and nontheistic versions of fullness. The cover terms *theism* and *nontheism* house many varieties within them, as the example of James who supports a limited God who contributes to the vitality of life makes apparent.

Does fullness really contrast that much with vitality, then? Taylor, I imagine, might say no, though at the conference in which a longer version of this interlude was presented he agreed that *fullness* had not entirely worked to provide the inclusive term within which contending traditions could be set. Taylor's own conception of a limited divinity as a caring co-presence with humanity in which both, apparently, have things to learn may even point toward a valorization of vitality, as rather similar themes clearly do in James and Whitehead. So there may be a difference of inflection here, amplified by somewhat different images of the cosmos in which the two formulations are set.

For some of us, vitality is a capacity to appreciate and cultivate to the extent we can because, first, it enhances our positive sense of attachment to a cosmos that is neither predesigned for us nor that susceptible to our control and, second, it is a gift we can draw sustenance from when new and unexpected situations arise. But, as already noted, it is an ambiguous gift if the world is not preorganized for us in either of the above two ways. The experience of vitality itself suggests an element of exaggeration in the idea of an organic fit between humanity and the world. Perhaps, as suggested in the first interlude, thinking itself requires exploratory conversations between voices within us, and perhaps the connection between us and the world is replete with constitutive dissonances and tensions. Vitality expresses those tensions. Do most of us also display tendencies to assume, upon waking up in the morning, that the fit is closer than that? Probably. Vitality deserves to be cultivated and respected as we act into a future replete with fragility and shifting degrees of real uncertainty.

CHAPTER 4 :: process philosophy and planetary politics

The future's not what it used to be. What's more, it never was. I steal this saying from the Weavers, a radical folk band of the 1950s and beyond, because it fits my thesis to a T. It means to me that dangers to the human estate itself press on the horizon during an era when capitalism has intensified and when encounters between it and a variety of nonhuman force fields with independent powers of metamorphosis have once again become dicey. It also means that to understand those dangers and possibilities we may need to recraft the long debate between secular, linear, and deterministic images of the world on the one hand and divinely touched, voluntarist, providential, and/or punitive images on the other. Doing so to come to terms more closely with a world composed of interacting force fields set on different scales of chronotime composing an evolving universe open to an uncertain degree. Such an image may better allow us to sense, feel, and engage both the fragility of things and our modest participation in modes of creativity that extend beyond the human estate.

Greek and Quantum Sources of the Vision

Nietzsche, if you bracket his statements about eternal return as the return of long cycles and attend to almost everything else he says, is one modern source of such a vision. Whitehead, if perhaps you *qualify* his discussions of "eternal objects," is another. What is interesting is that each thinker approached such a vision through a different set of engagements. Whitehead, writing during the advent of quantum mechanics, extrapolated from those ideas in ways that other leading practitioners did not. Nietzsche, writing before quantum theory was in the air, drew inspiration from Hesiod, Heraclitus, and Greek tragedians. In each case obdurate features of both Christian monotheism and Newtonianism had to be challenged. Indeed both detect the "remains" of a monotheism of omnipotence in some of the secular images of science they contest, though Nietzsche is the most blunt about saying so.

The different materials of inspiration for each make a difference to the position articulated. Nietzsche engaged both Hesiod and Heraclitus as a young man. Hesiod's multiple, interacting, and contending gods, as we have already noted, introduce modes of causality into the world that exceed any conception of efficient cause, that trouble a notion of fixed "laws" of nature, and that disturb in advance the Humeian idea that laws and causes are mere projections of human habit onto external processes. When Zeus lay with a human, Semele, and gave birth to Dionysus, the god of joy and the element of wildness in the world who entranced Nietzsche for his entire adult life, each event engendered a future that was not what it used to be projected to be. What's more, these "events" were marked by modes of sensuality, deceit, digestion, strange attractions, and uncertainties that make early modern ideas of mechanical cause and eternal laws of nature decreed by a distant god look sterile. How could the formation of life from nonlife, or species change, or a variety of complex civilizations emerge from such dry, bleached processes?

It was not that difficult, soon enough, to translate those gods from beings into natural forces of different sorts. Heraclitus starts the process, and the young Nietzsche is touched by him. He loves this formulation:

"This universe which is the same for all, has not been made by any God or man, but it always has been, is, and will be, an ever living fire, kindling itself by regular measures and going out by regular measures."[1] Consider a few statements from an early course by the young teacher on the ancient sage, replete with the exaggerations Nietzsche admired in the Greeks and poured into his own work so as to fix its effects upon our "entrails" as well as our more refined conceptual capacities:

> Nowhere does an absolute persistence exist, because we always come in the final analysis to forces, whose effects simultaneously include a desire for power [krafterlust]. Rather, whenever a human being believes he recognizes any sort of persistence in living nature, it is due to our small standards.

> Yet at the greatest level nothing absolutely unalterable exists. Our earthly world must eventually perish for inexorable reasons. The heat of the sun cannot last eternally.

> Well, this is the intuitive perception of Heraclitus: there is no thing of which we may say, "It is." He rejects Being. He knows only becoming, the flowing. He considers belief in something persistent as error and foolishness.

> The Passing Away is in no way a punishment. Thus Heraclitus presents a *cosmodicy*, over his great predecessor [Parmenides,] the teacher of the injustice of the world.[2]

The themes of cosmic innocence and becoming persist in Nietzsche too, so that as late as the *Twilight of the Idols* he complains about the lack of a historical sense among philosophers who continue to search for a stable resting place from which explanation can proceed, in which morality can be anchored, and through which the outlines of the future can be discerned. Such philosophers express "the hatred of even the idea of becoming. . . . All that philosophers have handled for millennia has been conceptual mummies; nothing actual has escaped from their hands alive."

> Death, change, age, as well as procreation and growth, are to them objections—refutations even. What is does not *become*; what becomes is not. . . . Now they all believe, even to the point of despair, in that which is. But since they cannot get hold of it, they look for reasons why it is

being withheld from them. . . . We've got it, they cry in delight, it is the senses! These senses, *which are immoral as well*, it is they which deceive us about the *real* world.[3]

In resisting the "Egyptianism" of philosophers who give too much priority to being over becoming, Nietzsche, like Henri Bergson, William James and Whitehead after him, suggests that the protraction, connectedness, and liveliness of our sensory experience suggests much about the course of the world beyond the human estate too.

What about the source of somewhat similar themes in Whitehead? He does pay attention to early Greek thought, in this case to the *Timaeus* of the later Plato that complicates the early Platonic emphasis on eternal ideas. But the main impetus to his exploration comes from the shock he received when the Newtonian science he had accepted as apodictic was shattered by the advent of quantum mechanics at a key moment in his intellectual development.

It (almost) goes without saying that I am not really competent to give an account of quantum theory, and only partly because it has been subjected to many contending accounts. I will say just enough to allow us to sense how it moved Whitehead to make adventurous cosmological extrapolations from it.

The official Newtonian world, though his experiments with alchemy may have belied this, was deterministic and linear, with space functioning as a container of things and the arrow of time potentially reversible by inverting the direction of causality. This universe was also created by a God who defined its fundamental laws and then left it to unwind. That explains why Whitehead rejects the Newtonian conception of laws as "impositional" in favor of an "immanent" conception. This is an important move, for it enables a conception of law-like relations that include noise, messiness, and disturbances within them, some of which might form part of an impetus to creative change at key conjunctions. The impositional ideal of Newton also explains why he was committed—secretly, but in letters and texts that survive—to the Arian heresy, in which a single God created the world and its eternal laws from scratch, rather than to the Trinitarian image, which makes Jesus divine from birth. All these Newtonian assumptions are contested by Whitehead, though he may have appreciated the long fascination of Newton with alchemy.

While multiple interpretations persist of the Heisenberg and Bohr approaches to quantum theory, we must remain "content" for now with this version. Bohr at first tended to treat the problem of not being able to discriminate in the same test procedure between the location of an electron and its momentum—what he calls the problem of complementarity—as an epistemological issue. It is due to the effect of our instruments on the phenomenon itself. He himself, however, also developed suspicions about what this inability indicates about the real character of "quantum entanglement," whether it suggests that the universe consists of entangled, active elements rather than discrete particles.[4] The closer one moves to the latter reading, the more active the potential effect of microscopic phenomena can be on macroscopic processes.

Heisenberg, on the Epperson account I am following, moves robustly beyond the confines of an epistemological reading of the entangled relation between the subject of experimentation and the object of experimentation. He gives an ontological rendering of quantum process. Here is a formulation by him about the complex relation between "potentia" and "actuality": "The question is no longer, 'What is the mechanism by which a unique actuality physically evolves from a matrix of co-existent actualities?,' but, rather, 'What is the mechanism by which a unique actuality evolves from a matrix of coexistent potentia?'"[5]

"Coexistent potentia." These potentia are real but inactual, in the sense that when they are most active and on the way, they have not themselves "decohered" into a fixed actuality or object. They are real but not actual unless and until decoherence occurs. And decoherence is apparently as dicey to understand as is the "coherence" of multiple potentia. Here is quotation from Epperson, who accepts Heisenberg's rendering, that may help to set a context to Whitehead's adventure: "For Heisenberg, again, potentia are ontologically significant constituents of nature that provide the means by which the facts comprising the system measured (and environment) are interrelated in quantum mechanics."[6]

For Whitehead, such potentia never disappear, and they are more or less active in real entities from time to time, depending on the circumstances. They help to drive real novelty into the universe. As Epperson says, "For Whitehead, the potentia driving novelty constituted a different species of reality, as they did for Heisenberg—realities that do not derive entirely from some particular antecedent actual datum but rather from a spatio-temporally generic, and therefore primordial, actuality."[7]

At this point we merely state three points that Whitehead draws from quantum mechanics. They are not "derived" either from the theory or from quantum reality, as the case may be. Whitehead contends that each cosmology carries a *speculative* dimension with it that is unlikely to be subtracted from it entirely. These are, then, themes that make sense as speculations if you take quantum mechanics seriously as a real phenomenon.

The first, perhaps the closest to the phenomenon itself, is Whitehead's articulation of the "fallacy of misplaced concreteness," a fallacy still committed in parts of philosophy, economics, political theory, and science. If Whitehead were writing today he would doubtless say that the fallacy refers in the first instance to those who still ignore that mysterious process by which two "particles," separated after having been adjacent, now shift together simultaneously, even when at a great distance from one another.[8] Nobody seems even now to have a deep account of this simultaneity. For Whitehead, misplaced concreteness means more broadly the tendency to overlook entanglements between energized, real entities that exceed any atomistic reduction of them, as when a climate pattern and ocean current system intersect and enter into a new spiral of mutual amplification, or when a cultural disposition to spiritual life befuddles the academic separation between an economic system and religion by flowing into the very fiber of work motivation, consumption profiles, investment priorities, and electoral politics. Misplaced concreteness thus downplays both entanglements and processes of self-organization on the way, depreciating how every thing is both enmeshed with others and metamorphizes according to the time scale appropriate to it. Such an image of multiple entanglements does not, therefore, devolve into a kind of organic holism, for that move would subtract the element of real creativity from the universe. The entanglements are close enough to exceed a philosophy of atomism consisting of either autonomous particles or larger entities; they are too messy, incomplete, and on the way to fit an image of holism. I call this, in honor of James, *protean connectionism*.

The second, related upshot is that space is not a mere container of things to Whitehead; it consists of relations of spatialization, engendered by formations as they unfold. This leads Whitehead to reduce the emphasis in European grammar on substantives and predicates—"the rock is solid;

the ocean is blue"—and to underline the importance of prepositions and conjunctions. The metaphysical suggestions of the preposition *in* are particularly misleading. Either the preposition should be dropped, which is very difficult to do, or its meaning should be extended beyond the sense of a container. So you move closer to Whitehead's thinking if you read the phrase "In the beginning" in the King James Bible so that the *in* involves the protraction of a moment interwoven with what came before and that which arrives next. Perhaps active verbs without definitive agents who *own* them entirely need to be emphasized in this philosophy too.

The interesting thing is that the style of writing actually adopted by Nietzsche heeds such injunctions more than that adopted by Whitehead, at least much of the time. Nietzsche, you might say, writes cinematically, allowing scenes to flow, bump, or meld, as the case may be, into each other so that things emerge during the protraction and dissonance of a "moment" that are related to the past but were not always "implicit in" it. And he uses ellipses often, allowing the three dots at the end of a sentence to suggest entanglements that exceed his articulation of them, inviting you as he does to pursue a line of thinking the thought suggests to you.

Whitehead also emphasizes not only entanglement but the persistence of "actual entities" before they perish under pressure and evolve into something new.[9] So it might be best to say that the ideal Whiteheadian style would be to shift back and forth between a grammar of things and a grammar of process, expressing in its mode the fluctuations between periods of slow and rapid metamorphosis that mark the lives of things.

Another difference of style between Nietzsche and Whitehead is pertinent. Whitehead, writing in the Cambridge-Harvard mode of the day, adopted a magisterial style that projects the presumption that the leading intellectual ideas of his day will eventually filter into the operative assumptions of the wider, democratic culture. Nietzsche, writing in a different context and challenging the dominant images of science and monotheism of his day more bluntly, often conveys a mood of trying to ward off a barbarism that repeatedly threatens to overwhelm modern culture. We will return to this difference in the last section.

Back to Whitehead. The third theme, more speculative yet but still entangled with the quantum theory under scrutiny, is the idea that real creativity is distributed differentially across the universe and "over" time. A world of becoming expresses the "agency" of real creativity lodged in the sometimes bumpy relations between real entities. It is this issue that we will explore further in Whitehead before Nietzsche reenters the fray.

Actual Entities, Vibrations, and Real Creativity

Creativity is an "ultimate term" in Whitehead's philosophy, meaning, I take it, that you can show when it occurs and point rather roughly to how it happens but not delineate the process in complete explanatory terms.[10] It happens within preconditions and constraints, so there is never creation ex nihilo. The constraints are explained in large part by the fact that at any moment in chronotime the universe is composed of "actual entities" of innumerable types which help to set preconditions for new events. An actual entity is any formation that has some tendency toward self-maintenance, such as, differentially, a rock, a cell, a tornado, a system of ocean currents, a continent, an organism, a civilization, and a mist. Creativity is not the simple product of an agent or subject. Rather it is embedded in processes that to varying degrees go through periods of what I earlier called teleodynamic searches. My intent here is to allow recent work in complexity theory noted earlier to fold into Whitehead's themes, wherever the former seems to support and coalesce with his general agenda. The creative process, at its most active, occurs in teleodynamic searches within and between entities whose relative equilibrium has been disturbed, and it draws upon the noise within and entanglements between entities. So insofar as Bergson thought of time as an independent force separate from space—and it is not perfectly clear that he did—Whitehead is at odds with him, even though the affinities between the two are otherwise close.[11]

It is through the periodic acceleration of "vibrations" within and between entities that novel formations emerge. As Whitehead says, "Newton would have been surprised at the modern quantum theory and at the dissolution of quanta into vibrations."[12] And, as we began to see earlier, Whitehead would have been surprised to see how entanglement exceeds his own theme of vibrations, though it does apply to many of the processes we are exploring. When elements from one entity press toward another there is the issue of whether, and if so in what ways, they will "ingress" into it. The receiving entity "prehends" some of its dimensions positively and others negatively, depending in part upon its prior organization and in part upon the creative responses it engenders. As the interinvolvement occurs, there is "feeling" on the part of the receiving entity, even if it is only "vector feeling" in the simplest cases.[13] And periodically a new "concrescence," or searching self-organization by the entity, of the prehended elements, alters it in an important way. In this period of accentuated movement back and forth, the present creatively draws upon the past without simply replicating it.

Although Whitehead, to my knowledge, does not expressly engage this issue, we might draw upon him as a guide to make a distinction between two ideas that are sometimes equated. Unpredictability and creativity are related but not identical processes. You can have unpredictability when there is an epistemic screen separating you from the real determinants. But creativity involves a mode of self-organization that brings something new into being. Whitehead challenges the speculative ontology that asserts that every inability to predict is due to a screen that hides full determination. Often such a common ontology is not articulated because it *is* so common and seems so obvious to its defenders. But it has never been proven. His counterontology of differing degrees of real, conditioned creativity is speculative, defensible, and grounded in some aspects of experience. The first chimp to filter chaff out of grain by floating the mess in water participated in a creative process, and that routine was then passed on to other chimps.

Whitehead, unfortunately, is surprisingly short on examples of creative change in nonhuman processes. So let's try out a contemporary and controversial one merely to allow some of his key concepts to be placed into operation. According to biologists, a bacterium needs phosphorus to survive. But in one experiment, with bacteria that had lived in the vicinity of arsenic, infusions of arsenic encouraged the bacteria to evolve so that arsenic replaced phosphorus to a great degree as the life-giving source.[14] From a Whiteheadian perspective, this creative development, if true, is complex: it involves a process of ingression, a "feeling" by the bacteria of some degree of affinity to the arsenic, and creative self-organization on the part of the bacteria as the "concrescence" by which it evolves into a mode of life—an actual entity—previously indiscernible on Earth.

Other elements might have been ingested, each resulting in decline or death. And bacteria that had not previously been surrounded by arsenic might fail in such an evolutionary process of creative self-organization. So there has to be a potential affinity between the bacterium and the newly intruded element. But the potential, neither felt by it before ingression nor knowable by us prior to the experiment, becomes discernible after the creative work has been accomplished. Who knows, such a new form of life might provide a base from which other novel species are launched.

It must be emphasized that this example remains at the center of experimental controversy. If it stands, it gives an operational sense of what Whitehead means by real creativity in the production of novelty. If that experiment is overturned, there are several more established instances that can be clarified through Whitehead's categories. *Symbiogenesis*—the process of horizontal gene transfer between organisms—constitutes a prime instance.

To read between the lines, it seems to me that the phrase *real creativity* fits Whitehead's image whenever a reductionist explanation of change fails, when something new is added to a preexisting environment, when the newness involves a degree of self-organization on the part of at least one of the entities involved, when that self-organization invokes a searching process in which the end pursued is cloudy at first and becomes consolidated later, and when the new mode of equilibrium was both promoted in part by the searching process and the result exceeds that search. It is true that I have added the term *self-organization* to the reading of Whitehead, but it does seem to me to fit what he says about "ingression" and "concrescence," and it speaks to recent work on the character of self-organization. My approach, again, is to work modestly upon Whitehead as I draw sustenance from him.[15]

The creative relation, to Whitehead, operates by *attraction* and *repulsion* within and between interacting entities; otherwise there would be little power of an entity to maintain itself. That often involves a process of teleosearching, in a way that parallels the more complex versions of self-organization in nonhuman processes discussed in the second interlude. It also means, and Whitehead is explicit about this, that an *aesthetic* element is in play within relations of ingression, prehension, and concrescence. This aesthetic element is not merely operative in human relations or in the human relation to things; it is involved in several thing-thing relations too. That is why he insists upon extending the word *feeling* to involve relations between entities beyond the human and organic estates.

Creativity for Whitehead, again, is not total, complete, or ever ex nihilo. It is always a conditioned creativity in which that which is created involves enabling and constraining relations of ingression and concrescence between actual entities. That is one reason, at least on my reading, he construes the creative process as one that may slow down in a domain for a time as the forces of self-maintenance prevail and then accelerate when an ingression poses a more severe shock. Whitehead is not a philosopher of things in perpetual flux, as some critics of a philosophy of becoming project upon its carriers, so that they do not need to think about it further. His notion of "actual entities" works against that.

His claim is that the play of attractions and repulsions becomes more sophisticated as entities become more complex, that is, as they become able to transfigure more incompatible or antagonistic elements into *contrasts* that are brought into some kind of harmony in the same entity. The more complex the contrasts brought into harmony the more the result is irreducible to simple unity. Whitehead is drawn to an evolving aesthetic of beauty more than to one of the sublime, though you might hear traces of the latter in those fecundities which help to set the new into motion. Does Whitehead also tend to read the beautiful as fragile? Some statements by him tend in this direction. The beauty to us of an orchid in bloom, you might say, is bound up with the premonition that the bloom is ephemeral.

Before we move to criticisms and further possible adjustments, it might be wise to ask whether anything more can be said on behalf of Whitehead's thesis about conditioned creativity. Well, it curtails the need to adopt a Kantian rendering of the world in which it must *appear to us* to be governed by mechanical laws while we must also *postulate* a human power of freedom that escapes those determinations as it also possesses almost magical power to act back upon bodily processes to guide behavior. It also makes more sense than Kant was able to do of those organic modes of self-organization which he himself talked about in which the whole acts upon the parts and the parts upon the whole. Indeed it deploys them to make sense of creative evolution, a process Kant eschewed. Finally, it relieves the postulate of the "anthropic exception" adopted by some physicists who project an entirely deterministic world, punctuated only by the capacities of those humans who conceive and experiment upon it. By adopting an axiom of real creativity distributed differentially through the world, neither of these strategies is required.

I will extrapolate again a bit beyond Whitehead's formulations to crystallize a pincer movement at work to some degree in his texts. The idea is to move back and forth between human experiences of apparent creativity and reasoned assumptions about nonhuman processes that may help to redeem those preliminary experiences. Pointing to putative human experiences of creativity in the plastic, poetic, and musical arts, Whitehead might say, "Isn't it probable that creativity in those domains expresses something real? If so, aren't such modes of creativity also apt to find *some* expression in ethics, politics, religion, and economic life? For why would such a process stop arbitrarily before infiltrating the latter activities? If you concede this much, is it not also likely—at least for those theists and nontheists who embrace a theory of species evolution and doubt that human beings are *unique* agents made in the image of a personal, omnipotent god—that there are degrees of creativity at lower levels of sophistication in force fields outside the human estate? If so, might there also be surprising intersections between some of the latter fields, out of which something new is created?"

A pincer movement is thus put into play by which you pursue the theme of differential creativity by moving through quantum theory to protean experiences of the human estate and then back again from protean human experiences to novel formations in nonhuman force fields. One pincer jaw clamps upward; the other clamps downward. It may take both jaws to render the argument most plausible. For *if* there is real creativity anywhere, it is apt to operate to some degree in both human and nonhuman venues. And it does seem difficult to participate in thinking without projecting creativity into that enterprise. This is a site at which we echo Kant without replicating Kant.

Such a pincer movement, then, does not produce a knockdown argument of the sort Kant attempted. There are counterspeculations available to cut it off. But these have not been proven either, and that awareness in conjunction with distinctive experiences of the time we inhabit may open more people to modes of experimental exploration as they bracket the most familiar alternatives. Whitehead's speculations, it should be acknowledged again, might be disproven someday by deterministic accounts that profit from new sophistications of conceptualization and experimentation. But this has not happened to date. And if his speculations continue to accumulate persuasive power in several domains, as a growing number of humanists and scientists think they are doing, the thesis of a cosmos of *differential degrees of creativity* may inform the ways we engage artistic activity, sports innovation, entrepreneurial invention, the activation of new social movements, scientific productions, species evolution, ocean current shifts, climate change, and civilizational evolution. The idea, again, is that the complexity of human feeling, agency, creativity, and evolution would probably not have evolved unless traces and aspects of such powers precede, infiltrate, and surround the human species. This is another aspect of conditioned creativity, one that functions to save cultural theory from the closures pushed upon it by the most reductive versions of biology, neuroscience, and social science.

The more complex, to Whitehead, arises from the less complex, even as its evolution means that some powers, skills, and sensitivities are lost along the way. The latter are the "scars" of creative evolution. Nonetheless terms such as *higher* and *lower* must be used with caution, partly because of the element of perceptual and ethical provinciality inside our species perspective. With respect to humanity, the goal is neither to deny a degree of species provincialism nor to allow its boundaries to be frozen by transcendental arguments, nor to assume that the objects of our apprehension and prehension are entirely constituted by us: the objective is to *stretch* human subjective capacities by artistic and experimental means so as to *respond more sensitively* to other force fields. To extrapolate, the objective is to replace both the Kantian idea of a universal constitution of the world by the human subject and simple realist images of it with an image of evolving codependence in which our *responses* to what is outside us can be stretched and amplified as we experiment upon ourselves and the world. The idea of real creativity challenges classical idealist and realist models alike with a notion of speculative and experimental realism. That is why it makes sense to place Whitehead's work into conversation with later scientists and philosophers discussed earlier in this text, such as Stuart Kauffman, Terrence Deacon, Lynn Margulis, and Evan Thompson.

Eternal Objects and an Impersonal God

What, more closely, holds things (and systems) together before they evolve into something new? One of Whitehead's most controversial ideas is that of "eternal objects." An eternal object is a potential on the way, not consolidated until it has been successfully absorbed and "realized" in a specific way by an entity. An eternal object is relational, emerging as an actual mode, "only when there is a potential ingression into an actuality."[16]

But what makes this potential an *eternal* object? There are strong and weak readings of the idea of eternity in Whitehead. Perhaps he himself fluctuated in this respect. On my reading of him, a "complex" eternal object is a potential pattern that could become instantiated. The repetition with variation of certain patterns in leaves, wings, and mammal limbs, the similarities in shape of a tornado and hurricane, these are patterns that subsist as potentials during "this cosmic epoch." As the new or novel comes into being, these patterns help to hold the new formation together. They are realized, as it were, after the fact rather than before. The new bacterium subsisted as cloudy pluripotentialities on the way rather than either operating as a fixed potential implicit in actuality or being the sole effect of antecedent, blind causes.

In my view, the emphasis by Whitehead on eternal objects throws a conundrum into his philosophy. If he postulates many that are too definite, the element of real creativity in process philosophy becomes cramped. If he dissolves eternality into pure potential—into intense, diffused energies sometimes entering into creative vibrations with each other—his philosophy may lose the sense of cosmic optimism that seems to permeate it. For Whitehead agrees that this or that tragedy can confront a human civilization in its interactions with itself, with nonhuman forces, and with other civilizations. But he also seems to think that the universe is progressing—creatively, as it were—from one period of complexity to futures of greater complexity. In this respect you can sense the melding of eternal objects into the developing nature of God in Whitehead, a God conceived by him as an impersonal entity within the evolutionary process that absorbs and collects creative impulses as they emerge. Here are a couple of things he says:

> But we have to ask whether nature does not contain within itself a tendency to be in tune, an Eros urging towards perfection.[17]

> This final phase of passage in God's nature is ever enlarging itself.

> It belongs to the goodness of the world that its settled order should deal tenderly with the faint discordant light of the dawn of another age.[18]

Whitehead may not emphasize the fragility of things enough. Immortality, for Whitehead, is embedded in the process by which aspects of the past are preserved in the formation and persistence of new entities. God is the impersonal agent of that preservation. The idea, if I understand him, is that the combination of creativity, evolving entities, eternal objects, and an impersonal God as spur and collector of creative "advance" ensures the progressive complexity of the universe, even though particular human civilizations will bite the dust and the human estate (my term) will itself eventually go under.

It might seem that Whitehead's sense of growing cosmic complexity denies the second law of thermodynamics, the drive over the long term for entropy to increase. I suspect he does deny it as an iron law, and I wonder to what extent he accepts it as a strong tendency. Perhaps it makes sense to say, to qualify Whitehead, that there are some systems in the cosmos that delay and defer tendencies to entropy, and that they are involved periodically in processes of real creativity. Organisms, organic evolution, and ecosystems would be good candidates. Nietzsche, I suspect, would be inclined to accept some version of the idea that entropy tends to increase and to focus more actively on a subset of systems and processes that work against this tendency.

To what extent does the march of real creativity in human and nonhuman processes require eternal objects to sustain them? It seems to me, now at least, that a universe of real creativity could be marked by flexible *tendencies* toward pattern that persist and evolve as the world changes.[19] These tendencies, for instance, could be embodied in what Kauffman calls "preadaptations," a pattern that has evolved in one system that is redundant or serves one function now and, under new circumstances, sets a preliminary condition from which creative change occurs. Thus the wings of primitive birds set preadaptations from which the limbs of animals and humans eventually evolved, as Brian Goodwin contends.[20] And the amygdala, the primitive brain node in reptiles, acquires new functions and abilities as it joins others in the human body-brain-culture network. Such preadaptations were not implicitly designed to become human limbs or brain nodes—though the name Kauffman gives to these uncertain preconditions may inadvertently suggest that—nor were they simply determined to do so by genetic mutations that were automatically "replicated."[21] They set flexible enabling conditions and limits from which creative evolution proceeded.

So I suspect that Whitehead, though he has a hand to play, overplays it. It may be that his doctrine of eternal objects both reduces the scope of possible creativity in the world and obscures some dimensions of real danger to the human estate in a cosmos composed of multiple, interacting force fields. That "may be" is pertinent, since I concur with Whitehead that a philosophy of becoming, as well as those with which it competes, contains a "speculative" element that can be defended comparatively by reference to evidence and argument but is unlikely to be susceptible to definitive proof.

On this latter point, the great logician and mathematician concurs in an uncanny way with the philologist Nietzsche before him, though he apparently did not read Nietzsche. The powers of logical proof are inflated by those who ignore the fermentation within many entities. That smoothing is doubled if the mobility and entanglements of thinking are themselves flattened into sealed identities from which definitive logical arguments proceed. A credible philosophy, Whitehead thinks, can seek rough coherence, but, given the interentanglements of things, thought, and language, it is inapt to be demonstrable. Classical logic and process do not mesh neatly, just as time and closed transcendental arguments do not. There are, however, apparently modes of logic and mathematics through which such complexity, entanglement, and openness can be better expressed.[22]

Will to Power and Constrained Possibility

If you read some of Nietzsche's experimental formulations, particularly those collected in the *Will to Power*, through the lens provided by Whitehead, some interesting things happen. For, first, the latter's concepts help to illuminate some things that Nietzsche, writing before the advent of quantum mechanics, was trying to say. And, second, we soon reach a point at which persisting differences between them can be seen more clearly, thus opening up issues that we can seek to negotiate.

In several notes Nietzsche focuses on creative condensations in the rush of action-oriented perception forward and the process of thinking.[23] These condensations occur *before* a tight logical argument starts to do its work. His formulations touch those made by Whitehead when the latter presents human consciousness as the afterglow of a complex organization that precedes it and also when he contends that the light consciousness can shine on itself is weak. But Nietzsche moves further. He suggests that modes of creative self-organization of simple organisms, and even of some nonorganic processes, display traces that find more complex expression in human feeling, perception, thinking, and judgment. In Whitehead's terms Nietzsche injects an aesthetic element of attraction and repulsion into the nonhuman world, that is, into nonhuman expressions of "will to power" from which the impetus to creative evolution proceeds. Here are a couple of formulations:

> "Thinking" in primitive conditions (pre-organic) is the crystallization of forms, as in the case of crystal.

> All thought, judgment, perception, considered as comparison, has as its precondition a "positing of equality," and earlier still a "making equal." The process of making equal is the process of incorporation of appropriated material in the amoeba.

> The fundamental inclination to posit as equal . . . is modified, held in check, by considerations of usefulness and harmfulness. . . . This whole process corresponds exactly to that external mechanical process (which is its symbol) by which protoplasm makes what it appropriates equal to itself and fits it into its own forms and files.[24]

It is wise not to move *too* quickly from the preorganic and organic instances Nietzsche cites to his critique of the philosopher's excessive trust in logic, though that upshot is pertinent too. Nietzsche's basic point parallels that made by Whitehead in pointing to modes of attraction and repulsion in some preorganic and simple organic processes that enable negative and positive prehensions. Moreover creative processes of self-organization in the receiving entities enable them not merely, say, to *represent* similarity as identity but to work upon the digested elements until they *become* more "equal," until they are actually "incorporated" or fit more closely "into its own forms and files."

This "absorbing and fitting" activity means both that the ingested elements change as they are metabolized and that the receiving, organizing entity changes too. The aesthetic and creative elements in a world of becoming are expressed together in these passages. Representational thinking, you might say, comes into play after the organic processes of absorption and equalization have occurred.

The most fundamental dimension of will to power is expressed in activities of creative relation and becoming, though the habitual Euro-American reception of that phrase obscures this dimension in favor of others also there, such as drives to domination and expansion. The phrase Nietzsche adopts, however, too readily suppresses the other pregnant dimensions rolling around in it, so that a post-Nietzschean with Whiteheadian affinities may find it wise to replace *will to power* with other expressions. Once these preliminary moves are made, a potential debate is now opened up between Whitehead and Nietzsche about the proportionate roles played by creative reception and creative expansion in the universe.

But before dropping the phrase, let's listen to a subtext operating *within* the Nietzschean theme of domination in relational processes, as we note again how for him too such creativity includes and extends beyond the human estate:

> Physicists believe in a "true world" in their own fashion, a firm system-atization of atoms in necessary motion, the same for all beings. . . . But they are in error. The atom they posit is inferred according to the logic of perspectivism of consciousness and is therefore a subjective fiction. This world picture that they sketch differs in no essential way from the subjective world picture: it is only construed with more extended senses [with microscopes, etc.] but with *our* senses nonetheless—And in any case they left something out of the constellation without knowing it: *precisely this necessary perspectivism by virtue of which every center of force—and not only man—construes all the rest of the world from its own viewpoint, i.e., measures, feels, forms, according to its own force* [empha-sis added].

> My idea is that every specific body strives to become master over all space and to extend its force (—its will to power) and to thrust back all that resists its extension. But it continually encounters similar efforts on the part of other bodies and ends by coming to an arrangement (a "union") with those of them that are sufficiently related to it: thus they then conspire together for power. And the process goes on—[25]

The resonances between Whitehead and Nietzsche are intense here. First, subjectivity is not a ground of being; it is a formation. Second, subjec-tivity and intersubjectivity are not only ineliminable; they find differential degrees of expression in numerous processes beyond the human estate that are entangled with it. Every "center of force" or "actual entity" expresses a "perspective" through which it receives and repels potential relations. It "measures, feels, forms, according to its own force." Third, that is why it is often wise for us to extend our capacities of sensitivity to other force fields, to the extent it is possible to do so. Fourth, Nietzsche, before the advent of quantum theory, joins Whitehead in advance in resisting the sufficiency of efficient causality and impositional laws of nature.

Doing these things, Nietzsche also becomes suspicious of the typical replies critical philosophers make to mechanistic theories, in which they merely point to an element of "chance" in change. Chance, you might say, is the only counter to invoke to others who conceive the world in mechanistic terms if you yourself both think that much of the universe is mechanistic and lack a philosophy of creative process. So Nietzsche, who rejects the sufficiency of *both* the organic and mechanical images, projects relations that exceed mechanical cause without reducing the excess *entirely* to chance. He says that we need "to recognize the active force, the creative force in the chance event—chance itself is only the clash of creative impulses."[26] He thus moves in advance toward the Whitehead idea that creative change is irreducible to chance, mere unpredictability, or efficient cause. Or if chance is in play, as the word *clash* seems to suggest, it is often the result of intense interactions between two exploratory processes. The intense vibrations back and forth between two entities that enter into relations of accelerated disequilibrium sometimes set new possibilities of being into play in which the result that emerges exceeds the pursuit of either or both in aggregate. This makes creativity an ultimate property of the universe, not entirely reducible to classic categories of explanation, not entirely assimilable to bits of chance within mechanical processes, and incompatible with finalist conceptions of being. It is probably the bogeyman of finalism that has discouraged many from exploring the teleodynamic processes periodically involved in real creativity.

You might say that Nietzsche embraces the idea of transcendence as that which goes beyond what has been, but he does not accept it as a *being* beyond, a divinity whose commands or love are separate from humanity and reach down into the world. The relations of connection and dissonance between Whitehead and Nietzsche at this point become delicate.[27]

Out of such periodic encounters between entities of different types a new "union" or "arrangement" is sometimes forged, bringing something new into the world: a new bacterium-arsenic bond, a new flu bird-human jump, a new weather pattern, a new climate system, a new social movement, a new religious practice, a new economic system. Finally, as the previous formulations by Nietzsche suggest, he and Whitehead concur that no entity beyond the most simple *merely* seeks to preserve itself. Both contend that such entities, though to varying degrees, exude excess energies, loose ends, and unsettled remainders which, when a new situation arises, may excite novel vibrations. Even protoplasm, Nietzsche says, does not aim just at self-preservation, "for it takes into itself absurdly more than would be required to preserve it."[28] This is the most fecund meaning of will to power, the aspect that I have elsewhere tried to adumbrate under the "powers of the false."[29]

So the affinities between these two thinkers are real, and each also helps us to highlight elements in the other that might otherwise slip away. The differences, however, are also notable. Nietzsche may not focus enough on the degree of responsiveness we must cultivate to allow something new to become creatively consolidated in our thought or lives, although there are places in *Thus Spoke Zarathustra* that move in this direction. Nietzsche also gives no sense of accepting something like Whitehead's notion of eternal objects that, first, help to mediate creative relations between mobile entities; second, help explain what holds things together; and third, set limits to creativity in concrete situations.

Finally, Nietzsche not only challenges an omnipotent God as a personal, moral Being who monopolizes creativity; he would also be wary of the Whiteheadian impersonal God who provides an impetus to creative unions and collects the complexities that emerge as the universe advances from lower to higher levels of complexity. He hesitates, perhaps out of concern for the history of uses to which the name has been put, to give the name God to such an impetus. Nietzsche is more attracted to the contending gods of Hesiod, translating them into a world of multiple, interacting force fields ungoverned by an overriding center, moving at different speeds and degrees of complexity. He, again, responds to them by including the idea of transcendence as a reaching and going beyond that is purely naturalistic.

Negotiating the Differences

I take Nietzsche to concur in advance with my attempt to qualify eternal objects with conditional processes of preadaptation that periodically set the platform for a new creative "union." He criticizes Darwinism, I think, because the version he received diminished or eliminated the creative element in species evolution.

Let's briefly compare him to Whitehead on aesthetic relations. In a discussion of the "Gift Giving Virtue" in *Thus Spoke Zarathustra*, Zarathustra speaks of an aesthetic drive to expand the "inflow" of experience and to allow that influx to become organized unconsciously by the human sensorium until a new sensitivity and excess of energy become available to bestow "gifts" of generosity upon others and the Earth. The "others" he has in mind are particularly those whose professions of faith, identity, self-interest, and moral imperative differ from ours in important respects. For nobility cannot be unless several nobilities, expressing different existential creeds, contend with and against each other in noble ways. Thus, to Zarathustra and Nietzsche, the ground of morality is not found in a transcendent command or a set of universal principles from which concrete imperatives are "derived." Such conceptions are too lazy and crude for a world marked by twists and turns that periodically challenge congealed habits. We need to cultivate presumptions of care and agonistic generosity to draw upon as we respond to new, unexpected situations. We need to pursue a "spiritualization of enmity" with others, to the extent they will allow it, in which each internalizes the discomfort the other poses, each accepts the agony of challenge to its heartfelt beliefs, and each also challenges the other. We also need to stretch our sensory, perceptual, experimental, and conceptual powers so that the species and cultural provincialisms with which we start can be tested and extended. This, at least, is one side of Nietzsche, though it is periodically compromised by other moods.

Whitehead would pursue such adventures more consistently. He expresses a debt to Wordsworth's nature poetry in which our sensitivity is enhanced by visiting protean scenes twice, the first time to receive the inflow of experience and the second to amplify its effect on memory and future powers of perception. From this perspective Nietzsche, despite his alter ego's love of the Earth, still may not do enough to cultivate heightened sensitivity to various aspects of the nonhuman world. The domination element in will to power sings too loudly. In a world composed of multiple attractions and repulsions that exceed our everyday practices of action-oriented perception, we need to work on ourselves to become more *responsive* to the artistry of whales who compose music as they travel, to the quantum complexity of birds' powers of sonar navigation, to the self-organizing powers of ocean currents, to the complexity of lava flows that issue in unpredictable patterns of granite, to the simple, unconscious intentionality of a bacterium as it adjusts its movement up a glucose gradient, and to yeast as the intense sounds it emits express feelings of pain when alcohol is poured on it. The aesthetic element of becoming finds expression in Nietzsche, but the human-nonhuman dimension of aesthetic relations is pursued even more sensitively by Whitehead.

Jane Bennett, Timothy Morton, Davide Panagia, Brian Massumi, and Anatoli Ignatov make valuable contributions to this dimension of being.[30] Today new scientific instruments and artistic endeavors—and often both together—can alert and extend our perceptual and relational capacities. They can sensitize us to some aspects of processes that were previously opaque to us, as when, for instance, biologists amplify the sounds of yeast first when it is at rest and then when alcohol has been poured on it that increases the intensity of its perturbations. Nietzsche, let us say, was *not enough* of a romantic in this respect, even if his Dionysianism carried him to the edge of that movement and even if he had reason to question *other* aspects of romanticism.

What are those "other aspects"? Nietzsche, much more than Whitehead, measured in advance cultural resistance to signs in favor of a world of becoming on the part of many who had imbibed Judaism, Islam, and Christianity for centuries and, in some cases, then unconsciously absorbed "the remains" of those theologies into Enlightenment and secular notions of linear, progressive time, a deterministic model of science, a moral image of the world, or the promise of human mastery. Moreover Nietzsche also detected resistance to an ungoverned cosmos of becoming in romantic drives to commune with a unity that subsists just over the horizon of everyday awareness. The romantic drive, he thinks, was to find a world predisposed in its largest compass to the human estate as such. Whether he is right about those judgments is an interesting issue. Perhaps it fits some cases and not others.

But regardless, Nietzsche, the modern philosopher of an ungoverned cosmos, was highly sensitized to subterranean currents of existential resentment that proliferate when many harbor suspicions that disrupt two familiar and contending images of cosmic reassurance. The issue of *ressentiment* now enters the scene, with the culturally embattled Nietzsche more alert to its modes of expression and cultural danger than the magisterial Whitehead.

The Cosmopolitical Dimension

It is serious enough to resent, first, human mortality and, second, time's "it was" in which you cannot reverse past events or actions you regret the most. A third, related dimension is activated when people who have imbibed traditional monotheisms and/or secular or humanist notions of human uniqueness encounter living evidence on behalf of a bumpy, multitiered world of becoming. Today such encounters can be resisted but perhaps not easily ignored. They are lodged in the accelerated pace of some dimensions of cultural life in dissonant relation to other slow processes, in the rapid, global, media communication of earth-shaking natural events, in scientific speculations about the evolution of the cosmos as well as solid evidence of species evolution, in renewed intensities of conflict between regionally anchored religions with contending claims to universality in a world of rapid communication, in recent research in neuroscience that makes the human body-brain-culture system look closer to a teleodynamic system oscillating between decoherence and coherence than to either a carrier of free will floating above earthly life or a system of mechanical causes, in impressive evidence of previously unexpected conjunctions between late capitalism and the acceleration of climate change which disturbs the idea of an autonomous nature either sufficient to itself or governed by God, in action-oriented films required to inflate human powers of heroism grotesquely to retain the image of mastery, and in widespread experiments in film and the new media that complicate action-oriented modes of perception with the uncanny complexity of duration. Such experiences can accumulate to cast doubt upon previous assumptions about the place of humanity in the cosmos. They can therefore amplify intensities of existential resentment in many, as those intensities surge *through* the issue of mortality and teeth gnashing over the "it was" *into* anxieties about the shaky place of the human estate in the cosmos.

Such cosmic issues have never been absent, as several religious traditions testify and as our short forays into the distinctive responses of Hesiod, Sophocles, Voltaire, Hayek, and Kant to different versions of them display. But the issue does wax and wane in its political expressions, and we are living through a global time when it waxes in a distinctive way, a period when every creedal minority in a world of minorities rubs shoulders more regularly and acutely with others.

When such existential issues are inflamed, they do not remain confined to the late-night anxieties of isolated individuals. They become burned into institutional practices and political conflicts, infusing media news reporting, church assemblies, compensatory consumption practices, investment routines, electoral campaigns, state priorities, military elites, action films, global conflicts, and the resonances between these venues. Such anxieties are not always *confessed*, for such confessions would too readily challenge official *professions* of secular or religious confidence. They are, rather, expressed variously and indirectly in the exacerbation of religious struggles, in the avoidance of certain issues, in hyperconfidence in the impersonal rationality of economic markets, and in the demonization of constituencies who call upon us to address the fragility of things. For today we need to slow down and divert human intrusions into various planetary force fields, even as we speed up efforts to reconstitute the identities, spiritualities, consumption practices, market faiths, and state policies entangled with them. Such a tension helps to constitute the contemporary fragility of things.

Today we encounter not just the issue of mortality, or the precariousness of a state, or cultural exclusions, or the severe challenges to this or that civilization. Those, as it were, continue, and they can be agonizing. Today we encounter intensely again the fragility of a human estate entangled by a thousand threads and resonances to a cosmos of multiple force fields, most of which are not first and foremost predisposed to our welfare. Our world has moved closer to that of Hesiod and Sophocles, and the issue of how to respond to it is unsettled. When you link the fatefulness of these imbrications to the acceleration, intensification, and globalization of neoliberal capitalism, the situation becomes yet more highly inflamed. For these planetary force fields set on different tiers of chronotime—such as climate patterns, glacier flows, viral evolution across species, bacteria in our guts, tectonic plate movements, water-filtering processes, the ocean conveyor belt, and processes of soil self-renewal—pose challenges to both received conceptions of time and to the anticipated trajectory of capitalism. Since both of these latter traditions are wound deeply into the ethos of modern life itself, the tension we have posed easily slides into a cul de sac: *the planetary fragility of things is increasingly sensed, as many protest against acknowledgment of that very sense to remain loyal to traditions of belonging woven into their bodies, role performances, and institutions.* Festering there, such anxieties *could* morph into concerted experiments to modify established patterns of attachment and belonging. But they can also become transposed into bellicose political movements of denial and deferral, movements joined to virulent attacks on any constituency that challenges the complementary modes of cosmic and civilizational assurance already in place. Witness the media attacks on scientists of climate change and proponents of sustainable energy. Or think about the dogmatism with which many impugn any notion of species evolution because it might open the possibility that neither a creator God nor military might nor benign capitalism really rules the world. Or think about those new atheists who dismiss with disdain every theological faith or concern for spiritual vitality. Or, again, think about the dismissiveness with which a subset of scientists, secularists, and religious leaders treat the hypothesis that we inhabit a cosmos of becoming. Or, finally, consider how carriers of the evangelical-neoliberal machine in the United States reject the legitimacy of every exploratory effort to rethink either the terms of capitalism or the creeds with which capitalism is closely entangled in that country. These examples could easily be extended to other places and domains. But we have perhaps cited enough to indicate how many "signs" available today cut against the reassuring historical set Kant identified at a high point of the Christian Enlightenment.

Nietzsche was prescient about the contemporary escalation of ressentiment as cosmic uncertainty rumbles again below cultural refusals to articulate it. He sensed the potential cul de sac in advance, as a seer traces one tendency in play among others to sense where it might go if it is not deflected. He also composed one alternative *response* to the existential suffering that comes with being alive and self-conscious. He calls it "my theodicy," the word *my* bringing out both its contestable character and his identification with it. Here is one way he put it:

> This type of *artist's pessimism* is precisely the *opposite* of that religio-moral pessimism that suffers from the "corruption" of man and the riddle of existence—and that by all means craves a solution. . . . The profundity of the tragic *artist* lies in this, that his aesthetic instinct surveys the remote consequences . . . , that he affirms *the large scale economy* which justifies the terrible, the evil, the questionable—and more than merely justifies them.[31]

Before we appraise the *double-entry* approach Nietzsche sometimes embraces to his own *theodicy*, we need to be clear about the entry he embraces in his own voice on the way to pursuit of a positive "spiritualization of enmity" with other voices. Nietzsche himself affirms "the large scale economy" of an ungoverned cosmos of becoming that includes and surpasses us. That is, he "more than justifies" it in the sense that he treats it as a condition of existence as such. We can affirm or resent this world but we are unable to change its most fundamental parameters. He does not take delight in human suffering and evil, though some love to deflect his challenge by pretending so. Nor does he merely *believe* in an ungoverned cosmos with fluctuating periods of relative quiescence and unruliness in its entanglements with the human estate. Rather he, first, acknowledges the experience of existential suffering that involvement in such a cosmos engenders; second, calls upon us to subdue and sublimate that suffering by tactical means; third, additionally appreciates some modes of suffering as possible conditions of creative thinking and action; and fourth, works to *affirm* the sweetness and vitality of life in such a cosmos. He treats the cosmos as a precarious condition of possibility for the sweetness of human life, attachment to the world, and the modest participation by the human estate in moments of creativity that range well beyond it. He seeks to drain existential resentment from existential experience to overcome or divert destructive and self-destructive human drives.

He admits on several occasions that his is only one positive "conjecture" by which to acknowledge and address the cosmic condition. The hope is that many who adopt other cosmic creeds will also affirm the gift-giving virtue in their worldly relations with other creeds, even though he came to doubt that a majority could or would do so. Given the more rapid minoritization of the world and the globalization of fragility since the time of Nietzsche, it is now even more urgent to forge a positive ethos of engagement between diverse and contending creeds.

Nietzsche, as I dramatize tendencies discernible in his work, adopts a two-pronged relation to other perspectives. He first evangelizes an ungoverned cosmos that exceeds the assumptions of providence, human uniqueness, and mastery. In doing so, he works upon us to *affirm* simultaneously (a) the sweetness and miracle of life in which mortality is unavoidable and extreme misfortune very possible, (b) the irreversibility of time and "it was," and (c) modest human participation in creative powers that extend into an ungoverned cosmos composed of multiple force fields. We are thrown into being within that world, amid the temporary enclosures we construct and maintain to provide sustenance in it. It too comes with pleasures, disruptions, and periods of creativity. As Nietzsche says in defense of a tragic *vision* of *possibility* and a critique of tragic *resignation*, "The faith that a good meaning lies in evil means to abandon the struggle against it."[32]

In a second gesture, however, Nietzsche affirms, when he is at his best, that the theodicy he embraces is not the only affirmative way to engage things. There are others. They become "noble" when practitioners of this or that *creed* of immanence or transcendence mix into it a spirituality of cosmic gratitude drawn upon to pursue positive assemblages with carriers of other creeds. So when he is not mesmerized by the judgment that only a very few noble ones in any faith will ever entertain relations of agonistic respect across difference, he offers his *theodicy* as *one* minority faith to press into comparative exchanges with others. Who knows, a potent pluralist assemblage could eventually emerge from such crossings and contestations, though Nietzsche's double, Zarathustra, himself eventually shied away from investing hope in politics.[33]

Dropping the phrase *will to power* and playing up more than he did the fragility of things, I otherwise embrace much in Nietzsche's vision of the cosmos and the human relation to it. I admire the double-entry approach he sometimes pursued in relations with other visions, and I seek to press it more consistently. And Whitehead? My double-entry stance in its first gesture pulls me a little distance from Whitehead's cosmic image of ever growing complexity, but it then expresses a welcome indebtedness in a second move to the way he pursues the question of creativity and the affirmative *spirituality* he brings to an open cosmos. My sense is that periods of real creativity in the evolution of worldly objects and systems may be even more robust at key junctures, for good or ill, than Whitehead imagined. This sense distances me to some problematic degree still to be worked out from his notions of eternal objects, automatic tendencies toward greater complexity, and an impersonal God who conveys new levels of complexity into the future, even as I accept the idea that previous modes of complexity set conditions of possibility from which new ones *may* evolve. So Whitehead has a hand to play here, but he may push it too far.[34] To accept it unrevised may be to underplay the dangers of human hubris, complacency, and ressentiment in late modern capitalism.

It must be emphasized that the positive spirituality Whitehead pours into his speculative philosophy is at least as affirmative as that of Nietzsche, and more consistently so. These two process philosophers are thus worthy protagonists from whom others can draw sustenance: they advance contending, overlapping cosmic creeds that speak to today; they address the spiritual quality through which a creed is lived in relation to others; and they throw up for grabs a set of established, complementary assumptions during a period when many constituencies both feel and suppress doubts about those assurances. Each, at his best, argues with the carriers of other creeds while inviting their proponents to fold positive spiritualities into their creedal relations.

When you fold intercoded concepts such as "the human estate," "a cosmos of becoming," "heterogeneous, intersecting planetary force fields," "a tragic vision of possibility," "existential resentment," "existential affirmation," "the fragility of things," and "the spiritualization of enmity" into interpretations and interventions that are *also pitched at the levels of local, state, interstate, and global politics*, political thought may approach the layered, exploratory engagements appropriate to the contemporary condition. Now interpretation becomes more multilayered so that dicey intersections between late capitalism, regional religious practices, and nonhuman, planetary forces with their own powers of metamorphosis become more closely defined *objects* of engagement. Not by striving to encompass everything about all of them in one totalizing system, for a philosophy of becoming engages multiple scales without enacting closure. You proceed, rather, by tracing a significant problem complex up and down its scales of intercalation and imbrication wherever such a slippery adventure takes it. You become a problem-oriented pragmatist while expanding the potential scope of fields relevant to those problems. This means, for instance, that sometimes you attend to how existential issues and anxieties infiltrate into specific political formations and at others you sink into how a glacier-amplification process and capitalism impinge upon one another. You engage the planetary dimension of politics when you explore how ocean current flows, climate patterns, regional patterns of drought and flood, water self-purification processes, hurricane patterns, and so on impinge upon us and how cultural processes impinge upon them. You touch the cosmic dimension when you consider how tacit and articulated images of the cosmos itself fold into established patterns of response to local, global, and planetary processes. Each must be engaged in relation to the others.

The existential tempers of ressentiment, hubris, and studied complacency, discernible as contending spiritual forces invested into the life of politics today, may not simply be distributed as diverse responses by different constituencies to larger world processes. It may be, as Sophocles showed in another era and Voltaire suggested with respect to the two theodicies he charted, that each temper often subsists as a minor chord in the others, so that today some evangelical and secular carriers of ressentiment are also activated by a degree of hubris, so that neoliberal and military purveyors of hubris often convey subtones of existential resentment, and so that many "moderate" carriers of studied complacency contain enough traces of the first two spiritualities to be more susceptible to contagion from them than otherwise would be the case.

To speak of a cultural constellation composed of multiple existential tones and subtonalities is to point to a generic feature of contemporary life. It secretes a shifting politics of surge and flow across diverse constituencies. The complex that emerges is not entirely reducible either to traits of individual character or to fixed cultural blocks. The entanglements and movements are too variable and invested in the vicissitudes of political life to succumb entirely to either mode of analysis. In *something like* the way the tones, themes, and refrains of a piece of music performed in a concert hall with excellent acoustics saturates the room as it waxes and wanes, so too do the shifting tones of hubris, ressentiment, and studied complacency inflect constituency and interconstituency relations. That is the danger. In the United States, at least, one strategic constituency singularly susceptible to allowing the first two tones to pour into its complacency calls itself the cadre of "moderates" and "independents."

Some of the dangerous combinations erupt during protean periods when interruptions shock established modes of identity and reassurance, as with the Lisbon quake during one moment, the introduction of Darwin's theory of evolution at another, the shock of the European Holocaust later, the dropping of nuclear bombs upon Japanese cities, and the slow burn of conjunctions between capitalism and climate change today. Such examples could be multiplied. Nonetheless, if and as extreme demands for the cosmic entitlement of the human estate are subdued, suitable spiritual arts are more widely adopted by more constituencies, and a politics of positive engagement with the fragility of things is actively pressed by a positive constellation of minorities, it may also be possible to expand the cadre whose political commitments express attachment to the planet. Besides the dangers they bring, some shocks and interruptions set conditions of possibility for positive modes of creative action. We can take the examples listed in chapter 2 as instances of the latter. At some level, many already exude differential degrees of gratitude for the vitality of human existence, the modes of attachment it makes available, and the creative adventures it opens.

This, then, is a *cosmic* dimension folded into contemporary politics, in part because it speaks to a time when several planetary force fields become entangled densely with several aspects of daily life, in part because our capacities to explore and respond politically to such imbrications with affirmative intelligence are severely challenged, in part because dangerous existential dispositions surge and flow again into defining institutions of late modern life, and in part because these very intersections convey the need to rethink the contemporary condition.

Nietzsche and Whitehead articulate the planetary and cosmic dimensions in diverse concepts and affective tones that also touch, though neither may have anticipated how densely planetary processes with differing degrees of self-organizing power are entangled today with local, regional, and global issues. Each expresses, in his inimical way, a spirit of deep attachment to a cosmos of dispersed, conditioned processes; each, if he were to confront the contemporary condition, might appreciate the potential contribution an ethos of existential gratitude forged across territories, constituencies, and existential creeds could make to addressing the fragility of things. Or so I project into the magisterial Whitehead and the agonistic Nietzsche. The task, merely launched here, is to draw selective sustenance from each to think our place in the cosmos, to come to terms with the fragility of things at local, regional, global, and planetary sites, and to fend off the existential resentment that threatens to become severe under late modern conditions.

postlude :: role experimentation
and democratic activism

As already suggested, the quality of existential orientations to the human predicament plays a significant role in ethical, political, and economic life. Such a sensibility does not simply infuse individual life. A gratitude for being overflowing suffering, duties, and tasks can broaden the positive connections and presumptive generosities of interinvolved constituencies, as it is communicated back and forth between them. Such an ethos bumps into politics as it invites relations of selective affinity and agonistic respect with the collective moralities of divine law, subjective command, negative theology, and teleological finalism. A positive pluralist assemblage is likely to draw energy from several of these sources. On the other hand, existential resentment readily finds expression in vengeful cultural orientations to crime and punishment; in stingy conceptions of distributive justice; in narrow definitions of self-interest that squeeze generosities of character and experiences of interconnectedness out of it, in an eagerness to hear and spread dismissive stories about those who are down and out; in severe accusations against those outside your country, class, ethnicity, faith, or sexuality; and in refusals to acknowledge and address the fragility of things. The official source of an ethic and the existential orientation invested in it, then, are interinvolved elements that both shape and form the quality of an ethos.

To probe differences in sensibilities is to see how the right-wing media today does not simply manipulate its target audience, driving that audience to contradict its self-interest. Self-interest is more complex than that. Rather a resonance machine is forged between a will to believe among the primary audience and the media messages relayed to it. That is why factual correction is often insufficient to counter the emanations from such a machine. The best hope is to mobilize a counterconstituency as you also tap into subordinate strains of sensibility among those on edge of that machine, seeking to draw out more noble tendencies as you correct misstatements of fact. Such a combination is not always easy to enact. That is one reason we live during a dangerous time.

The above summary still conceals complexities. First, it is partly through our vulnerabilities that we appreciate and respond to the suffering of others. The experience of suffering plays a role in existential gratitude, making the interplay between gratitude and suffering delicate. That element of fragility, then, is wired into the human predicament as such. Suffering, of course, can often turn us in a different direction. The experience of severe abuse or collective terror, for instance, can incite obstinate desires to take abstract revenge on others. So, as we saw in the first interlude, existential vulnerability and gratitude are delicately interwoven. Another complexity is that existential gratitude, as already suggested, is underdetermined by creed and/or social position in ways that unsettle attempts to chart correlations between the formal positions of class, creed, or ethnicity and ethicopolitical stances. Moreover there are always incipient dispositions that can break in several directions. The accentuation of existential anxiety, for instance, might be pulled toward existential affirmation by artful means or toward *ressentiment*. The same goes for shame. It can provide a spur to bring our aspirational selves closer to our operational selves or, if overwhelming, a prod to conceal a will to revenge under expressions of piety so as to take others by surprise attack. Catholic nuns who resist Vatican authority to support same-sex relations provide noble examples of the former. A subset of priests who exude piety while preying on young boys provides distressing examples of the latter. Perhaps sexual identities and spiritual dispositions are particularly subject to such ambiguities, but other practices are not exempt.

Finally, some who act out of presumptive generosity may hesitate to cultivate such an ethos further; they may fear that cynics are right who commonly associate such an ethos with naïveté or the "myth of positive thinking" or a lack of sophistication about the world. But that is a mistake. Existential gratitude is not tied by necessity to either cosmic or historical optimism; it can go hand in hand with a tragic view of human possibility and a refined sense of the fragility of things, as it does in several strains of thought already consulted in this text. People are tricky, with regard to their relations with each other and their layered complexities. Culture is layered too, replete with zones of opacity within each layer and shaky modes of communication across them.

Nonetheless an ethos exuding existential gratitude, amid the vitality and vulnerabilities that mark life, can help to render us alert to the fragility of things as we also allow the sweetness of existence to sink into our pores. It can, for instance, help to mobilize surplus energies needed to work experimentally upon the institutional roles that now help to situate us culturally. In the late modern era we bear a responsibility to the future to cultivate existential gratitude to the extent our position in the world makes it possible to do so and to renegotiate the modes of political activism in play today.[1] The "we," here as elsewhere, is invitational.

:: :: ::

My procedure will be to address segments of the populace who pursue a critical perspective and feel tremors of gratitude for existence itself. If those who deny feeling such tremors nonetheless participate in the efforts to be explored, so much the worse for my preliminary perspective and the better for the project. For I am not certain about the asserted connections between temper and action, and I am happy to be disproven by action. There are points at which the hermeneutics of decipherment break off and experimental politics ensues.

We begin by noting a dilemma haunting electoral politics in several countries. (1) It is tempting for critics to forgo electoral politics because it is so dysfunctional. But to do so cedes too much independent power to corporate action and the radical right with respect to state power. The right loves to *make* politics dysfunctional to make people lose confidence in it and to transfer their confidence to the private sector. (2) Yet the logic of the media-electoral-corporate system does spawn a confined grid of electoral intelligibility that makes it difficult to think, experiment, and act outside its parameters. Think of the market initiating/state veto power of corporations, of media talking heads concentrating on differences between candidates, of the primacy of electoral strategists, of focus groups, of the role of scandal in the media and electoral politics, of the strategic location in elections of inattentive "undecided voters," of billionaire super PACs, and so on. The electoral grid cannot be ignored or ceded to the right, but it also sucks experimental pursuits and bold ventures out of politics. How can we renegotiate this dilemma of electoral politics? That is the problematic within which I am working. I do not purport to have a perfect response to it. Perfect answers are suspect.

It may be wise to *start* with the positive possibilities of micro-experimentation on several fronts. One thing that connects individuals, constituencies, and institutions is the roles that constitute an institutional matrix. The word *connection* is actually too weak. We are partly constituted by the array of roles we perform, and those performances resonate with the larger institutions in which they are set. You are, say, a teacher, an athlete, a lover, a parent, a middle-aged child of an aging parent, a student, a worker, a voter, a churchgoer, a film addict, a citizen, a consumer, a member of a political party, an investor, a blogger, a musician, an artist, and so on endlessly. You are, in part, a composite of the roles in which you participate, even though you overflow that composite. Subcategories, of course, multiply within each abstract category. A "worker" may repair computers, cook hamburgers, serve tables, advise clients on investments, sell furniture, teach elementary school kids, give Sunday sermons, be a TV producer, be a film director, and so on. As a devotee, you may be an evangelical Christian, a Catholic, a reform Jew, an orthodox Jew, a Unitarian, a devotee of nontheistic reverence, a Muslim, a Hindu, or a follower of the kind of Buddhism that eschews a personal God. The degree of intensity within each of these modes of identification will also vary.

Many role performances are tacit, as when you follow accepted rules of eye contact on an urban street, stop automatically at a red light on the way to work, chew your food a set number of times before swallowing, unconsciously participate in a settled practice of consumption, watch and listen quietly to a film at the theater, glance at an attractive gym partner through the mirror rather than staring directly, close the door when you are in the bathroom, adopt a distinctive stride during casual walks, or never pick your nose in public. To break that last restraint would be disgusting, reminding us how tacit role performances are infused with affective judgments. Such practices have become habitual, often in ways that condense previous relations of overt power.

Other role performances are more clearly laden with degrees of power, as when you obey an order from a boss, pay your taxes on time, arrive at work punctually, bow your head during prayer to minimize family tensions, avoid eye contact with a cop, give your earnings to the pimp who oppresses you, obey the terms of your probation, buy a car because no other mode of transportation is available, conform to the pace of work on an assembly line, or conceal drugs from prison officials.

Erving Goffman is brilliant at disclosing the tacit character of many shared role performances, as Judith Butler is in thinking about how they help to constitute a culture of gender practices. Here is one statement from Goffman, as he collects examples from multiple sources, exposing a series of tacit role performances that define and secure the modern sense of bodily integrity:

> How very intimate the bodily sense is can be seen by performing a little experiment in your imagination. Think first of swallowing the saliva in your mouth, or do so. Then imagine expectorating it into a tumbler and drinking it! What seemed natural and "mine" suddenly becomes disgusting and alien. Or picture yourself sucking blood from a prick in your finger; then imagine sucking blood from a bandage around your finger! What I perceive as separate from my body becomes, in the twinkling of an eye, cold and foreign.[2]

"In the twinkling of an eye." Butler, in *Gender Trouble*, focuses on how experimental performances bring out tacit practices that constitute the dominant experience of gender. Here is what she says in an early book about the ambiguity of drag: "In imitating gender, drag implicitly reveals the imitative structure of gender itself—as well as its contingency. Indeed, part of the pleasure, the giddiness of the performance is in the recognition of a radical contingency in the relation between sex and gender in the face of cultural configurations of causal unities that are regularly assumed to be natural and necessary . . . ; we see sex and gender denaturalized by means of a performance." It is of course debatable how far such denaturalization proceeds, and drag does not guarantee, as Butler knows, which responses will be made to its strategy of denaturalization. But denaturalizing performances do open the door to new possibilities of enactment, as they disclose inner, nuanced relations between cultural performance and gender constitution. As another quote from Butler in a later edition of the same book reveals, the culturally infused sense of bodily integrity and disgust in Goffman's example carries implications for the unconscious norms of sexual experience historically built into this culture: "Those sexual practices in both heterosexual and homosexual contexts that open surfaces and orifices to erotic signification or close down others effectively reinscribe the boundaries of the body along new cultural lines. Anal sex among them."[3] To reinscribe the cultural play of disgust and pleasure with respect to bodily fluids and orifices is to participate in the micropolitics of gender and sexual practice.

As these two thinkers reveal, there are significant relays between role performance, self-identity, and the formation of larger political constellations. Not in the sense that minor shifts in a series of role performances could by itself transform an entire political regime but in the sense that large-scale cultural investments in a set of role expectations tend to express and support the priorities of an established regime, while large-scale role experimentations can both make a difference on their own *and help to set preconditions for constituency participation in more robust political movements*. The domains of gender and sexuality are important on their own, and recent success in these domains carries suggestions of how to act in others as well. The creative politics of gender and sexuality during the past forty years displays how potent the play back and forth can be among role experimentations, occupational practices, local assemblies, teaching routines, church struggles, state policies, judicial decisions, and legislative enactments. Here I focus on protean connections between role experimentation, self-identity, economic performance, and macropolitical actions.

:: :: ::

To condense the flow chart, an institution is an organized hierarchy of roles in relation to energies and activities that overflow them, such as gossip, backdoor deals, confusion, whistle-blowing, care, revenge, and secrecy; roles mediate between identities and institutions; there is often a degree of slack within institutions as to how a role is to be performed; an accumulation of role experimentations in several venues can make a direct difference in politics; role experimentations by some can also set examples for others; and such experiments can filter into the sensibilities, beliefs, identities, and larger political activities of those who initiate and respond to them.[4] A series of shifts on this register, for instance, may dispose you to listen attentively to new proposals for large-scale political action. Powerful subterranean currents thus flow back and forth between role performance, existential orientation, belief, and larger political actions. Indeed as such oscillations proceed, moments of stuttering, unfocused shame, laughter, and hesitation periodically arise, drawn from the element of noise that inhabits the spaces between roles and role bearers.

There is no zone of complete neutrality in a world of role performances. Obedient performances in cumulative effect tend to support the existing regime as they insinuate its dictates into our collective habits of perception, judgment, and action. Unless a dissident group of workers meticulously "works according to rule" to disrupt production through excruciating obedience in a way that discloses how tangled formal rules can become. Or a group creatively improvises on the performance of Bartleby the Scrivener, posing endless questions about the orders given to it until the machine overflows itself or is jammed. These indeed are creative role experimentations. So was the practice in Eastern Europe during the late stages of Soviet rule to clap endlessly when a Soviet stooge spoke, until the bewildered speaker was moved to sit down amid the roar around him. I recently attended a faculty meeting with the president of my university at which the entire faculty remained silent after his CEO-style talk ended and he departed slowly up the aisle. Sometimes silence sends a message to power.

Our lives are messages.[5] Role experimentation can disrupt and redirect the flow of authority, habit, institutional regularity, and future projection. It can also encourage others to look more closely at their own performances in this or that domain. Such experiments can also set the stage for more adventurous and larger scale actions. My examples will be limited to constituencies who are the most apt to read this book, though they could easily be adjusted to a broader array.

Suppose a constellation of students, studying to enter professional life, forms study groups to explore more closely how those professions presuppose and enforce a set of practices that contribute to the fragility of things as they simultaneously draw attention away from that contribution. The students may pose untimely questions in their political science, economics, engineering, medical, business, legal, and biology classes. If in a secular institution, they may seek out courses that complicate the assumptions of secularism. If in a religious school, they may organize a group to explore the history of atheism or of minority faiths that eschew the theme of a personal God. They can engage experimental artistic work that stretches their habitual patterns of perception and judgment. The nature- and soundscape compositions of John Luther Adams have salutary effects on many in this respect. Such activities can also prime you to experiment with other role performances once you enter professional life. If a lawyer, you may organize to rethink your connections to the ugly prison system and to adjust your practice to protest its ugliness. Or you may give a portion of your time to challenge corporations, localities, and states that defile the environment. If a doctor, you may organize voluntary medical care for the poor and publicize what you are doing. In both cases these experimentations make a modest difference on their own, prime our capacities for more sensitive perception in other domains of life, and may prepare us to participate with others in yet more adventurous activities. These are minor moments, but an accumulation of minor moments can jostle settled habits of perception; they can encourage a readiness to become more exploratory; and they can extend the time horizon within which we think and act.

Suppose, now, you are middle- or upper-middle-class citizens in a polity that has competitive elections. You have become increasingly dissatisfied with the course your society is taking. Voting, while pertinent, seems radically insufficient to the issues involved. Its time horizon is too short and the strategic place of ill-informed undecided voters in electoral politics skews campaigns too sharply. Inequality has been extended. The lower reaches of society are left out in the cold and often blamed for the suffering they undergo. The news media are organized around scandal and a brief time horizon. Racial differences are exploited to break up potential coalitions on the left. A large slice of the population is periodically susceptible to war fever. Climate change is widely subjected to deferral, denial, or formal acceptance disconnected from action. And the right wing actively promotes filibusters and legislative stalemates to encourage more and more people to withdraw from citizenship and to tolerate the privatization of more and more of life.

The sciences and professions with which you are familiar are often too narrowly defined. Too many churches either provide refuges from the world or serve as sites of aggressive attack on ecological concerns, homosexuality, carriers of alternative faiths, or poor minorities. You know what political party you support; you vote regularly; and you give time and money to your party. But you also find it difficult to connect the sentiments you profess to the role expectations sedimented into your practices of work, church, consumption, neighborhood association, investment portfolio, children's school, artistic pursuits, and local news reporting. Now is the time to join others in becoming role experimentalists.

You may actively support the farm-to-table movement in the restaurants you visit; you may support the slow food movement; you may frequent stores that offer food based on sustainable processes; you may buy a hybrid or, if feasible, join an urban zip-car collective, explaining to friends, family, and neighbors what effect such choices could have on late modern ecology if a majority of the populace did one or the other; you may press your neighborhood association and workplace to buy solar panels and install them yourself; you may use writing and media skills developed in school to write for a blog; you may shift a large portion of your retirement account into investments that support sustainable energy; you may withdraw from aggressive investments that presuppose an unsustainable growth pattern, threaten economic collapse, and/or undermine the collective future; you may bring new issues and visitors to your church, temple, or mosque to support rethinking about interdenominational issues and the contemporary fragility of things; you may found, join, or frequent a repair club, at which volunteers collect and repair old appliances, furniture, and vehicles to cut back on urban waste and increase the longevity of these items; you may probe and publicize the multimodal tactics by which twenty-four-hour news stations work on the visceral register of their viewers, as you explore ways to counter those techniques; you may travel to places where unconscious American assumptions about world entitlement are challenged on a regular basis; you may augment your pattern of films and artistic exhibits attended to stretch your habitual powers of perception and to challenge some affect-imbued prejudgments embedded in them; you may seek out new friends who are also moving in these directions. You may regularly relay pregnant essays you encounter to friends, colleagues, and relatives. A series of minor role experiments.

As we proceed our aspirational selves may now begin to exceed our operational selves, and the shame we feel about the discrepancy between these two aspects of the self may generate energy to enter into yet new modes of role experimentation.[6] We thus begin to make ourselves and our engagements more experimental rather than simply falling into a ready-made set of role expectations. We have begun to become what Nietzsche calls "our own guinea pigs" rather than merely being the guinea pigs of those in charge of these institutions.

As such experiments accumulate, the ice in and around us begins to crack. First, the shaky perceptions, feelings, and beliefs with which we started these experimentations now become more refined and more en-trenched. Second, we are now better situated to forge connections with yet larger constituencies engaging in similar experiments. Third, as these con-nections accumulate we may be more inspired to join macropolitical move-ments that speak to the issues. Fourth, as we now join protests, slowdowns, and confrontational meetings with corporate managers, church leaders, union officials, university officials, and neighborhood leaders, we may now become more alert to the institutional pressures that propel these constitu-encies forward too. They are also both enmeshed in a web of roles that en-able and constrain them and often more than mere role bearers. These roles too exhibit varying degrees of pressure and slack as they link the details of daily conduct to the strategic practices of the larger political economy.

One advantage of role experimentation by several constituencies at mul-tiple sites is that it speaks to a time in which the drive to significant change must today be mobilized by a large, pluralist assemblage rather than by a single class or other core constituency. Such an assemblage must be primed and loaded by several constituencies at many sites. Role experimentations and the shape of a pluralist assemblage thus inflect one another.

We must condense some of the steps involved. But perhaps the multi-dimensional pluralist assemblage in which you have now begun to partici-pate approaches a tipping point—crystallized, say, by movement back and forth between role experiments, shifts in the priorities of some strategic in-stitutions, and a change in the contours of electoral politics. Now a surpris-ing event may occur, allowing these emergent energies to be crystallized. At this point some will enter the scene to say that no kind of "reformism," no matter how extensive, is acceptable. We must wait for a bigger, more total transformation, they will say. Such an account will be offered at precisely this tipping point as the only sophisticated reading of the world. But it is not. Yes, roles, institutions, events, constitutive acts, and larger structures are interinvolved, with each enabling and limiting others. Yes, we do inhabit a world of multiple entanglements and interconnections. Yes, the primacy of capitalist markets and private ownership does give owners and high-rolling investors key advantages in setting the agenda of the state. Yes, states subject to public elections are also limited by systemic relations to corporate structures and the threat of capital strikes. Yes, extreme inequality, combined with legislative and court decisions inspired by neoliberal ideology, do disenfranchise many as they release billions of dollars to right-wing electoral campaigns. Yes, private ownership of the media does give great advantages to the corporate establishment. Yes, dependent workers do face uphill battles in limiting capital through labor organization. Yes, the limited reach of semisovereign states in the global economy exerts corporate pressure on them, just as, inside the United States at least, the right-wing Supreme Court's devolution of authority to states in a federal system forces states to compete with each other for corporate favors. Yes, elected representatives are dependent on campaign money and their desires to find jobs as lobbyists after they leave office. Yes, there are pressures on many in the lower middle class to identify with the vision of the future publicized by those above them. It may therefore appear that there are no cracks and fissures in these interconnected processes. It may seem that you must either embrace the system with fervor, withdraw as much as possible from it, or wait for an explosion that changes everything rapidly.

The hegemony of neoliberal ideology reinforces such a reading of the alternatives, in its way, even as it otherwise emphasizes our inability to have a bird's-eye view of the system. It offers a bird's-eye view of the whole whenever it insists that market self-organization means impersonal market rationality. But repeated experience belies such an equation. There are numerous examples of surprising economic meltdowns, often ushered into being by submission to that very ideology. And periodically critical movements emerge, as if from nowhere, to challenge existing priorities at vulnerable sites. There is, for starters, the surprise of the Arab Spring, with its ambivalent possibilities; the emergence of a New Left in Euro-American countries in the 1960s and 1970s; the birth of feminist and gay rights movements in those same countries that have probed soft spots in churches, the media, corporate benefit packages, universities, state policy, and families; there is the "slut walk" by which young women challenged the idea that how they dress determines whether they deserve sexual assault; there is Tiananmen Square, which revealed currents of energy and protest in China that are still festering; there is the Occupy movement, springing as if from nowhere, to galvanize previously isolated pockets of dissatisfaction and unrest; there is the civil rights movement, which has reenergized itself several times; there are several ecological movements, mobilizing diffuse dissatisfactions with the direction neoliberal regimes have taken. Each of these events and movements exposes soft spots, cracks, uneven edges, and leakages in "the system," through which new lines of creative activity can form and pass.

While under way, these become creative forays with differing degrees of self-organization built into them. If and as their success grows, they may expose yet more seams and cracks in a system that is far more replete with rough edges between its subsystems than either its most ardent ideologues or some of its structural critics may acknowledge. The cracks, edges, fissures, noise, and renegade flows in these processes, hidden by this or that streamlined view, are often rendered visible by such experimental actions. One creative thing about that slut walk is how it incited erotic energy and recruited that energy for critical politics. More such experiments of this sort are needed in other domains. There is no reason in the world to allow sensual desire to flow into the advertisement, sale, and purchase of cars, clothing, perfume, vacations, and jewelry but yet to purge it from areas in which it could help to instigate and mobilize productive political activism. Except a self-denying Puritanism within radicalism itself.

:: :: ::

It is impressive how Karl Polanyi, writing in the mid-1940s after the collapse of classical market theory due to the Great Depression and before the later hegemony of neoliberalism, saw how rickety and leaky economic systems are. He identifies dangers that accompanied the great meltdown in 1929, exploring how the Great Depression unleashed or intensified a number of fascist movements in the Euro-American world. He resists both the story of sufficient market rationality and any critical theory that either explains everything in terms of conflicts of class interest or waits for a total revolution. As wider bands of culture and nature are incorporated into economic processes the limits, fractures, and contingencies of economic assemblages multiply too. Political and economic thinking, he contends, must thus become more "situational," wary of its own tendencies to postulate closure when several degrees of slack, contingency, and surprise may be in play. We too readily become too confident about our ability to give complete explanations, he says. We must fold modesty about the "situational character" of economic life into the operational assumptions of theory and practice. A "situation is created, as a rule, by external causes, such as a change in climate, or the yield of crops, a new foe, a new weapon used by an old foe, the emergence of new communal ends, or, for that matter the discovery of new methods of achieving traditional ends."[7]

While we would today add items to Polanyi's list—attending to pockets of noise within and sharp edges between the subsystems that constitute an assemblage and emphasizing even more the nonhuman forces that impinge upon it in so many ways—Polanyi's insight is crucial to contemporary engagements with political economy. The outside periodically carries potent forces into the inside, upsetting a consummate theory of impersonal market rationality or a critical theory of capitalism that purports to exhaust its essence. Indeed the differential powers of the outside render such assumptions dangerous.

Pressures to postulate either a self-regulating rationality or a closed system of exploitation can arrive from several contending sites. There are those who, plagued and exhausted by the demands of everyday life, yearn for a story that assures them that everything would work smoothly if *only* states, politicians, unions, and disruptive social movements receded from the scene. The very burdens they face may predispose them to neoliberal ideology. Some in more favorable social positions may feel entitled to democracy but resist the need to invest more of their energies in it so that it can flourish. They want democracy to be automatic.[8] Additionally there are social scientists filled with the existential demand to posit a world fully susceptible "in principle" to their explanatory prowess. And there are critics who sense that *if* the world is to be susceptible to revolutionary overhaul, it must now take the shape of a tight, contradictory structure. These are merely tendencies, replete with significant exceptions and variations of degree. But together they may distract attention from a world composed of heterogeneous, interacting systems with variable powers of self-organization that are resistant to consummate rationality, explanation, or control. Much of late modern experience attests to that latter image, while numerous pressures and desires arise to efface it in this or that way.

Today it is palpable both that things are fragile and that the multiple systems in which we participate are less closed, rational, or integrated than they appear from an abstract perch high above them. We engage life in the middle of things. On the ground, the back and forth between role experimentations, enhanced sensitivity to noise, and larger political actions periodically shows promise. Of course, you don't *know* noise while it *is* noise. You may, however, periodically draw uncanny drafts of creative energy from this or that incipience on the way as you respond to a new, unexpected situation. Those drafts can make a difference to the creative thinking that emerges. That is why films, music, spiritual exercises, and theatrical erotica are all pertinent to the energy of a critical movement. They sometimes encourage new thoughts to surge forward as if from nowhere and then to become infused into critical action. Who will be the musicians whose performative experiments do for our day what, say, the Weavers, Joan Baez, and Bob Marley did for several constituencies during another time? Who will be the film directors? The bloggers?

In the scenario I visualize, active minorities in several sections of society escalate and extend their strategic role experimentations, pressing the numerous institutions in which they are located to become more responsive. They increase nonviolent disruptions of business as usual on several fronts. They then make new inroads into electoral politics that would not have been feasible without those activities. As such pressures accumulate, this or that event may erupt, emerging from the world of periodic volatility in which we participate. The combination of the event and a many-fronted social movement that reaches down into role experimentations and up into public actions could help to spark a yet more militant movement, *if* the groundwork has been laid. The movement will act at multiple sites, including electoral politics, church assemblies, public protests, corporate boycotts, media interventions, and union meetings.

Yes, as such a movement unfolds it could be overwhelmed or folded back into the fractured, rickety, leaky assemblage in which it participates. In a multitiered world of conditioned becoming there are no guarantees. But the story that, short of a violent revolution, absorption is always necessary or unavoidable flies in the face of a recurrent history of natural events, political disruptions, and creative changes. Unless the mode of change envisioned is so total and complete that it is supposed to bring the trials, frictions, struggles, and surprises of history to an end. In a world of becoming there is no such future. What structural Marxist in, say, the 1950s or early 1960s prophesied the disruptive link between neoliberal capitalism and climate change? What Keynesian did the same, or explored critically the relation between the infrastructure of consumption and the constriction of consumption possibilities?[9] Which secularists in the mid-1970s, including those as diverse in voice, ideology, and stature as Rawls, Elster, Habermas, Williams, Althusser, Shklar, Laclau, Foucault, Wallerstein, Hayek, Lukes, Wolin, Connolly, and Dahl, anticipated the rapid rise of an evangelical-neoliberal resonance machine in America within a very few years? Such situational features, we now know retrospectively, rendered problematic the explanations and responses each did offer. Some of the elements listed above were solid actualities outside the line of vision of those who insisted that, say, economic life must correspond to the conceptual boundaries of an economics department. Other cloudy processes, however, festered as pluripotential *incipiencies* that could have broken in more than one direction. These processes limit in principle the predictive power of the human sciences and social movements alike, particularly when considered in relation to the powers of nonhuman force fields that impinge upon human life.

I do not pose such examples to criticize the failure to anticipate such events but to both dampen the hubris of those who think they know in advance what the limits of democratic social movements must be and to lend support to an experimental politics of militant action operating at several intercoded sites. The significant spread of role experimentations by more constituencies into new venues can provide important catalysts to broader political action. If our role performances become frozen, so do our beliefs, identities, and larger modes of political experiment. You are indeed then apt to become nervous and resentful of any mode of experimentation initiated elsewhere. You are apt to call critical experimentalists *hypocritical* if they do not break completely with the web of roles in which they are enmeshed and to call them *irrelevant* if they seek to do so. Such tactics place democratic activists in a double bind. The charge conveys either a cynical, narrow image of *self-interest* as the only real basis of action or, less often, an image of *moral purity* as the only worthy source. But we inhabit an entangled world in which the best hope is to extend and broaden our identities, interests, and ethos of interconnectedness as we multiply the sites of political action.

Do not, then, underestimate the potential power of subterranean flows back and forth between sensuality, identity, faith, perceptual powers, role performance, institutional life, electoral politics, and social movements. That would be to underplay the potential of self-organization in politics. When creative shifts in the performances of many are enacted, the stage may be set for a self-amplification system to emerge, with each initiative inflating some of the others. Such a creative resonance machine is one thing the Occupy movement has called us to again, as movements at other times and places have too. Its instigators and initiators are often lodged in the interstices of cultural life as liberal arts students, sexual minorities, marginalized workers, academics outside the mainstream, women, the newly unemployed, artists, independent film directors, bike commuters, those undergoing spiritual transformation, ethnic minorities, and on and on. That is why the right regularly attacks such constituencies as vagrant.

Can the dilemma of electoral politics be broken as we work both outside and inside its terms to alter its grid of political intelligibility? I do not know. But an orientation that focuses upon the potential interplay between productive actions at numerous sites does provide a strategic entry into the task of renegotiating that grid of intelligibility. This is especially so in a world in which more and more people sense both the fragility of things and feel the resistance within courts, corporations, electoral politics, and our souls to address it.

:: :: ::

Let us suppose that progress is made on the intercoded fronts of role experimentation, changes in the infrastructure and ethos of political economy, and pressure for new state policies. I will treat the instances reviewed in chapter 1 to exemplify the interim state policies needed. Clearly, as movements from the antiapartheid actions in the 1980s to Occupy in recent years have shown, a *cross-state citizen dimension* is also needed. Such a dimension applies pressure to states, corporations, workers, investors, consumers, churches, voters, and universities from both inside the state and outside it. If and as such cross-state citizen fermentation arises again, the interlocking constituencies may need a beacon to help orient our energies and actions. It may be that those who both appreciate the fragility of things and hear a call for democratic militancy at several sites can be further energized by connecting these critiques, proposals, and actions to such a beacon. Whitehead would call it a "lure," to infuse a sensual dimension into its temporal horizon and categorical shape. Perhaps an appropriate lure today is to prepare, by the multiple means noted above, a set of interacting minorities in several countries for the time when we coalesce around a general strike launched in several states simultaneously. Perhaps it could be a graded strike at first, with one-day actions followed by longer actions if the demands are ignored. If, once preliminary support for more militance has reached a tipping point, such actions were organized by citizen activists across several countries, the odds that any single country could defeat the strike by itself would be reduced. The overriding goal is to press international organizations, states, corporations, banks, labor unions, churches, consumers, citizens, and universities to act in concerted ways to defeat neoliberalism, to curtail climate change, to reduce inequality, and to instill a vibrant pluralist spirituality into democratic machines that have lost too much of their vitality.

ACKNOWLEDGMENTS

Several presentations at different universities have helped me to think and rethink the themes of this book. I note a talk at the University of Essex in the fall of 2010, one to the Humanities Center at Brown University in the fall of 2011, a keynote to the national graduate student theory conference at Cornell in the spring of 2012, a talk to a symposium on *A World of Becoming* in London in December 2011, a conference on my work at the University of Nottingham in the spring of 2012, a keynote at an Oxford University conference on Becoming and Creativity, and another at the *Millennium* Conference on Global Politics and the New Materialism. There were rich and even fecund discussions at each of these meetings, and the final product that has emerged is very much an outgrowth of these discussions.

I should also note the blog *The Contemporary Condition*. Jairus Grove and I launched it in the winter of 2010, and it has grown into a rich forum for presentations on major issues of the day. Several of the themes in this book first found expression in one of my postings on that blog. I am indebted to Jairus Grove both for the work he does for *The Contemporary Condition* and his explorations of these ideas with me. Tim Hanafin and Steve Johnston have now become comoderators of that blog, and discussions with them have also been very useful.

Many colleagues inside and outside the Department of Political Science at Johns Hopkins University provide impressive support for the theory enterprise in general and this project in particular. I note Jane Bennett, Sam Chambers, Jennifer Culbert, Nicolas Jabko, Siba Grovogui, Katrin Pahl, Paola Marrati, Naveeda Khan, and Veena Das as key members of that cohort. People beyond Hopkins, such as Bonnie Honig, Lars Toender, Mike Shapiro, Tom Dumm, Mike Hanchard, Catherine Keller, Kathy Ferguson, Alex Livingston, Davide Panagia, Bhrigu Singh, John Buell, John Thatamanil, Aletta Norval, Paul Patton, David Howarth, and Nathan Widder, have also been very kind to read and comment thoughtfully on sections of this book as it has evolved. Indeed, Bonnie Honig, Paul Patton, and Catherine Keller have given close readings of large portions of this text, and their comments have been invaluable.

A couple of Hopkins graduate seminars helped me to consolidate these themes. One was the seminar "Political Economy and Complexity Theory" that Nicolas Jabko and I cotaught in the spring of 1012. I thank Nicolas for his thoughtful engagements with these issues. Anatoli Ignatov, Patrick Giamario, Adam Culver, Tripp Rebrovik, Drew Walker, Katie Glanz, Chris Forster-Smith, Derek Denman, Jairus Grove, Stephanie Fishel, Chad Shomura, and Ben Meiches are current or very recent students whose thinking now plays a role in my own. Anatoli, Adam, and Derek offered critiques of some of these chapters that proved to be particularly helpful. Eleanor Gardner, an impressive undergraduate, prepared the initial draft of the bibliography in a precise way.

Two of these chapters are greatly expanded and augmented versions of essays that appeared in previous publications. I thank Princeton University Press for permission to reprint "Shock Therapy, Dramatization, and Practical Wisdom" from *The Joy of Secularism*, edited by George Levine (Princeton: Princeton University Press, 2011), 95–210. The version published here explores more closely the relations between Kantian postulates about automatic regulative processes between nations and within nature and assumptions about politico-economic life. I also thank the publisher of *theory&event* for permission to republish "Steps toward an Ecology of Late Capitalism," which appeared in that journal in February 2011. "*Melancholia and Us*" first appeared as a post in *The Contemporary Condition*.

Patrick Giamario has not only discussed these chapters with me in thoughtful ways, he has done yeoman work in preparing the index, working on the notes, and completing the bibliography. Jane Bennett and I taught two seminars together that speak to these issues. She has also read each chapter in an early form, helping me to consolidate and sharpen themes. I am deeply appreciative to her for the kind of person she is, the intellectuality she emanates, and, well, her partnership in life.

Prelude

1 Quoted in Hamblyn, *Terra*, 28. Much of my description of the Lisbon event is taken from this study.

2 A fine essay that compares the Kantian "optimistic" reading of the shock of the sublime under the influence of Lisbon to the more wrenching readings by Lyotard and Adorno under the shadow of the Nazi Holocaust is Ray, "Reading the Lisbon Earthquake." I engage Kant in chapter 3 of this study.

3 Voltaire, "On the Lisbon Disaster."

4 Doubtless the Voltaire satire does not do justice to the philosophy of Leibniz. Leibniz, for instance, does not promise that every *individual* will eventually flourish after suffering. In this best of all *possible* worlds many are apparently doomed to lives of hell. His is a philosophy, insofar as I understand it at this point, in which God has engineered the best world out of a fairly bad set of possibilities. Even with that proviso, however, Voltaire calls upon us to focus

on how the demand to vindicate such a God can recoil back to stifle concern for suffering and victims. For a thoughtful account of the Leibniz theodicy, see Nadler, *The Best of All Possible Worlds*.

5 Voltaire, *Candide*, 25.

6 Voltaire, *Candide*, 25–26.

7 Perhaps the first time I explored this theme was in a reading of the Book of Job in 1993. Here is a quotation from that essay: "This God [in Job] is not the designer of a cosmic womb that envelops the little circle of human categories, wishes, fears and hopes in its care. It is the instigator of a strange, vast world of internal energies and external forces; they clash, collide, converge, and career through, over and against one another in multifarious ways. Their multiple lines of intersection often produce unexpected effects" (Connolly, *The Augustinian Imperative*, 10).

8 The seed for this book was sown in a posting in *The Contemporary Condition* on August 16, 2010, entitled "The Fragility of Things." The discussions I have had with people since that posting have helped me to refine the tensions identified there more closely. See http://contemporarycondition .blogspot.com/search?q=The+Fragility+of.

9 I have profited from the following books in considering neoliberalism in comparative perspective: Brenner and Theodore, *Spaces of Neoliberalism*; Harvey, *A Brief History of Neoliberalism*; Blyth, *Great Transformations*; Jabko, *Playing the Market*. The task would be to link those studies of each neoliberal regime examined to the differential powers of self-organization in numerous force fields with which the regimes intersect.

10 In *Capitalism and Christianity, American Style*, I explore how neoliberalism and evangelicalism form a powerful resonance machine in the United States today. That book also examines in chapter 4 an *interim* set of movements and state policies that could speak both to ecological concerns and counter neoliberalism. Those policies, in turn, reach beyond the confines of Keynesianism in the way they are to be promoted, in the relations between state action and public ethos they project, and in their contents. I view this book as a companion to that one, adding themes to it.

Chapter I

1 See Foucault, *The Birth of Biopolitics*. He focuses on that period between 1935 and 1960, when neoliberalism became consolidated as an econopolitical philosophy, covering figures such as Friedrich Hayek, Ludwig von Mises, Walter Lippmann, and Milton Friedman. See also Blyth, *Great Transformations*. Today we can add Alan Greenspan, the *Wall Street Journal*, several fig-

ures on TV financial news shows such as Larry Kudlow on CNBC, Stephen Moore, and a number of right-wing talking heads such as Sean Hannity, Glenn Beck, and Bill O'Reilly, who combine extreme cultural conservatism with inordinate confidence in market rationality. That latter combination is not as surprising as it might seem at first. The most fervent devotees of both neoliberalism and the cultural right convey extreme senses of special entitlement, the first for economic privilege and the second that their own sexual, gender, family, religious, and linguistic identities be confirmed by the behavior of those around them. Neoliberalism and the confined nation are siblings under the skin, even as they enter into family feuds when the interests of neoliberal globalization press against those of cultural nationalism. It was not surprising, therefore, when the neoliberal prime minister of the United Kingdom, David Cameron, came out as a critic of "multiculturalism." For an account of how neoliberalism uses new shocks to enact its programs through the state, see Connolly, "The Shock Doctrine and Neoliberalism" in *The Contemporary Condition*, http://contemporarycondition .blogspot.com/2010/04/shock-doctrine-and-neoliberal-imaginary.html.

The claims of that essay were, of course, verified later, when the Tea Party held the United States hostage to the threat of a national default until it accepted its programs to "starve the beast."

2 Neoliberalism is a large and shifting set of orientations. To condense the discussion I focus here more on its American version. For an account that digs deeply into the Chicago school, see Peck, *Constructions of Neoliberal Reason*. For an account of the internal relations between neoliberalism, inequality, and intensive discipline in America today, see Wolin, *Democracy Incorporated*. The next chapter is entitled "Hayek, Neoliberalism, and Freedom." If radical neoliberalism presents one set of themes, Hayek advances a more moderate set. I address his themes about emergence, spontaneity, and complexity while extending them into sites well beyond the market to contest his utopian model of market rationality through self-organization. Everything changes when you do that. I thank Davide Panagia for calling my attention to this dimension of Hayek's thought.

3 Because of health issues my brother-in-law retired early from General Motors, before it went into bankruptcy in 2009. After the bankruptcy occurred, General Motors was saved, a good thing because it encouraged the company to reorganize itself to produce a better product and saved the jobs of many workers. But the bankruptcy agreement resulted in the retiree's pension, one he had earned over thirty years of work and had been part of a binding collective bargaining agreement, to be cut in half. He and his wife now struggle to make ends meet. There are millions like him in similar positions.

A good law would have protected retirees, or if some adjustment had to be made to save the company, would have guaranteed a return to the earlier level as soon as recovery was accomplished. Today *austerity* is another name for transmitting the costs of retrenchment to those at the lower levels of the hierarchy.

4 There are several brands of Marxism. Speaking very broadly, I am closest to those that translate a literal reading of the labor theory of value and fetishism into a polysemic discourse emphasizing the power of capitalism to proliferate new modes of compensatory meaning. "Capitalism: A Horror Story (or the Return of the Commodity Fetish)," a paper by Ivan Ascher on this topic at the 2011 Western Political Science Association meeting, was thoughtful. I also agree with Jane Bennett, cited later in this chapter, that Marx missed something important when he decided not to build upon the Epicurean and Lucretian ideas of swerves in nature. I thus engage a wider notion of nonhuman force fields with powers of metamorphosis than is found in some versions of Marxism. While I am obviously a critic of what might be called "exclusive humanism," with its tendencies to ignore or diminish our intimate relations with other force fields, I do not identify with "posthumanist" versions of Marxism, partly because our attention to the fragility of things is pursued through *care* for the human estate in its variety of entanglements with nonhuman force fields. Finally, I do not reject, as posthumanists tend to do, the alienation themes in Marx. I am the son of a factory worker and have seen those processes of alienation close at hand. Rather I would include the themes Marx elaborates under that heading (with adjustments) and *extend* the theory of alienation to come to terms with the issues of mortality, time, and the place of the human estate in the cosmos. This is the dissonant site at which Marx, Nietzsche, Whitehead, and Deleuze meet. That means, to put it too briefly, that some modes of alienation need to be resolved and others need to be *transfigured* into modes of existential affirmation so that the politics of *ressentiment* does not seep too deeply into church activity, theory construction, consumption practices, work processes, micropolitics, and state priorities.

5 See Hirsch, *The Social Limits to Growth.*

6 Simmel, *The Sociology of Georg Simmel*, 236–37.

7 For an account of the "pressure cooker" within which many white working- and middle-class families are caught, with the pressures it exerts on their orientations to race and gender and the political formula of the right to capture them, see Connolly, *Capitalism and Christianity, American Style*, chapters 1 and 2.

8 For a symposium on that book, in which several symposiasts touch upon

both the role that Christianity plays inside capitalist practices and the question of how the "evangelical-capitalist resonance machine" retains its hegemony, see Howarth, ed., "A Symposium on William Connolly's *Capitalism and Christianity, American Style*." The symposiasts are Catherine Keller, David Howarth, Kathy Ferguson, Philip Goodchild, and I.

9 If you emphasize imbrications between nondiscursive force fields and capitalist processes, as I am going to do, some readers may take the word *nondiscursive* to mean that you deny the importance of meaning, intersubjectivity, interpretation, discourse, narrative, and so forth in social life. As the earlier interpretation of sources of working-class support for neoliberalism already discloses, that is false. Meaning and interpretation are always in play, and indeed they even seep into living beings beyond the human estate. (Ticks pursue meaning; so do clusters of bacteria.) Neoliberalism is an interpretation embedded in a set of practices. In addition, the account of a cosmos of becoming partly defended and partly presupposed here is itself an interpretation both grounded in experience and projecting a speculative component to be placed in dialogue with others. Moreover I treat discursive practices as complex mixtures of words, architecture, bodily disciplines, and so on. So what weight, then, *is* given to the term *nondiscursive*? First, some (but not all) of the force fields noted in this chapter are not themselves discursive, even as they impact upon life and the established terms of discourse. Aspects of many are also outside our established terms of discourse even while making a difference to them, though this can best be shown after a new experiment or discovery alters those terms. Second, when the effect upon us of a nondiscursive force field is severe and rapid, the resulting *shock* can introduce new pressures into the world and *trigger* a shift in feeling, thinking, discourse, or narrative. The resulting reinterpretation, if it occurs, is not determined by the shock. It is *started* by it. You may, for instance, take account of the force field in a new way, as the devastating 1755 Lisbon earthquake encouraged many to predict the imminent arrival of end times, a few to launch a new science of seismology, and others yet to explore Enlightenment thought more carefully. My point is that neoliberalism tends either to downgrade the importance of nonhuman force fields to contemporary capitalism or to pretend that markets will take care of their effects in time. These responses protect the intercoded desires of neoliberals to treat nature as a deposit of resources and to minimize state regulation of markets. My sense is that some other theories as well, while folding nonhuman processes and things into the field of discourse, tend either to minimize the importance of human imbrications with nondiscursive fields or to reduce nature to a set of laws that curtail their (fields) powers of metamorphosis. A focus on imbrica-

tions between nonhuman force fields and cultural practices does not, then, eliminate meaning, subjectivity, narrative, discourse, and so forth from life. It *complicates* them, calling attention to how thinking itself involves a torsion between *trains of thought* and periodic *shocks* that throw a train off course. Creative thinking depends and draws upon such delicate imbalances. Such an approach plays down the hubristic idea that we simply "constitute" the world we interpret and plays up the need to participate in artistic and experimental practices that stretch and enliven the *receptive side* of our engagements. It is beyond the scope of this chapter to discuss how such an image of discourse does not fit a dialectical image well.

10 See Margulis and Sagan, *What Is Life?*

11 One place to start, at least with respect to biological systems, is with Clarke and Hansen, *Emergence and Embodiment.*

12 Some of the texts I draw upon for these examples are Hamblyn, *Terra*; Fortey, *The Earth*; Orsenna, *Portrait of the Gulf Stream*; Pearce, *With Speed and Violence*; Morton, *The Ecological Thought*; Hamilton, *Requiem for a Species*. The Hamblyn study reviews four earth-changing events: the Lisbon earthquake of 1755, the Iceland volcano of 1783 that changed the weather in Europe for two years, the Krakatau volcano of 1883, and the Hilo tsunami of 1946, paying attention in each case to the event, its sources, its cultural effects, and theoscientific accounts of it at the time. We could add to such a list the 1995 Kobe earthquake in Japan, Hurricane Katrina, the 2004 earthquake and tsunami in the Indian Ocean, the 2009 earthquake in Haiti, the 2010 volcano in Iceland, the 2010 oil spill in the Gulf of Mexico, and the 2011 quake, tsunami, and nuclear disaster in Japan. Stay tuned.

13 I review affinities between several of these thinkers, while assessing their most important differences, in Connolly, *A World of Becoming.*

14 Besides the reference to Foucault listed earlier, see Kauffman, *Reinventing the Sacred*; Deleuze and Guattari, "The Apparatus of Capture" in *A Thousand Plateaus*; Althusser, *Philosophy of the Encounter*; Wallerstein, *World-Systems Analysis*. For a thoughtful reading of the later Marx, showing him moving hesitantly in this direction, but without recourse to a cosmology of force fields, see Balibar, *The Philosophy of Marx.*

15 I explore this tendency with respect to Alan Greenspan in a March 1, 2010, posting in *The Contemporary Condition* entitled "Climate Change, Spirituality, and Neoliberalism," http://contemporarycondition.blogspot.com /2010/03/climate-change-spirituality-and.html.

16 For a close reading of Marx on this point, see Bennett, *The Enchantment of Modern Life*, chapter 3.

17 This dimension is explored at length in chapter 5 of Connolly, *A World of*

Becoming. I think of this chapter as a companion to that one and will not discuss the question of terrorism further here.

18 See Delaplane, *Crop Pollination by Bees*; Heinrich, *Bumblebee Economics.*

19 See Andresen et al., "Rapid Response of Helheim Glacier in Greenland to Climate Variability over the Past Century."

20 See Nettles, "Questions for an Ice Quake Expert." For a more extensive account, see Nettles and Ekström, "Glacial Earthquakes in Greenland and Antarctica."

21 See Kunii, "Predicting Earthquakes."

22 For a more extensive account of the infrastructure of consumption in the American context and potential ways to restructure it by a combination of state policy and citizen-initiated changes in the ethos of consumption, see Connolly, *Capitalism and Christianity, American Style,* chapter 4.

23 In *The Great Transformation,* Karl Polanyi shows how the Great Depression helped to fuel a whole series of fascist movements in several countries. He also thought that the market sources of that worldwide depression would prohibit the reemergence of radical market theory as a viable doctrine. He was right, at least on the first count.

24 I am indebted here and elsewhere in this essay to conversations with David Howarth, who cotaught with me a Spring 2010 seminar at Johns Hopkins, "Rethinking State Capitalism." I am also indebted to presentations by several students in that class and to comments made by Kathy Ferguson to an earlier version of this piece presented at the APSA, Fall 2010. Some of the seminar conversations were triggered by readings of Marx, Polanyi, and Deleuze, as well as a book we read by Lipietz, *Towards a New Economic Order.*

25 Keynesianism commits you to deficit spending during a downturn; it promotes unemployment insurance; it favors labor unions; it supports a progressive tax system, it uses government policy to reduce inequality. It is infinitely preferable to neoliberalism. Still, it does secrete serious limits. It tends to miss how the infrastructure of consumption makes ecological responses more difficult politically and how the current structure makes it more difficult for lower- and middle-class constituencies to make ends meet. It does not pay nearly enough attention to the variable capacities of nonhuman force fields to morph. It does not attend to how the current *ethos* of investment, saving, expenditure, and political involvement interacts with the infrastructure of the economy. Its proponents, often oriented to a top-down politics, evince too little appreciation of the need to generate a positive amplification machine out of movements back and forth between role experimentations and larger social movements. So it too needs critique. Nonetheless we would

be in a better situation if Keynesianism rather than neoliberalism were the hegemonic stance in need of critique. For a book that reviews the long-term debate between Keynes and Hayek, see Wapshott, *Keynes Hayek*.

First Interlude

1 I have entitled this interlude "*Melancholia* and Us" to emphasize audience responses I felt, heard, and observed at the theater, as well as in conversations with others shortly after seeing the film. In that respect, I particularly appreciate thoughts exchanged with Jane Bennett, Katrin Pahl, Nicolas Jabko, Libby Anker, Nick Tampio, Steve Johnston, Tom Dumm, and Paulina Ochoa. This interlude is not entitled "*Melancholia* and von Trier," in part because of an appalling interview with him about the film at the Cannes Festival in 2011. One might *perhaps* slide over his joking comments about the disposition to depression of one of his stars and the comparative sexual prowess of the other. But when he jokes his way through questions as to whether he is a Nazi sympathizer, that becomes too much. Some modes of denial are inconsistent with irony. And then, with no trace of humor, he invokes Albert Speer as a figure he does admire. I see nothing to admire in Hitler's minister of armaments and war production. Even Speer's "apology" after defeat is filled with denials and cover-ups. When many of *us* see the film we begin to think about the ambiguity of melancholia and our entanglements with planetary processes. I will not try to decipher von Trier. But at the end of the Cannes interview, which I saw after experiencing the film, as the interviewees were unhooking their microphones and beginning to move around, Kirsten Dunst leans toward him and says in a frustrated voice, "Ohhhh, Lars." Yes. Perhaps he should see *The Cave of Forgotten Dreams*.

2 Perhaps this is a timely moment to note some affinities and differences between Butler's *Precarious Life* and this study. Butler is courageous and compelling in her engagements with Israeli and American Zionism while expressing a deep appreciation of the ethical power of the Jewish tradition. Her account of how encounters with the face of the other can either incite an ethical response or instigate a desire for violence speaks to an uncanny element in human life. It makes me shudder. Her discussion of how the media so often frame some faces so that the relation between their and our vulnerability is effaced is timely and evocative. I hope I have internalized something from these encounters. There are, perhaps, two differences of emphasis between us, though they are no more than differences of emphasis. I seek to oscillate between fostering a love of the sweetness of human life that exceeds the specific roles in which we are engrossed and appreciating the vulnera-

bility of life, particularly the uneven ways in which that vulnerability is distributed. I agree, and insist, that you must be lucky to appreciate the first side. But that appreciation, when it is possible and joined to a sense of vulnerability, contributes something important to the energies needed to participate ethically in micro- and macropolitics. To me, Spinoza had a rather tough life. He was both excommunicated by Jews in Amsterdam and called a "Jewish philosopher" by Christians. And yet he emphasized and lived the positivity of an ethical life infused with a love of being. I do not know to what extent Butler and I disagree on these points, nor am I that confident about the specific balance between them I myself should pursue. There is only a possible difference of emphasis on this register, then. The second? Butler helps us to become more sensitized to others, enabling us to expand our perceptions and identifications even in the face of organized attempts to efface the other. My goal is also to extend sensitivity, to varying degrees depending on the situation and forces involved, beyond the human estate itself to a variety of nonhuman forces with which the species is closely entangled. I do not believe that there is a "rupture" between humanity and the rest of the world; there are rather multiple entanglements and significant differences of degree, not all of which point in the same direction. I say that we have "distinctive" characteristics, some of which are shared to differential degrees with a variety of nonhuman organisms and entities. I seek to be neither an exclusive humanist nor a posthumanist. Precariousness and fragility, then. I realize that my agenda raises at least as many issues as it resolves. But that effect, at least, is one Butler would not shy away from either. She articulates an ethic of cautious exploration and experimentation, not one composed of final criteria and settled orders. If there are differences of emphasis between us, they retreat amid that affinity.

Chapter 2

1 Friedman, *Why Government Is the Problem*, 6.
2 For a history of neoliberal shocks and hostage takings over the past forty years, see Klein, *The Shock Doctrine*. Klein sometimes acts as if these shocks are always intentionally produced. For another take, indebted to her and written before the intentional legislative hostage taking around the debt ceiling crisis in the United States, see Connolly, "The Shock Doctrine and the Neoliberal Imaginary."
3 Lindblom, *The Intelligence of Democracy*.
4 Hayek, *Rules and Order*, 36.
5 Hayek, *Rules and Order*, 37.

6 Hayek, *Rules and Order*, 39.

7 Hayek, *Rules and Order*, 51.

8 Hayek, *The Road to Serfdom*, 108.

9 Hayek, *The Road to Serfdom*, 86.

10 Hayek, *The Road to Serfdom*, 86.

11 Hayek, *Rules of Order*, 58.

12 Hayek, *The Road to Serfdom*, 223–24.

13 See Deleuze and Guattari, *A Thousand Plateaus*, plateau 12; MacKenzie, *An Engine, Not a Camera*. It would be fascinating to see what would happen to MacKenzie's thoughtful engagement with how financial theory and technologies became incorporated into financial markets as an "engine" if he connected that analysis to the robust engagements with "machines" in the work of Deleuze and Guattari. One of the things that would fall out is the notion of the disconnected or noninterventionist social scientist; MacKenzie seems aware of this, but that awareness may not be sufficiently incorporated into the acceptance in pragmatism of social science as also a mode of social activism. My sense, however, is that Hayek, with his appreciation of the role of ideology, does appreciate a cool variant of such a role definition. Just not the one I embrace.

14 Hayek, *The Constitution of Liberty*, 424, 500–502, 424.

15 Hayek, *The Constitution of Liberty*, 452.

16 Hirsch, *Social Limits to Growth*. See also Connolly, *Capitalism and Christianity, American Style*, chapter 4. That chapter includes several examples of "inclusive goods" that could circumvent the paradox of consumption that Hirsch identifies. But they will require the state to intervene in different ways in the established, publicly supported infrastructure of consumption.

17 Connolly, *The Ethos of Pluralization*, chapter 6.

18 For one account of uneven global exchanges, see Wallerstein, *World-Systems Analysis*. I try to augment and modify this perspective in Connolly, *A World of Becoming*, chapter 5.

19 Habermas, *Legitimation Crisis*.

20 For a discussion of the scope of the problem and various ways to try to respond to it, see Hamilton, *Requiem for a Species*. Hamilton contends that the most dramatic assumptions about probable climate change have received the most new evidence in their favor over the past ten years.

21 See Connolly, *Capitalism and Christianity, American Style*; Harvey, *A Brief History of Neoliberalism*; Gibson-Graham, *The End of Capitalism (As We Knew It)*.

22 The classic essay on this topic is Berlin, *Two Concepts of Liberty*. I discussed these notions comparatively in Connolly, *The Terms of Political Discourse*,

chapter 4. Chapter 5 of that book, "Conceptual Revision and Political Change," provides the seedbed, I now think, for the perspective developed in this section.

23 For a discussion of philosophy of "protean connectionism" that draws upon William James and Alfred North Whitehead, see Connolly, *A World of Becoming*, chapter 1. This doctrine both appreciates our interconnections and leaves room for elements of partiality, uncertainty, and real creativity (spontaneity) in those connections. We return to this issue in the last chapter.

24 See Johns Hopkins University, "This Is Your Brain on Jazz: Researchers Use MRI to Study Spontaneity, Creativity," February 26, 2008, http://www.hopkinsmedicine.org/news/media/releases/this_is_your_brain_on_jazz_researchers_use_mri_to_study_spontaneity_creativity. I thank Davide Panagia for calling my attention to this site.

Second Interlude

1 In a commentary on my *Christianity and Capitalism, American Style*, Philip Goodchild illustrated the notion of "resonance" developed in that book through reference to the Millennium Bridge. I am indebted to him for the example and for other comments he made. See Howarth, ed., "A Symposium on William Connolly's *Capitalism and Christianity, American Style*," with thoughtful commentaries by Kathy Ferguson, Philip Goodchild, Catherine Keller, and David Howarth and a response by me.

2 Schneider and Sagan, *Into the Cool*, 136.

3 For a close account of the life-world of the tick, see Uexkull, *A Foray into the Worlds of Animals and Humans*. This text, originally published in 1934, contains a rich study of relations between subjective experiences of numerous plants and animals and the worlds those experiences make available to them. As Dorion Sagan shows in his excellent introduction, Uexkull himself attributes all this to a master plan that exceeds the interacting worlds displayed rather than to interacting systems with differential degrees of self-organizational power. Nonetheless the examples themselves are endlessly absorbing and compelling. And Uexkull is superb at showing how perception and world are interwoven for each plant and animal explored.

4 Bennett, *Vibrant Matter*; Latour, *Pandora's Hope*.

5 Bassler, "Discovering Bacteria's Amazing Communication System."

6 Sagan, "The Human Is More than Human."

7 Deacon, *Incomplete Nature*, 359.

8 Deacon, *Incomplete Nature*, 273.

9 Deacon's account of the teleodynamic process has some things in common

with the discussion of *autopoiesis* in Clarke and Hansen's edited collection, *Emergence and Embodiment*. The authors in some of these essays distinguish autopoiesis from more simple processes of self-organization. My tendency is to speak of differing levels of self-organization.

10 Deacon, *Incomplete Nature*, 416.

11 Thompson, *Mind in Life*, 181.

12 See Juarrero, *Dynamics in Action*. In general, she thinks teleological behavior which involves a searching element could sometimes occur just one time. She uses the example of a student: "Suppose a student with nothing to lose, flatters his teacher to get a higher grade even though S is well aware that it is for the most part the wrong thing to do. . . . But S has a hunch it might work just this once" (68). It tends to work with me, and yet not always. . . . This is a fine book to explore to bring complexity theory and the human sciences closer together.

13 Deacon, *Incomplete Nature*, 415. Some reviewers of Deacon's book are critical of his writing style and the places where he purports to account for things that still remain mysterious. There is something to these critiques. He may sometimes ignore gaps in his own account, but there are also places where he emphasizes the speculative and preliminary character of his claims. Thompson, in *Mind in Life*, is perhaps even more clear about where the gaps are in his own version of such an account. His critiques of computer and connectionist models of human thinking and perception in favor of a "dynamic model" are on the same wavelength as Deacon's. Particularly useful are Thompson's discussions of how phenomenology and neuroscience need each other, a theme also supported in chapter 2 of Connolly, *A World of Becoming*. Here is merely one quotation from Thompson that suggests his affinity with Deacon: "Dynamic-system explanations focus on the internal and external forces that shape such trajectories as they unfold in time. Inputs are described as *perturbations* to the system's intrinsic dynamics, rather than as *instructions* to be followed, and internal states are described as self-organized compensations triggered by perturbations, rather than as representations of external states of affairs" (11, my emphases). That all being said, Deacon's notion of "teleodynamism" is very suggestive.

14 For a rich discussion of preadaptations, see Kauffman, *Reinventing the Sacred*. The concept is explored in Connolly, *A World of Becoming*, chapter 1. I will suggest in chapter 4 that such a concept, already operative in Whitehead, could be amplified further to reduce Whitehead's dependence on "eternal objects."

15 This argument is pursued in chapters 1 and 2 of Connolly, *Capitalism and Christianity, American Style*.

16 In *The Politicized Economy*, first published in 1976, Michael Best and I argued that a large segment of the white working class could easily defect to the right unless the new pluralizing movements, which we also strongly supported, built a definite class dimension into their initiatives. That part of our thesis was ignored by the pluralizing left. We did not, however, anticipate the rapid turn to a politically active evangelicalism by a segment of this class.

17 See Panagia, *The Political Life of Sensation* for an exploration of how strong narrative approaches undercut attention to the organization of perception out of disparate senses and how this activity often enough creates remainders that both disrupt the narrative process and create triggers to help turn it in new directions. The ugly word *explanatocracy* is coined here as a parallel term to indicate how several deterministic and probabilistic conceptions of explanation distract attention from creative moments in politics and other domains.

18 For an engagement with Alan Greenspan see Connolly, "Neoliberalism, Spirituality and Climate Change," in *The Contemporary Condition*, http://contemporarycondition.blogspot.com/2010/03/climate-change-spirituality-and.html. Several posts in that blog speak to the issues we are engaging here.

Chapter 3

1 Hesiod, *Theogony*, 56, 58, 66, 67, 78, 79. The introduction by Brown is superb. Some will resist this myth on the grounds that it glorifies human violence. But my sense is that while *The Odyssey* and *The Iliad* may do that, Hesiod himself does not. His commendations to Greek farmers in "Works and Days" point toward coping peacefully and wisely with an unruly universe. Others may say that the Olympians smooth out the world of the Titans. Perhaps. But does not Dionysus soon creep in from the East, and was not Sophocles alert to a continuing conflict between these two sets of gods? That being said, I still have much to learn about Hesiod. My goal is not a return but a use. For the essay cited above, see Athanassakis, *Hesiod*.

2 Vernant, *Myth and Thought among the Greeks*, 395.

3 Serres, *The Birth of Physics*.

4 Williams, *Shame and Necessity*.

5 Damasio, *Descartes' Error*. For a more recent analysis that takes into account the revolution in neuroscience occasioned by the discovery of "mirror neurons," see Damasio and Damasio, "Minding the Body."

6 Giacomo Rizzolatti's discovery of mirror neurons, while still controversial in some circles, fits remarkably well with the account of passive syntheses in

Deleuze. The latter explores how cultural tendencies become embodied from the earliest age, and the former uncovers the biological processes in which such syntheses are forged. All of this puts a lot of pressure on the apodictic starting points, to be reviewed later, from which Kantian transcendental arguments proceed. Indeed, as we shall also see, there are some themes in Kant himself that touch these points. One could productively read Kant against himself at this and other junctures, though, for the most part, I will not try to do that here. The pertinent texts are Rizzolatti and Sinigaglia, *Mirrors in the Brain*; Deleuze, *Difference and Repetition*.

7 Shaviro, *Without Criteria*, 13.

8 Kant, *Critique of Judgment*, 249, 253.

9 Romilly, *Time in Greek Tragedy*, 88.

10 Augustine, *Concerning the City of God*, 503.

11 Augustine, *The Confessions*, 197.

12 Augustine, *St Augustine: Select Letters*, 315.

13 Augustine, *On Christian Doctrine*, 30.

14 Kant, *Critique of Practical Reason*, 48–49.

15 Kant, *Critique of Practical Reason*, 49.

16 In *The Twenty Five Years of Philosophy*, Eckart Förster puts the point this way: "For though Kant's starting point in the Second Critique is not a sensible perception, he does start with the *experience* of the moral law as a fact of reason that is as certain as perception, and this distinguishes his procedure here from that of the First Critique" (122). Eckart's book came out while mine was in production. I have already dipped into it enough, however, to see that it is a superb study, all the more fascinating in that its agenda is different from the one pursued here.

17 I take a postulate to be a possibility that is not foreclosed by other aspects of reason and that we must project in order to sustain the logic of morality, a logic that is apodictic at its starting point. There is more to be plumbed in the idea of a postulate, particularly since different ones seem to carry different standings. But I will not attempt to pursue this topic here.

18 Kant, *Religion within the Limits of Reason Alone*, 32.

19 Kant, "On the Proverb," 86.

20 I came across the fascinating book by Louden, *Kant's Impure Ethics*, after the first version of this chapter was published. Louden argues that the purity of Kantian morality must be connected, as it is in Kant, with facts about that side of human nature and culture that are impure. Otherwise morality, in Kant's view, will not progress historically. He thus makes contact with the discussion of "gymnastics" in this chapter. The differences between us are, first, that he does not call into question the apodictic character of the

pure dimension of morality and, second, that he treats Kant's orientations to women, race, and non-European countries as *prejudices* that do not touch the universal core of the philosophy. I contend that the connection between his postulate of universal progress and the need for "signs" in empirical history that display it in historical actuality deepens the problem of his universalism. At any point in history, you might say, this demand for a universal morality of law contains the potential to deepen and harden prejudices of the day by attaching them to a sense of universal progress demanded by the philosophy. Louden should pay more attention to the signs taken to provide indispensable support to the initial, "pure" aspects of Kantian morality. Despite these differences, the richness of the Louden book speaks to the themes explored in this chapter. For a dissertation near completion that explores the role of race in Kantian philosophy, see Culver, "Race and Vision."

21 Kant, *Religion within the Limits of Reason Alone*, 110.

22 Kant, *The Conflict of the Faculties*, 75.

23 Kant, "Perpetual Peace," 120, 124. As Kant makes clear, "nature" does not refer in this instance to those processes known by the cognitive understanding but to postulates we must make about what underlies and undergirds them if morality is to progressively approach its own end. This latter demand, in turn, is needed if our commitment to morality is to be as secure as it can be now. And we must see "signs" of this underlying process in the things we do observe. The wisdom of Kant, however, also finds ample expression in this essay, as when he says "Since the earth is a globe, they [human beings] cannot scatter themselves infinitely, but must, finally, tolerate living in close proximity" (118). This essay is wonderful both for what it reveals about the underpinnings of the Kantian system and for what it reveals about Kant's aspirations for the human estate.

24 Kant, "The End of All Things," 97.

25 Habermas, *The Future of Human Nature*, 115.

26 All three statements come from *Critique of Practical Reason*, 153. For a book that explores the role that humiliation plays in the crystallization of practical reason and the willingness to submit to it, see Saurette, *The Kantian Imperative*.

27 See Whitehead, *Adventures of Ideas*, chapter 7, "Laws of Nature."

28 The elements of practical wisdom articulated here represent the next stage in a briefer, less contextualized version advanced in Connolly, *A World of Becoming*, chapter 3. The revisions represent improvements, I hope, after discussions with others about that chapter.

29 Freeman, Libet, and Sutherland, eds., *The Volitional Brain*.

30 I have discussed elsewhere *how* to proceed, particularly in *Neuropolitics*. For

a book that carries such explorations to a higher pitch yet, see White, *The Ethos of a Late Modern Citizen*.

31 Nietzsche, *Twilight of the Idols*, 73. See also "At Noon" in *Thus Spoke Zarathustra*.

32 See Sophocles, *The Oedipus Plays*, translated by Paul Roche. The Roche translation is valuable because of its attention to the rhythms of the text and its attempt to capture in English something of the multiple meanings installed in key terms. My reading and use of Sophocles on the tragic comes out most sharply, perhaps, in *Capitalism and Christianity, American Style*, chapter 5. While I have not yet read the whole study, since it was not published when this book was in production, I have heard and read some of the chapters in Honig's *Antigone Interrupted*. Her focus on the minor figures is particularly apt, and I draw sustenance from it.

Third Interlude

1 Taylor, *A Secular Age*, 5, 6.

2 Taylor, *A Secular Age*, 7, 10.

3 Taylor, *A Secular Age*, 655.

4 Whitehead, *Process and Reality*, 94.

5 Proust, *Time Regained*, 247–48. I also draw upon this instance from Proust in Connolly, *A World of Becoming*, chapter 4. There the focus is on differing, interacting registers of memory, including strange memories of incipiencies that have not become actual. Here it is on what vitality becomes when one of its essential dimensions falls out of precarious balance with the other.

6 See Nietzsche, *Thus Spoke Zarathustra*, #22, "The Gift Giving Virtue."

7 I discuss these issues in detail in chapter 2 of *Pluralism*, "Pluralism and Relativism." It would be a mistake to think that a vibrant ethos of pluralism and pluralization does not itself pose limits. There will be strong barriers against, say, including rapists, murderers, and child molesters in such an ethos of pluralization, even though the sources of that commonality will vary across different constituencies. Such an ethos also requires a degree of economic equality as one of its preconditions that allows all citizens to participate in modes of consumption and cultural life generally made available. That means, as discussed in *Pluralism* and even more in the texts that followed upon it as worries about neofascist movements became more urgent, that occasions arise when it is essential to mobilize a militant pluralist assemblage to amplify the ethos of pluralism, to ward off drives to religious, ethnic, or linguistic unitarianism, and to curtail economic inequality. The idea is that the same ethos of engagement that supports plurality is also the

one most apt to support drives to economic equalization. Such an ethos sets limits, then, but perhaps not in the direction that unitarians of various stripes seek. I believe, by the way, that Taylor and I move close together on these themes, illustrating at the level of intellectual life how a pluralist alliance can be forged between those who honor different ethical sources in the first instance.

Chapter 4

1 Nietzsche, *The Pre-Platonic Philosophers*, 64.

2 Nietzsche, *The Pre-Platonic Philosophers*, 60, 62, 62, 63.

3 Nietzsche, *Twilight of the Idols*, 35. How, it is surely to be asked, does this formulation and innumerable others like it in several Nietzschean texts, square with the idea of eternal return as the return of long cycles, in which everything that becomes during one cosmic cycle returns in exactly that mode in future cycles? There is no tension if this idea is merely posed as an existential test: "Would you choose life again if everything in it repeats?" But Nietzsche, besides treating it as only a test sometimes, also experiments with long cycles as a metaphysical theme. To me that theme is incompatible with a real philosophy of becoming: while it might appear during each cycle that what becomes has a creative element in it, the fact of its exact recurrence would suggest to an observing god viewing the cycles the necessity of each item within each cycle. The assumption Nietzsche makes about the finitude of matter and infinity of time is the key problem here, one that Whitehead—without reference to Nietzsche, whom he apparently did not read—contests. For time is embedded in actual energy and matter processes, rather than being separable from them. So to the extent Nietzsche supports a philosophy of long cycles, I oppose that philosophy. I am drawing upon the numerous other elements in his exploratory thinking.

4 See Barad, *Meeting the Universe Halfway*. Barad contends that Heisenberg's rendering of the "uncertainty principle" is corrected by Bohr in a way the former eventually accepts. And that Bohr replaces his own early account with a reading that becomes increasingly ontological, in which the "complementarity issue" becomes more central, that is, the inability to detect both position and momentum in the same test procedure. The entanglement of test and object, she says, signifies the entangled character of becoming itself rather than merely expressing an effect of limited human instruments of detection upon a world otherwise following classical laws.

5 Epperson, *Quantum Mechanics and the Philosophy of Alfred North Whitehead*, 56.

6 Epperson, *Quantum Mechanics and the Philosophy of Alfred North White-head*, 51.

7 Epperson, *Quantum Mechanics and the Philosophy of Alfred North White-head*, 102.

8 As Stuart Kauffman summarizes the claim, "After the particles are entangled they can separate to arbitrary distances at speeds up to the speed of light and remain entangled, and if one of the particles 'is measured' as having a given property the other particle instantaneously has a corresponding property. This deeply puzzling feature of quantum mechanics gave Einstein the gravest concern. . . . The implied instantaneous correspondence has now been confirmed experimentally, and is called nonlocality" (*Reinventing the Sacred*, 221).

9 Whitehead can be called both a process philosopher and a speculative realist. The latter term speaks to the speculative element explicitly invested in his philosophy and the important role that the persistence of "actual entities" plays in it before they undergo change. These terms speak not only to Whitehead but to an interesting group of philosophers who until recently had called themselves "object-oriented" philosophers. Some now call themselves speculative realists. One leader is Graham Harman, whose book *Prince of Networks: Bruno Latour and Metaphysics*, is very rich. It distinguishes itself from the work of thinkers such as Deleuze by labeling them "lump ontologists" and radical "relationists." Latour and Whitehead come out a bit better in this text, though they too are criticized for being too relationist. My sense is that Whitehead has it about right on this score. He focuses on the *entangled* stability of "actual entities" as they periodically form new entanglements and morph. He also comes to terms with excesses in each actual entity. For a recent discussion of the issues with which I largely agree, see Jane Bennett's response to interesting essays by Harman and Morton, "Systems and Things." More exploration is needed of the connections and differences between these two traditions.

10 Whitehead, *Process and Reality*, 7.

11 Whitehead is not shy about using the terms *metaphysical* and *cosmological* because he thinks such modes of reflection are essential to thought about science, ethics, human culture, and nonhuman forces that impinge upon all of these. He presents his distinctive ontocosmology as speculative in a way that presses others to come to terms more reflectively with the ontocosmologies they hold. His can be coherently developed in relation to recent scientific findings and cultural experiences, but it is unlikely to be proven definitively. It is, in my terms, *defensible* in that it brings forward arguments and evidence to support it and *contestable* in that some other readings could cred-

ibly make sense of the processes under review. In a recent book, *The Lessons of Rancière*, Sam Chambers draws upon Jacques Rancière to challenge the pertinence of *any* ontodimension to political theory, saying such a dimension *depoliticizes* and *dehistoricizes* too much of life. Others have suggested to me that to attend to Rancière's later work on aesthetic theory is to identify such elements in his work too. At any rate, I contend that to ignore the ontopolitical (and the metaphysical, too, since those two terms have become increasingly interchangeable) is to ignore an essential dimension of politics. Theorists such as Rawls and Habermas, who once bracketed key issues by defining themselves to be both "postmetaphysical" and "secular," missed important dimensions of politics and history. A specific theospiritual complex in American evangelicalism, to take one instance, now infuses its politics and the character of its alliance with neoliberalism. Postmetaphysical types missed this development when they pretended their own desire to keep religion in the private realm actually represented a sharp division in the world. They underestimated how diverse spiritual orientations fold into political struggle. On the "dehistoricization" front, take the long, violent struggle in the Mediterranean during the fourth century between Trinitarianism and Arianism. The victory of the former (in which Arianism was officially defined as a heresy to be punished, with suspect ties to Judaism) had a lot to do with the long, immensely destructive relation Christendom bore to both paganism and Judaism. Is it really possible to think of trinitarianism as *merely* an epiphenomenon with no *independent* power? Attention to the ontotheological and atheological dimensions thus deepens engagements with politics and history. If the suggestion is that the *theorist*, at least, should avoid ontological assumptions (in order to make theory more precise and demonstrable), the range of ontopolitical stances to be resisted actually noted turn out to be instances of what Deleuze calls the "Royal" and "Arboreal" traditions of European metaphysics. Epicurus, Lucretius, Spinoza, Nietzsche, James, Thoreau, Kafka, and Deleuze, on the other hand, have historically challenged these with "minor" or "nomadic" modalities. Deleuze, who for this reason refused the title "postmodern" some tried to foist on him, contends that critical theory must articulate positive counterconceptions to challenge the royal traditions. Negative critique does not suffice, since "deterritorialization" is followed by unconscious "reterritorialization." The minor tradition (in its various guises) contests things in the royal tradition, including a dominant conception of time, tendencies toward narrow anthropocentrism, restrictive views of how morality *must* be "grounded," distrust of an ethos of pluralist engagement that is more rhizomatic in character, suspicion of the politics of pluralization by which new identities and rights erupt, and a linear concept of cause. The more I read about the ontopolitical assumptions Rancière is said to reject, the more it seems that he both *flirts with* the minor tradition and *refuses to articulate* it relationally. That is perhaps why, in the conference I attended on him around 2007, he refused to relate his work to several others with whom speakers thought it had affinities. I continue to be wary of the hesitancy to explore how the quality of the *ethos* of different ("police") regimes speaks *differentially* to the possibilities of pluralization (as I call it) by which new movements, rights, and identities surge into being and the apparent tendency to a cultural internalism in which opposition to "anthropocentrism" merely means rejection of a founding human subject rather than *also* appreciation of variable powers of metamorphosis in nonhuman force fields. *The Ethos of Pluralization*, in which the term *ontopolitics* was introduced in 1995, explored with examples how *new* rights, identities, and movements periodically surge into being without always being already "implicit" in a culture. The claim was that a minor tradition crystallizes such political processes in a way that challenges both the fiction of postmetaphysical thought and dialectical ontologies of recognition. There is a point at which Chambers and I may converge. To focus on the *onto* dimension *alone*, which some theorists do find tempting, makes you always getting ready to stake out a political stance and never actually doing so. For a superb book that probes these issues—engaging political theories that suppress the onto dimension, those that affirm it and ground their own with too much confidence, and those that affirm one and address the relational contestability of the ontopolitical stance they propel forward—see White, *Sustaining Affirmation*.

12 Whitehead, *Process and Reality*, 94.

13 The question arises: How deep into organic and nonorganic process do traces of creativity sink? The quotation about vector feeling suggests that the traces sink far indeed for Whitehead. In *Incomplete Nature*, discussed in the second interlude, Terrence Deacon distinguishes between thermodynamic, morphodynamic, and teleodynamic processes. He would probably reserve the word *creative* for organic processes with teleodynamic capacities. He defines *autogens* as intermediate, autocalytic processes of an unusual complexity that most probably allowed life to emerge from nonlife. I want to keep the issue of creativity relatively open for now, once we proceed beyond systems that clearly express a teleodynamic dynamic. The Helheim self-amplification system, for instance, is creative along one criterion, as it introduces a new pattern and result into the world; it is not creative, however, in the sense of displaying teleodynamic tendencies. As we develop new concepts appropriate to forge new experiments (and vice versa) we may become more capable of generating detailed answers to these questions.

14 Richards, "Scientists Discover a Bacteria That Can Grow in Arsenic."

15 Stengers, in *Thinking with Whitehead*, admirably works upon the texts as she charts changes that emerge as his work proceeds and as he does not go back to identify that a change has been made. A thinker in process. I add to that a bit here by trying to fold some recent work in complexity theory into Whitehead wherever it fits the spirit of his endeavor. The goal is to create a reading that can both help to explain recent work and is sustained by some of its conceptual and experimental innovations.

16 Whitehead, *Process and Reality*, 291.

17 Whitehead, *Adventures of Ideas*, 251.

18 Whitehead, *Process and Reality*, 349, 339.

19 Ball, in *The Self-Made Tapestry*, explores a whole host of patterns that recur in different domains of nature and culture, as they also evolve into new forms. This quote may give a sense of his project and the way in which it could open a promising conversation with Whitehead on eternal objects: "Competition lies at the heart of beauty and complexity in pattern formation. If the competition is too one-sided all form disappears, and one gets either unstructured, shifting randomness or featureless homogeneity. . . . Patterns live on the edge, in a fertile borderland between these extremes, where small changes can have large effects. . . . Pattern occurs when competing forces banish uniformity but cannot quite induce chaos. It sounds like a dangerous place to be, but it is where we have always lived" (253).

20 Goodwin, *How the Leopard Changed Its Spots*. Here is a sample of what Goodwin says: "The first is a hind limb that belonged to a fossil fish *Ichthyostega*, from the Devonian period. The second is the hind limb of a salamander. Then there are the wings of a bird and a bat, the front leg of a horse and a human arm" (142). His point is that, when you observe these similarities and differences of pattern, you detect how the latter could have evolved from the former. Some may have set preliminary conditions from which others evolved.

21 Thompson, in *Mind in Life*, provides an excellent review of critiques of the "genocentric" model in recent biological work. I came across this book as my study was nearing completion. The more I sink into it, the more it seems to complement and enrich the thinking pursued here. I agree, for example, that neuroscience and phenomenology need each other. I pursue that issue in an essay, "Experience & Experiment," and in chapter 2 of *A World of Becoming*.

22 In *Reinventing the Sacred* Kauffman charts several processes that are not susceptible to algorithmic treatment now and, he suspects, will not be in the future. In *Essays on Deleuze*, Dan Smith writes a chapter entitled "Mathematics and the Theory of Multiplicities: Deleuze and Badiou Revisited." He shows how Badiou's commitment to set theory is inappropriate for engaging

the mathematics of turbulent fluids and flows Deleuze draws upon. I am a consumer in this area and appreciate the insights both Kauffman and Smith provide.

23 Nietzsche, *The Will to Power*, #501, 512, 514, 515, 516, 517.

24 Nietzsche, *The Will to Power*, #499, 501, 510.

25 Nietzsche, *The Will to Power*, #636.

26 Nietzsche, *The Will to Power*, #673.

27 My thinking on this point is sharpened by an email from Catherine Keller in 2012 suggesting that transcendence does not have to be merely a being beyond; it can also be a going beyond. I concur, noting only how the pair immanence and transcendence now becomes a very tricky pair, with each maintaining some distance on some renderings of transcendence—*being* beyond, the outside as *divine*—while at least partially flipping into the other on a couple of other readings: the *outside* and *going* beyond. Whitehead and Nietzsche have more affinities with each other across distance than either does with strong finalism or determinism.

28 Nietzsche, *The Will to Power*, #651.

29 Connolly, *A World of Becoming*, chapter 4.

30 Bennett, *Vibrant Matter*; Morton, *The Ecological Thought*; Panagia, *The Political Life of Sensation*; Massumi, *Semblance and Event*; Ignatov, "Practices of Eco-Sensation."

31 Nietzsche, *The Will to Power*, #852.

32 Nietzsche, *The Will to Power*, #1019.

33 In *Identity\Difference*, I examine the metaphors Zarathustra uses to justify a world in which "passing by" those who seek to pull down a spiritual nobility is possible and politics is avoidable. The argument is that those spatial metaphors of relative isolation no longer carry the same weight in a world in which distance has become compressed, the pace of many processes has accelerated, and the interinvolvement of everyone with everything has intensified. This chapter presupposes those arguments.

34 In a 2010 exploratory seminar I taught on Whitehead and Nietzsche, some students argued that Whitehead had, at least by the time of *Adventures of Ideas*, softened the presentation of eternal ideas so that they assumed a character close to pure potential. This reading does mesh with Whitehead's presentation of the aesthetic dimension of the prehensive relation. But I do not detect such a radical shift, and other students concurred in this second reading. I suspect that Whitehead would doubt the possibility that the universe could devolve from higher to lower complexity. On the other hand, Whitehead does evince a sense that the human estate will eventually dissolve as the universe evolves. So the issue remains open to some degree. I

merely say that *insofar* as Whitehead retains a strong reading of eternal objects and an impersonal God, I contest that reading while also respecting it. On the other hand, those (like me) who support a more open rendering of the cosmos still have to cope more closely with the question "What, then, holds evolving things together?" I would like to express my appreciation to the students in the 2010 seminar for the contributions they made to our collective understanding of issues posed by the conjunctions and disjunctions between Nietzsche and Whitehead. This chapter is indebted to those debates and discussions.

Postlude

1 I have explored "tactics of the self" and "micropolitics" to promote this end in Connolly, *Neuropolitics*, particularly chapter 4. This postlude focuses on exchanges between role performance and political life. From the day Deleuze and Guattari introduced the idea of micropolitics in plateau 9 of *A Thousand Plateaus*, it has been clear that the micro- and macropolitics are interdependent modes. That, however, did not stop many from missing the connection, focusing only on the dimension that had been unfamiliar to them.

2 Goffman, *Relations in Public*, 53–54. The statement itself is a quotation from Gordon Allport. Goffman himself often proceeds by accumulating quotations from others, which in cumulative effect reveal the dense and extensive microphysics of cultural life, depriving the reader of those large structural formulae that pretend to capture the essence of things.

3 Butler, *Gender Trouble* (1990), 137–38; (1999), 169. For a thoughtful review of how Butler's ideas about the relation between performativity and gender practice have developed, see Chambers and Carver, *Judith Butler and Political Theory*, especially chapter 7.

4 In *Identity\Difference*, I argue that every collective formation of identity is constituted in part by the differences it seeks to define and manage, both within and outside itself. It is relational. The danger of collective identity is thus that in its attempt to consolidate itself, it may succumb to the temptation to convert difference into otherness to be marginalized, punished, or attacked. This feature of relational identity too forms part of the fragility of things. That book explores mostly religious and sexual identities as sites of this temptation. And what, some people asked, allows you to distinguish a dangerous identity in need of limits from one that can be acknowledged? As also developed in chapter 3 of this study, one answer lies in an ethic of cultivation attuned to situational developments in a world composed of multiple force fields. It is not a perfect answer, only an excellent one to pursue

if you have lost confidence in transcendental and transcendent sources of ethical responsibility and think that they need another competitor to keep them honest. Of course, a militant pluralist assemblage will combine carriers from several of these traditions. That is what "deep pluralism" means.

5 A word to the wise. To say "A swan is white" does not mean that it is white and nothing else. For example, it is capable of flying. Such a misreading, however, is relatively common among those who make their careers looking for self-contradictions to identify and correct, always pretending they are merely using the words of those they correct. *Is* is a complex word.

6 Nietzsche and Bernard Williams pay close attention to the positive potential of shame in this respect. For a thoughtful, recent study under the influence of Nietzsche and Stanley Cavell which probes the political bearing of such relations, see Norval, *Aversive Democracy*.

7 Polanyi, *The Great Transformation*, 159.

8 In "The Real Entitlement Crisis," posted on *The Contemporary Condition* in the summer of 2012 (http://contemporarycondition.blogspot.com/2012/08/the-real-entitlement-crisis.html), I contended that neoliberal chants about an entitlement crisis in the areas of Social Security and Medicare function as a smokescreen to cover up the most severe entitlement crisis of all: the demand among the superrich to pay a low percentage of taxes, to siphon off a huge portion of collective wealth, to be coddled by the media, to run their enterprises with minimal regulation, and to have a free hand in funding elections as they see fit. Romand Coles, reading that post, suggested to me that there is another entitlement issue too, a tricky one. Today too many affluent citizens who prize democracy think they are entitled to have it without investing a portion of their energies in grasping the issues, participating in movements, and holding officials accountable in an informed way. I exempt the Tea Party from this charge. It is just that they celebrate market rationality and demonize the social movements that are the most important.

9 I am not saying that either of these two theories denied the role of noise and unpredictability. Certainly Keynes played up the role of "animal spirits," and Althusser late in the day came to terms with aleatory processes in material practices. I am reminding us that there are often relevant things on the way that we are not in touch with yet. Drawing upon artistic practices to extend perception and render it more sensitive to incipient processes on the way is thus always pertinent. So is engaging techno-artistic modes of enhancing perception and engaging explorations in the sciences of complexity of how densely the human estate is entangled with heterogeneous forces both inside and outside its skin.

Althusser, Louis. *Philosophy of the Encounter: Later Works, 1978–1987*. New York: Verso, 2006.

Andersen, Camilla S., Flammetta Straneo, Mads Hvid Ribergaard, Anders A. Bjørk, Thorbjørn J. Andersen, Antoon Kuijpers, Niels Nørgaard-Pedersen, Kurt H. Kjær, Frands Schjøth, Kaarina Weckström, and Andreas P. Ahlström. "Rapid Response of Helheim Glacier in Greenland to Climate Variability over the Past Century." *Nature Geoscience* 5 (2012): 37–41. http://www.nature.com/ngeo/journal/v5/n1/full/ngeo1349.html.

Ascher, Ivan. "Capitalism: A Horror Story (or the Return of the Commodity Fetish)." Paper presented at Western Political Science Association annual meeting, 2011.

Athanassakis, Apostolos N. *Hesiod: Theogony, Works and Days, Shield*. Baltimore: Johns Hopkins University Press, 1982.

Augustine. *Concerning the City of God: Against the Pagans*, translated by Henry Bettenson. Middlesex, U.K.: Penguin, 1984.

―――. *The Confessions of St. Augustine*, translated by John K. Ryan. New York: Image Books, 1984.

―――. *On Christian Doctrine*, translated by D. W. Robertson. New York: Macmillan, 1958.

―――. *St Augustine: Select Letters*, translated by James Baxter. Cambridge: Harvard University Press, 1930.

Balibar, Etienne. *The Philosophy of Marx*. New York: Verso, 2007.

Ball, Philip. *The Self-Made Tapestry: Pattern Formation in Nature*. 2nd ed. 1999; Oxford: Oxford University Press, 2004.

Barad, Karen. *Meeting the Universe Halfway: Quantum Physics and the Entanglement of Matter and Meaning*. Durham: Duke University Press, 2007.

Bassler, Bonnie. "Discovering Bacteria's Amazing Communication System." *TED Talks*, April 2009, http://www.ted.com (accessed May 2010).

Bennett, Jane. *The Enchantment of Modern Life: Attachments, Crossings, and Ethics*. Princeton: Princeton University Press, 2001.

―――. "Systems and Things." *New Literary History*, Spring (2012): 205–24.

―――. *Vibrant Matter: A Political Ecology of Things*. Durham: Duke University Press, 2010.

Berlin, Isaiah. *Two Concepts of Liberty*. Oxford: Clarendon Press, 1958.

Best, Michael, and William Connolly. *The Politicized Economy*. 2nd ed. Lexington, Mass.: D. C. Heath, 1983.

Blyth, Mark. *Great Transformations: Economic Ideas and Institutional Change in the Twentieth Century*. Cambridge: Cambridge University Press, 2002.

Brenner, Neil, and Nik Theodore, eds. *Spaces of Neoliberalism*. New York: Wiley Blackwell, 2003.

Butler, Judith. *Gender Trouble: Feminism and the Subversion of Identity*. New York: Routledge, 1990.

―――. *Gender Trouble: Feminism and the Subversion of Identity*. 2nd ed. New York: Routledge, 1999.

―――. *Precarious Life: The Powers of Mourning and Violence*. London: Verso, 2004.

Chambers, Samuel. *The Lessons of Rancière*. Oxford: Oxford University Press, 2013.

Chambers, Samuel, and Terrell Carver. *Judith Butler and Political Theory: Troubling Politics*. New York: Routledge, 2008.

Clarke, Bruce, and Mark Hansen, eds. *Emergence and Embodiment: New Essays on Second Order Systems Theory*. Durham: Duke University Press, 2009.

Connolly, William E. *The Augustinian Imperative: A Reflection on the Politics of Morality*. Newbury Park, Calif.: Sage, 1993.

———. *Capitalism and Christianity, American Style*. Durham: Duke University Press, 2008.

———. "Climate Change, Spirituality, and Neoliberalism." *The Contemporary Condition*, March 1, 2010, http://contemporarycondition.blogspot.com /2010/03/climate-change-spirituality-and.html (accessed March 2010).

———. *The Ethos of Pluralization*. Minneapolis: University of Minnesota Press, 1995.

———. "Experience & Experiment." *Daedalus* 135, no. 3 (2006): 67–76.

———. *Identity\Difference: Democratic Negotiations of Political Paradox*. Ithaca: Cornell University Press, 1991.

———. *Identity\Difference: Democratic Negotiations of Political Paradox*. 2nd ed. Minneapolis: University of Minnesota Press, 2002.

———. *Neuropolitics: Thinking, Culture, Speed*. Minneapolis: University of Minnesota Press, 2002.

———. *Pluralism*. Durham: Duke University Press, 2005.

———. "The Shock Doctrine and the Neoliberal Imaginary." *The Contemporary Condition*, April 18, 2010, http://contemporarycondition.blogspot.com /2010/04/shock-doctrine-and-neoliberal-imaginary.html (accessed April 2012).

———. *The Terms of Political Discourse*. 1974; Princeton: Princeton University Press, 1983.

———. *A World of Becoming*. Durham: Duke University Press, 2011.

Culver, Adam. "Race and Vision: A Tragic Reading." PhD diss., Johns Hopkins University, 2013.

Damasio, Antonio. *Descartes' Error*. New York: Avon Books, 1994.

Damasio, Antonio, and Hanna Damasio. "Minding the Body." *Daedalus* 135, no. 3 (2006): 15–23.

Deacon, Terrence W. *Incomplete Nature: How Mind Emerged from Matter*. New York: W. W. Norton, 2012.

Delaplane, K. S. *Crop Pollination by Bees*. London: CABI, 2000.

Deleuze, Gilles. *Difference and Repetition*, translated by Paul Patton. Minneapolis: University of Minnesota Press, 1994.

Deleuze, Gilles, and Félix Guattari. *A Thousand Plateaus*, translated by Brian Massumi. Minneapolis: University of Minnesota Press, 1987.

Epperson, Michael. *Quantum Mechanics and the Philosophy of Alfred North Whitehead*. New York: Fordham University Press, 2004.

Förster, Eckart. *The Twenty Five Years of Philosophy*, translated by Brady Bowman. Cambridge: Harvard University Press, 2012.

Fortey, Richard. *The Earth*. London: HarperCollins, 2010.

Foucault, Michel. *The Birth of Biopolitics: Lectures at the College De France, 1978–79*, translated by Graham Burchell. New York: Palgrave Macmillan, 2008.

Freeman, Anthony, Benjamin Libet, and Keith Sutherland, eds. *The Volitional Brain: Towards a Neuroscience of Free Will*. New York: Imprint Academic, 1999.

Friedman, Milton. *Why Government Is the Problem*. Stanford: Hoover Institution on War, Revolution and Peace, 1993.

Gibson-Graham, J. K. *The End of Capitalism (As We Knew It): A Feminist Critique of Political Economy*. Cambridge Mass.: Blackwell, 1996.

Goffman, Erving. *Relations in Public*. New York: Colophon Books, 1971.

Goodchild, Philip. "Response to *Capitalism and Christianity, American Style*, by William Connolly." *Political Theology* 12, no. 2 (2011): 195–201.

Goodwin, Brian. *How the Leopard Changed Its Spots: The Evolution of Complexity*. Princeton: Princeton University Press, 1994.

Habermas, Jürgen. *The Future of Human Nature*. Oxford: Blackwell, 2003.

———. *Legitimation Crisis*, translated by Thomas McCarthy. Boston: Beacon Press, 1975.

Hamblyn, Richard. *Terra: Four Events That Changed the Earth*. London: Picador Press, 2010.

Hamilton, Clive. *Requiem for a Species: Why We Resist the Truth of Climate Change*. London: Earthscan, 2010.

Harman, Graham. *Prince of Networks: Bruno Latour and Metaphysics*. Melbourne: re.press, 2009.

Harvey, David. *A Brief History of Neoliberalism*. Oxford: Oxford University Press, 2005.

Hayek, Friedrich A. von. *The Constitution of Liberty*. Chicago: University of Chicago Press, 1960.

———. *The Road to Serfdom*. Chicago: University of Chicago Press, 1944.

———. *Rules and Order*, vol. 1 of *Law, Legislation and Liberty: A New Statement of the Liberal Principles of Justice and Political Economy*. Chicago: University of Chicago Press, 1976.

Heinrich, Bernd. *Bumblebee Economics*. 2nd ed. Cambridge: Harvard University Press, 2004.

Hesiod. *Theogony*, translated by Norman O. Brown. Englewood Cliffs, N.J.: Prentice Hall, 1953.

Hirsch, Fred. *The Social Limits to Growth*. London: Blackwell, 1977.

Honig, Bonnie. *Antigone Interrupted*. London: Cambridge University Press, 2013.

Howarth, David, ed. "A Symposium on William Connolly's *Capitalism and Christianity, American Style*," with essays by Kathy Ferguson, Philip Goodchild, Catherine Keller, and David Howarth, *Political Theology* 12, no. 2 (2011): 180–236.

Ignatov, Anatoli. "Practices of Eco-Sensation: Opening Doors of Perception to the Nonhuman." *Theory & Event* 14, no. 2 (2011).

Jabko, Nicolas. *Playing the Market*. Ithaca: Cornell University Press, 2006.

Juarrero, Alicia. *Dynamics in Action: Intentional Behavior as a Complex System*. Cambridge: MIT Press, 1999.

Kant, Immanuel. *The Conflict of the Faculties*, translated by Mary J. Gregor. Lincoln: University of Nebraska Press, 1979.

——. *Critique of Judgment*, translated by Werner Pluhar. Indianapolis: Hackett, 1987.

——. *Critique of Practical Reason*, translated by Lewis White Beck. New York: Library of Liberal Arts, 1993.

——. "The End of All Things." In *Perpetual Peace and Other Essays*, translated by Ted Humphrey. New York: Hackett, 1983.

——. "On the Proverb: 'That May Be True in Theory but Is of No Practical Use.'" In *Perpetual Peace and Other Essays*, translated by Ted Humphrey. Indianapolis: Hackett, 1983.

——. "Perpetual Peace." In *Perpetual Peace and Other Essays*, translated by Ted Humphrey. New York: Hackett, 1983.

——. *Religion within the Limits of Reason Alone*, translated by Theodore H. Greene. New York: Harper, 1960.

Kauffman, Stuart. *Reinventing the Sacred: A New View of Science, Reason and Religion*. New York: Basic Books, 2008.

Klein, Naomi. *The Shock Doctrine: The Rise of Disaster Capitalism*. New York: Picador, 2007.

Kunii, Irene M. "Predicting Earthquakes: Japanese Scientists Aren't So Sure Anymore. 1997." *Plate Tectonics*, September 1997, platetectonics.com/article.asp?a=1&C=1 (accessed May 2010).

Latour, Bruno. *Pandora's Hope*. Cambridge: Cambridge University Press, 1999.

Lindblom, Charles Edward. *The Intelligence of Democracy: Decision Making through Mutual Adjustment*. New York: Free Press, 1965.

Lipietz, Alain. *Towards a New Economic Order: Postfordism, Ecology and Democracy*, translated by Malcolm Slater. New York: Oxford University Press, 1992.

Louden, Robert. *Kant's Impure Ethics*. New York: Oxford University Press, 2000.

MacKenzie, Donald. *An Engine, Not a Camera: How Financial Models Shape Markets*. Cambridge: MIT Press, 2006.

Margulis, Lynn, and Dorion Sagan. *What Is Life?* Berkeley: University of California Press, 1995.

Massumi, Brian. *Event and Semblance: Activist Philosophy and the Occurrent Arts*. Cambridge: MIT Press, 2011.

Morton, Timothy. *The Ecological Thought*. Cambridge: Harvard University Press, 2010.

Nadler, Steven. *The Best of All Possible Worlds*. Princeton: Princeton University Press, 2008.

Nietzsche, Friedrich. *The Pre-Platonic Philosophers*, translated by Greg Whitlock. Chicago: University of Illinois Press, 2006.

———. *Thus Spoke Zarathustra*, translated by Walter Kaufmann. New York: Penguin, 1978.

———. *Twilight of the Idols*, translated by R. J. Hollingdale. New York: Penguin, 1968.

———. *The Will to Power*, translated by Walter Kaufmann and R. J. Hollingdale. New York: Vintage Books, 1967.

Nettles, Meredith. "Questions for an Ice Quake Expert: Meredith Nettles on Tumbling Glaciers and Rising Seas." *Popular Mechanics*, October 1, 2009, http://www.popularmechanics.com/science/4302636 (accessed Fall 2010).

Nettles, Meredith, and Göran Ekström. "Glacial Earthquakes in Greenland and Antarctica." *Annual Review Earth Planet* 38 (May 2010): 467–91.

Norval, Aletta. *Aversive Democracy*. Cambridge: Cambridge University Press, 2007.

Orsenna, Erik. *Portrait of the Gulf Stream*. London: Haus, 2008.

Panagia, Davide. *The Political Life of Sensation*. Durham: Duke University Press, 2009.

Pearce, Fred. *With Speed and Violence: Why Scientists Fear Tipping Points in Climate Change*. Boston: Beacon Press, 2007.

Peck, Jamie. *Constructions of Neoliberal Reason*. Oxford: Oxford University Press, 2010.

Polanyi, Karl. *The Great Transformation: The Political and Economic Origins of Our Time*. Boston: Beacon Press, 1944.

Proust, Marcel. *Time Regained*, vol. 6 of *In Search of Lost Time*, translated by Andreas Mayor and Terence Kilmartin. New York: Modern Library, 1993.

Ray, Gene. "Reading the Lisbon Earthquake: Adorno, Lyotard, and the Contemporary Sublime." *Project Muse*, Spring 2004, http://muse.jhu.edu/journals/yale/summary/v017/17.1ray.html (accessed July 2012).

Rizzolatti, Giacomo, and Corrado Sinigaglia. *Mirrors in the Brain: How Our Minds Share Actions and Emotions*, translated by Frances Anderson. Oxford: Oxford University Press, 2008.

Romilly, Jacqueline de. *Time in Greek Tragedy*. Ithaca: Cornell University Press, 1968.

Sagan, Dorion. "The Human Is More than Human: Interspecies Communities and New 'Facts of Life.'" *Cultural Anthropology*, November 1, 2011, http://www.culanth.org/?q=node/513 (accessed February 2013).

Saurette, Paul. *The Kantian Imperative: Humiliation, Common Sense, Politics.* Toronto: University of Toronto Press, 2005.

Schneider, Eric D., and Dorion Sagan. *Into the Cool: Energy Flow, Thermodynamics and Life.* Chicago: University of Chicago Press, 2005.

Serres, Michel. *The Birth of Physics*, translated by Jack Hawkes. Manchester, U.K.: Clinamen Press, 2000.

Shaviro, Steven. *Without Criteria: Kant, Whitehead, Deleuze, and Aesthetics.* Cambridge: MIT Press, 2009.

Simmel, Georg. *The Sociology of Georg Simmel*, translated by Kurt H. Wolff. New York: Free Press, 1950.

Smith, Daniel. *Essays on Deleuze.* Edinburgh: Edinburgh University Press, 2012.

Sophocles. *The Oedipus Plays of Sophocles: Oedipus the King, Oedipus at Colonus, Antigone*, translated by Paul Roche. New York: Penguin, 1996.

Spence, Lester K. *Stare in the Darkness: The Limits of Hip-hop and Black Politics.* Minneapolis: University of Minnesota Press, 2011.

Stengers, Isabelle. *Thinking with Whitehead*, translated by Michael Chase. Cambridge: Harvard University Press, 2011.

Taylor, Charles. *A Secular Age.* Cambridge: Belknap Press of Harvard University Press, 2007.

Thompson, Evan. *Mind in Life: Biology, Phenomenology, and the Sciences of Mind.* Cambridge: Harvard University Press, 2007.

Uexkull, Jakob von. *A Foray into the Worlds of Animals and Humans*, translated by Joseph D. O'Neil. 1934; Minneapolis: University of Minnesota Press, 2010.

Vernant, Jeanne-Pierre. *Myth and Thought among the Greeks*, translated by Janet Lloyd and Jeff Fort. New York: Zone Books, 2006.

Voltaire. *Candide*, translated by Lowell Bair. New York: Bantam Classic, 2003.

———. "On the Lisbon Disaster." In *Toleration and Other Essays / Poem on the Lisbon Disaster*, translated by Joseph McCabe. Wikisource, April 16, 2011, http://en.wikisource.org/wiki/Toleration_and_other_essays/Poem_on_the_Lisbon_Disaster (accessed February 28, 2012).

von Trier, Lars. "Cannes Interview on *Melancholia*." www.youtube.com (accessed July 2012).

Wallerstein, Immanuel. *World-Systems Analysis.* Durham: Duke University Press, 2004.

Wapshott, Nicholas. *Keynes Hayek: The Clash that Defined Modern Economics.* New York: W. W. Norton, 2011.

White, Stephen. *The Ethos of a Late Modern Citizen*. Cambridge: Harvard University Press, 2009.

———. *Sustaining Affirmation: The Strengths of Weak Ontology in Political Theory*. Princeton: Princeton University Press, 2000.

Whitehead, Alfred North. *Adventures of Ideas*. New York: Free Press, 1933.

———. *Process and Reality: Corrected Edition*, edited by David Ray Griffin and Donald W. Sherburne. 2nd ed. 1929; New York: Free Press, 1978.

Williams, Bernard. *Shame and Necessity*. Berkeley: University of California Press, 1993.

Wolfe-Simon, Felisa, Jodi S. Blum, Thomas R. Kulp, Gwyneth W. Gordon, Shelley E. Hoeft, Jennifer Pett-Ridge, John F. Stolz, Samuel M. Webb, Peter K. Weber, Paul C.W. Davies, Ariel D. Anbar, and Ronald S. Oremland. "A Bacterium That Can Grow by Using Arsenic Instead of Phosphorus." *Science* 332, no. 64 (June 2011): 1163–1166.

Wolin, Sheldon S. *Democracy Incorporated: Managed Democracy and the Specter of Inverted Totalitarianism*. Princeton: Princeton University Press, 2010.

Absolutism, 137–39

Accidents: causality and, 7–8

Actants, 74, 84–85

Activism, 6, 11, 39, 41, 66, 90, 95, 195; ethos of cultivation and, 6; neo-liberal versions of, 94; role experimentation and, 19, 181, 190, 193; state versions of, 21–22

Actual, 95, 193; entities and, 143, 153–59, 166, 218n9; "eternal objects" and, 161–62

Adams, John Luther, 186

Aesthetics: becoming and, 165, 170; judgment and, 98–99, 103, 105–6;

Nietzsche and, 169–70, 173; teleo-dynamism and, 158; Whitehead and, 158–59, 169–70; will to power and, 164–65

Agency, 9, 14, 25, 101, 127–30, 135, 138, 160–61; ambiguity of, 75; creativity and, 155–56; force fields and, 142; freedom and, 73–80; God and, 162; Kant's view of, 16, 106–7, 113–14; micro-agents, 85; reflexive element in, 139; vitality and, 145

Agonistic respect, 146–47, 169, 179; across faiths and, 47, 51, 118–19, 138, 175; ethos of, 78, 133

Althusser, Louis, 30, 193
Amygdala, 163
Anaximander, 102
Anthropocentrism, 26. *See also*
    Hubris
Antigone, 139
Apartheid, 78, 194
Arab Spring, 77, 189
Arendt, Hannah: cosmology of, 30
Armageddon, 46
Assemblage, 19, 21, 35, 126, 138; book
    as, 12–13; capitalism as, 70; eco-
    nomic, 191; human/nonhuman, 49,
    85; neoliberal, 22; pluralist, 38, 41,
    137, 175, 179, 188, 192, 216n7, 224n4.
    See also Problematic
Atheism, 22, 186; "new atheism," 47,
    173
Augustine, 27, 108, 128, 142; Hesiod
    and, 110; Kant and, 108–9, 142
Austerity, 33, 79, 204n3
Autogens, 86, 220n13

Bacteria, 10, 29, 81, 92, 143, 162, 172;
    agentic capacities of, 49, 84–85,
    169–70; creative self-organization
    and, 79, 157, 167
Ball, Philip, 221n19
Barad, Karen, 29–30, 217n4
Bassler, Bonnie, on quorum sensing
    of bacteria, 85
Bateson, Gregory, 30
Becoming: aesthetic element of, 165,
    170; Nietzsche and, 151–52, 164–70,
    174; philosophy of, 29–30, 107, 142,
    159, 176, 217n3; Whitehead and,
    142, 150, 152, 159, 163–64; will to
    power and, 165–68. *See also* World
    of becoming

Bennett, Jane, 30, 84, 170, 204n4,
    218n9
Bergson, Henri, 145, 156; philosophy
    of becoming and, 29, 142, 152
Bifurcation points, 34, 71, 113
Biopolitics: neoliberalism and, 53, 59
Biosphere, 97; self-organizing power
    of, 81–82, 87
Bohr, Niels, 153, 217n4
Boycott, Thomas, 77
Bush, George W., 21, 67
Butler, Judith, 208–9n2; role perfor-
    mance of gender and, 183–84

Calvinism, 142
Cameron, David, 21, 67, 203n1
Campaign finance, 21, 62–63, 92, 189
Candide, 4–7
Capitalism, 6, 71, 173, 189; as assem-
    blage, 70; climate change and,
    30–32, 136, 171, 177, 193; fascism
    and, 39–41; globalization and, 69,
    137, 172; laissez-faire and, 20–21;
    neoliberal version of, 10–11, 20,
    22–23, 33–36, 39–42, 89, 136, 172,
    193; nonhuman entanglements
    with, 7, 14, 26–30, 37, 67–68, 70,
    149, 176, 205n9; as open system,
    25–26, 191; *ressentiment* and, 175
Care for the world, 80, 99, 124–26,
    129–32, 134–35, 138, 204n4
Catholicism, 2, 3, 95; nuns and, 180–
    81; Vatican and, 3, 22, 126, 180
Causality, 15, 78, 138, 184; efficient/
    mechanistic, 6–9, 31, 74, 85, 101–2,
    106, 111, 114, 116–17, 120, 127, 150,
    152, 162, 167, 171; emergent, 8, 127–
    28; finalism and, 7–8, 167; Hesiod
    and, 16, 100–102, 150; Kant and,

16, 102, 106, 111, 114, 116–17, 119–20;
nonhuman organisms and, 85, 88,
106, 114, 162; teleodynamism and,
85, 88. *See also* Self-organization

Cave of Forgotten Dreams, The, 50,
208n1

Chambers, Samuel, 219–20n11, 223n3

Chance, 8, 102; creative processes
and, 87, 157

Christianity, 22, 102, 113, 119, 139, 150,
170, 173, 182; Augustine and, 109;
neoliberalism and, 21, 24, 202n10;
Taylor and, 140–42

Civil rights movement, 190

Class, 15, 19, 28, 137, 180, 186, 188, 190;
investment and savings, 90–94;
military, 96; neoliberalism and,
33, 71, 89–97; white working and
middle, 22–24, 65, 89, 93–95, 117,
189, 207n25, 213n16

Climate change, 22–23, 28, 33, 93, 126,
136–37, 143, 171–73, 176, 186, 191;
creative evolution of, 141, 154, 160,
167; evangelical-neoliberal resonance machine and, 68; Habermas
and, 69; Hayek and, 69; political
economy and, 30–32, 67–69, 177,
193; responses to, 35, 39–40, 50, 70,
96, 136–37, 186, 195

Communitarianism, 79, 105

Complexity theory, 8, 14, 29, 83, 106–
7, 119, 156, 221n15

Conscience, 129–30; Kant and, 111

Constitution of Liberty, The, 61. *See
also* Hayek, Friedrich

Consumption, 51, 69; binds, 22,
65–66; ethos of, 12, 26, 40, 131;
infrastructure of, 12, 21–22, 35,
38–39, 40, 66, 71, 96, 131, 137, 172,

193–94; practices of, 30, 32, 36,
38–39, 41, 80, 96, 136–37, 154, 172,
183, 187, 193

Cosmic optimism, 3–5, 9, 93, 170, 173,
181; Whitehead and, 162. *See also*
Providence, belief in

Cosmopolitical, the, 176–79, 219–
20n11

Cosmos, 31, 40, 127; Augustine's
image of, 108–10; of becoming,
29–30, 36, 139, 141–42, 170, 173–74,
176, 205n9; contestability views of,
126, 139; creativity in, 11, 160, 163;
Hesiod's image of, 16, 100–102, 110,
120; human mastery and, 77, 103,
136, 148, 171, 174; Kant's image of,
16, 108, 110, 120, 127; of multiple
interacting force fields, 7–8, 11, 25,
49, 51, 81, 97, 99, 147, 163, 172, 175;
Nietzsche and, 170, 175, 178; philosophies of, 27, 51, 125–26, 139,
148, 177; post-Voltaireian image of,
6; practical wisdom and, 125–26;
speculative dimension and, 154,
160; Whitehead's image of, 31, 123,
143, 152, 154, 175, 178, 218n11. *See
also* Cosmopolitical, the

Creativity, 16, 29, 62, 68, 70, 72,
98–99, 123, 127, 133, 135, 138, 152,
192–93, 220n13; evolution and,
88, 141, 157, 159–61, 163, 165, 168;
freedom and, 14, 18, 74–80, 129;
human estate and, 10, 17, 76, 160,
174–75; improvisation and, 78–79;
and incompleteness of explanation, 54; language and, 78; markets and, 14–15, 54–57, 60, 66, 93;
Nietzsche and, 164–68, 174; nonhuman forces and, 9–10, 18, 27, 31,

Creativity (*continued*)
79, 150, 157, 160, 163–64; politics
and, 14, 38, 51, 66–67, 77–80, 95,
132, 137, 147, 178, 184–85, 190, 194;
question of its extent in the cosmos, 220n13; real, 9, 11, 13, 15, 18,
34, 75, 79, 92, 119, 145, 147, 154–56,
158–63, 167, 175; self-organization
and, 8, 25, 72, 87, 154, 157–58,
164–65; teleodynamism and,
85–87, 92, 156–58, 167; uncertainty
and, 75–77; vitality and, 18, 143–47;
Whitehead and, 143, 155–63, 175.
See also Noise
Critical responsiveness, 135
Critical theory, 141, 190–91, 219n11
Critique of Judgment, The, 103, 105–7,
122. *See also* Kant, Immanuel
Critique of Practical Reason, The, 105.
See also Kant, Immanuel
Cultural internalism, 48–49, 220n11
Cultural theory, 25, 161

Damasio, Antonio, 104
Darwinism, 168, 177; neo- , 87
Deacon, Terrence, 83, 161, 212n13,
220n13; teleodynamic processes
and, 85–88, 92
Death: memory and, 45
Debt ceiling crisis (2011), 54, 203n1
Deep ecology, 23, 31, 37, 41
Deleuze, Gilles, 145, 210n13, 214n6,
219n11; Kant and, 105; philosophy of becoming and, 29–30, 142;
political economy and, 30; species
evolution and, 86; "this world"
and, 125
Democratic politics, 10–11, 118, 136–
37, 178; critique and, 37, 41–42; experimental action and, 19, 36–37,

181–90, 192–94; militancy and, 17,
31–36, 125, 192, 195; neoliberalism
and, 36–42, 54; practical wisdom
and, 124–26; self-organization and,
14, 66–67, 194; vitality and, 195
Democritus, 102, 108
Denial, 43–45, 47–49, 51, 173, 208n1;
climate change and, 68, 186
Dennett, Richard, 47
Desire, 38, 48, 128–31, 133, 180, 190;
freedom and, 73–77, 79; Kant and,
111–13; neoliberalism and, 11, 23,
60, 92–93, 118, 189, 192, 205–6n9;
nonhuman, 29, 49
Dionysus, 100–101, 150, 170, 213n1
Disequilibrium, 167; periods of, 27,
101, 134–35, 156; vitality and, 143,
146
Dramatization, of cloudy processes,
12–13, 47, 49–51, 95, 113, 131, 137,
139, 174; flashpoints and, 16, 99,
100, 113, 121–24; fragility and, 32,
97

Electoral politics, 59, 136–37, 154, 188,
192; dilemma of, 19, 41, 181–82, 194
"End of All Things, The," 118. *See also*
Kant, Immanuel
Enlightenment, the, 173; Lisbon
earthquake and, 3; time and, 170
Entropy, 83–84, 87, 163
Epicurus, 32, 111, 204n4
Epperson, Michael, 153–54
Eternal objects: critique of, 163–65,
167–68; Whitehead and, 150, 161–
64, 168, 175, 221n19, 222–23n34
Eternal return: Nietzsche and, 150,
217n3
Ethical life, 16, 50, 99, 120, 124, 129,
161, 179–80, 208–9n2; creativity

and, 160; cultivation and, 17, 104, 130–38, 147, 223n4; fragility of, 17, 131–33; judgment and, 105; luck and, 132–33

Ethnicity, 63, 89, 137, 180, 194

Ethos, 11, 24, 26, 39, 103–4, 125, 131, 172, 180; of agonistic respect, 78, 133, 146; of consumption, 12, 38, 40, 66; of courage, 133; of cultivation, 6, 130–31; of diversity, 146; of engagement, 67, 138–39, 147, 174, 216–17n7; of existential gratitude, 178, 181; political economy and, 36, 68–69, 71, 194; of presumptive generosity, 133, 181; of responsibility, 17, 80, 133

Evangelicalism, 12, 24, 35, 39, 119, 126, 136, 142, 177, 186; neoliberalism and, 22, 68–69, 92–95, 117–18, 173, 193

Evangelical-neoliberal resonance machine, 68–69, 117–18, 173, 193; teleodynamism and, 93–95

Evil, 3–4, 6–7, 135, 142; Augustine and, 109; Kant and, 113, 129; Nietzsche and, 173–75

Evolution, 89, 97, 177; aesthetic element in, 164–65; bacterial and viral, 143, 157, 172; climate and, 141; cosmic, 171; creativity in, 79, 85–88, 141, 157, 159–63, 168, 175; God and, 162; Nietzsche and, 164–70; species, 13, 15, 27–28, 46, 55–56, 58, 67, 81–82, 84, 85–88, 92, 160, 168, 171, 173; teleodynamic processes in, 85–88, 92; Whitehead and, 160–64, 168–70

Existential affirmation, 28, 174, 176, 178, 180

Existential gratitude, 175, 178–81

Existential resentment, 18, 28, 125, 127, 133, 138–39, 147, 170–80. *See also Ressentiment*

Experimental action, 36–37, 72, 128, 134–36, 146, 161, 169, 172; role performances and, 19, 27, 38, 40, 42, 50, 129, 181–90, 192–94

Faith, 11, 16, 29, 32, 76, 80, 92, 113, 118, 127, 129, 131–32, 134, 137–38, 146, 169, 173, 180, 182, 187, 194; Augustine and, 109–10, 119; contestability of, 47, 120, 123, 175; neoliberal ideology and, 23, 95, 172; Taylor and, 140–42

Fascism, 39–40, 60, 74, 93, 136, 190, 207n23, 216n7

Finalism, 8, 167, 179

Flashpoints: Kant and, 16, 99, 106, 110–11

Financial crisis (2008), 23, 97

Force fields, 34, 143; agency of, 142; cosmos of multiple, interacting, 7–8, 11, 25, 36, 49, 51, 81, 97, 99, 138, 141, 147, 149, 163, 168, 172, 175, 204n4; gods and, 101–2, 168; Hesiod and, 27; interactions between, 27–31, 67–68, 79, 81–82, 125, 154, 168, 176, 178; nonhuman, 7, 9–10, 12, 14, 17, 26–27, 30–31, 36–37, 67, 74, 79, 105, 125, 141, 143, 149, 160–61, 166, 175, 193, 205–6n9; an outside to, 30, 141; planetary, 176, 178; Sophocles and, 27; temporal scales of, 27–29, 125, 133, 138, 149, 172

Förster, Eckart, 214n6

Foucault, Michel, 11, 193; neoliberalism and, 20–21, 30, 202n1

Fox News, 33, 93

"Fracking," hydraulic, 32, 78

Fragility, 6, 23–24, 124, 148, 174, 178; beauty and, 159; democratic militancy and, 10, 31–41, 194–95; of ethical life, 17, 131–33; examples of, 32–33; of human estate, 46, 48, 99, 143, 145, 172, 180; of identity, 89, 94, 223n4; Kant and, 17, 99, 103; of markets, 28, 60, 81–82, 97; of memory, 45; of neoliberalism, 97; palpability of, 19, 37, 192, 194; planetary, 172, 174; practical wisdom and, 17, 132; precariousness and, 7, 223n4; of things, 7, 10–12, 14–15, 19, 26, 29, 31–32, 34, 36, 41, 51, 71, 99, 103, 118, 132, 143, 149, 162, 172, 175–76, 180–81, 186–87, 194–95; Whitehead and, 159, 162

Freedom, 7, 17, 20, 79, 135; Augustine and, 109; creative element in, 14–15, 18, 74–80, 123, 129, 145; Hayek and, 57, 71–74; the implicit and, 74; Kant and, 102, 106, 109, 112–14, 120, 124, 136, 159; positive vs. negative, 72–73, 79, 145; reflexivity and, 75–76; vitality and, 18, 145; Whitehead and, 123; the will and, 17, 127, 129

Friedman, Milton, 27; Hayek and, 52, 60, 67, 78; involvement in Chile, 54; radical neoliberalism and, 52–54

Fullness: Taylor and, 18, 140–42, 147–48; vitality and, 17–18, 77, 140–48

Gay rights, 77, 132, 181, 189–90

Gender, 89, 137, 183–84

Genealogy: of the present, 102; of reason, 99

General Motors, 203n3

General strike, 39, 96, 195

"Gift Giving Virtue, The," 145, 169. See also Nietzsche, Friedrich

Glaciers, 30, 33–35, 40, 141, 143, 172, 176

Globalization: of capitalism, 32, 40, 53, 67, 69, 137, 172, 189; of fragility, 174

God, 1–4, 6, 10, 29, 46–47, 49, 51, 68, 122, 127, 129, 138, 148, 152, 171, 173, 182, 186, 202n7; Augustine and, 108–9, 119, 142; Kant and, 102, 107, 109, 111–13, 116, 119, 136; Nietzsche and, 29, 142, 168; Taylor and, 48, 142; Whitehead and, 29, 160–62, 142, 175, 223n34

Gods, ancient Greek, 27, 100–102, 107, 139, 150, 168

Goffman, Erving; tacit role performances and, 183–84, 223n2

Goodwin, Brian, 163, 221n20

Grace, divine, 17, 109, 111, 113–14, 120, 128, 132, 136, 142; fullness and, 141; human history and, 115–16

Great Depression, the, 40, 190

Greenspan, Alan, 27, 97

Habermas, Jürgen, 103, 108, 119, 193, 219n11; climate change and, 69

Haemon, 139

Hamilton, Clive, 210n20

Hayek, Friedrich, 27, 171, 193; democracy and, 60, 66–67; environment and, 61–62, 69; freedom and, 71–74, 79–80; Friedman and, 52, 60, 67, 78; ideology and, 14, 56, 58–63, 68, 71–72, 94; labor unions and, 63–65; moderate neoliberalism and, 13, 54–71; rational choice theory and, 72; self-organization

and, 14–15, 55–58, 62, 66–68, 74;
the state and, 57–62
Heisenberg, Werner: ontological
quantum theory of, 153, 217n4
Heraclitus: Nietzsche and, 150–51
Herzog, Werner, 50
Hesiod, 17, 172, 213n1; Augustine and,
110, 121; cosmology of, 27, 122,
100–103, 120, 150, 171; Kant and,
16–17, 100, 104, 106–8, 110, 121–22,
124, 136; Nietzsche and, 107, 150,
168; time and, 107
High-frequency trading, 90–92
Hirsch, Fred: consumption binds
and, 22–23, 65, 72
Honig, Bonnie, on minor tragic figures, 220n13
Hubris, 95, 97, 206n9; anthropocentric, 26, 175; democratic social
movements and, 193; "exclusive
humanism" and, 49; existential
force of, 18, 39, 177; neoliberalism
and, 24, 177; "new atheism" and, 47
Human estate, 18, 28, 37, 99, 117, 125,
142, 152, 170–71, 176–77, 222n34;
creativity within, 9, 76–77, 160,
165–66; entanglements with nonhuman processes, 7, 13, 26–27, 31,
35, 47, 49–50, 142, 149–50, 163,
166, 174, 178, 204n4, 209n2, 224n9;
fragility of, 46, 48, 99, 143, 172;
priority given to, 49–51. See also
Humanism
Humanism, 46–47, 141, 160, 171;
anti-, 50; "exclusive humanism,"
13, 46–50, 204n4, 209n2; post-, 13,
50, 204n4, 209n2
Human sciences, 8, 16, 94–95, 193,
212n12; cultural internalism and,
48–49; expanded image of, 11

Hume, David, 150
Hurricanes, 28, 162, 176; self-
organization and, 58, 67, 82–84

Ideology, 36, 38–39, 48, 80, 90–91,
193; Friedman and, 54; Hayek and,
14, 56, 58–63, 68, 71–72, 94; neoliberal, 7, 11, 13–14, 16–17, 22–23,
25, 31–32, 37, 51, 54, 58–63, 67–68,
72–73, 89, 92–94, 96–97, 117, 189,
191
Ignatov, Anatoli, and techno-artistic
explorations, 170
Immanence, 175, 222n27
Immigration, 24, 33, 35, 137
Immortality, of the soul, 109, 111–12
Implicit, 16, 85, 91, 131–33, 137, 147, 155,
162–63, 183, 220n11; freedom and,
73–75, 77; fullness and, 143–44;
Kant and, 122. See also Incipience
Improvisation, 76, 78–79, 143, 185
Incipience, 27, 128, 135, 180, 192–93;
contrasted to the implicit, 91, 122;
dramatization of, 122; and half-
second delay, 128, 144, 192; Kant
and, 120, 122; teleodynamism and,
91; vitality and, 143–44
Individualism: freedom and, 74, 79,
105; market, 58–59; methodological, 13, 73
Induction, cultural: Kant and, 120–24
Inequality, income, 22, 59, 68, 71, 89,
195, 216n7; neoliberalism and, 21,
57, 59, 61, 63, 90, 93–94, 97, 126,
137, 186, 189
Infrastructure of consumption, 12,
21–22, 35, 38–39, 40, 66, 71, 96, 131,
137, 172, 193–94
Interim agenda, 37–38, 41–42, 80,
194, 202n10

James, William, 154; God and, 147–
48; "litter" and, 145; philosophy of
becoming and, 29, 107, 142, 152
Jazz, 78–79, 143, 211n24
Jocasta, 102, 139
Juarrero, Alicia, 88, 212n12
Judaism, 95, 170, 208n2
Judgment, 14, 101–2, 104, 120; aesthetic, 98–99, 103, 105–6; ethical,
105, 130; Nietzsche and, 134–35,
164–65, 170, 175; role performances
and, 183, 185–87; situational, 17,
91–93, 126, 129; teleological, 106
Justice, pursuit of, 147

Kant, Immanuel, 126, 132, 134–35,
160–61, 173, 215n23; aesthetic judgment and, 98–99, 103, 105–7, 111;
apodictic starting points of, 15–16,
99, 103, 110–14, 120–24, 126, 214n6;
Augustine and, 109–10, 113, 119,
121, 135; care for this world and, 17,
99, 124; causality and, 16, 102, 106,
111, 114, 159; cosmology of, 103–4,
109, 111, 120, 127, 171; cultural induction and, 120–24; existential
anxiety and, 99, 116–18, 122–23;
flashpoints in, 16, 99, 106, 110–11;
fragility and, 17, 99, 103; Hesiod
and, 16–17, 100, 104, 106–8, 110,
121–22, 124, 136; and "gymnastics,"
121–24; marketlike processes, and,
16, 114–18; morality, and, 111–17,
121–26, 131, 133, 136, 214–15n20;
neoliberalism and, 16–17, 117; nonhuman systems and, 16, 83, 99,
106–7, 111, 114, 117, 128, 159; postulates of, 16–17, 44, 101–4, 107–12,
114–20, 122–23, 127, 133, 136, 139,
159, 198; practical reason and, 17,

98–99, 102–4, 109–14, 119, 121–23,
125, 127, 138; progress and, 44, 112,
114–17, 119–20, 130, 136, 138–39;
self-organization of organisms
and, 84, 106–7, 119, 128, 159; the
sublime and, 3, 17; transcendental
arguments and, 110–12, 118, 121–23,
214n6; the will and, 109, 111–14,
127–28
Kauffman, Stuart, 29–30, 83, 161, 163,
218n8, 221–22n22
Keller, Catherine, 29; two modes of
transcendence and, 222n27
Keynesianism, 7, 11, 25, 27, 42, 52, 70,
74, 79, 193, 207–8n25, 224n9
Klein, Naomi, 209n2

Labor unions, 95; Hayek and, 61,
63–65, 70, 72
Laissez-faire: vs. neoliberalism,
20–22
Language, 104, 132, 164; creative
innovations in, 76–78; evolution
of, 56, 58; Habermas and, 119
Latour, Bruno, 84
Law, moral, 103–4, 130; Kant and,
111–16, 121–23, 130
Laws of nature, 119, 122–23, 150, 167
Leibniz, Gottfried, 3–4, 201–2n4
Libet, Benjamin, 128
Limbaugh, Rush, 24
Lindblom, Charles, 55
Lisbon earthquake (1755), 1–8, 50,
91, 177
Louden, Robert, 214–15n20
Luck: ethical life and, 132–33

MacKenzie, Donald, 210n13
Markets, 27, 36, 38–39, 67, 97, 137; as
"abstract" processes, 60, 64, 70;

consumption binds and, 22–23, 65–66; creativity of, 54–57, 60, 76–77, 93; desire for, 24–25, 117; financial, 15, 88–94; fragility of, 28, 60, 81–82, 97; Hayek and, 54–62, 68–72; impersonal rationality of, 6–7, 11–12, 15, 24–25, 51–53, 55–59, 61–62, 66, 72–73, 93, 95, 97, 118, 172, 189–191; innocence of, 41; Kant and, 16, 114–18; masculinity and, 24, 93; nonhuman processes and, 95–96, 118, 205n9; providential view of, 39, 92, 95, 118; self-organizing power of, 12, 14–15, 25, 31–32, 54–56, 64–66, 81–83, 88–89, 92, 94, 97, 189; self-regulating power of, 20, 22, 25, 30, 36, 51–52, 55–58, 64–65, 95, 136, 189; the state and, 20–21, 23, 40, 52–54, 58, 60–63, 65, 189; teleodynamism and, 88–89; volatility of, 25–26, 28

Marxism, 25, 27, 79, 193; neoliberalism and, 11, 22, 52; nonhuman systems and, 32, 204n4

Masculinity: markets and, 24, 93–94

Mastery, human, 7, 26, 29, 101, 103, 120, 125, 138–39, 145, 148, 170–71, 174; creativity and, 14–15, 75, 77; neoliberalism and, 24, 39

Media, 40, 61, 74, 76, 120, 128, 171–72, 180, 186; corporate ownership of, 21, 38, 63, 182, 189; democratic politics and, 26, 38–39, 41–42, 90, 137, 182, 187, 190, 192; neoliberalism and, 12, 20–24, 33, 58–60, 63, 70–71, 90–91, 94–95, 173, 190

Melancholia, 13, 43–50, 208n1

Melancholia, 44, 48–49

Memory, 46, 49, 129, 135, 169, 216n5; death and, 45; as layered, 45

Metamorphosis, 15, 34, 134, 154–55; difference from teleodynamism, 15, 83–87; powers of, 26, 30, 36–37, 71, 97, 125, 143, 149, 176

Micropolitics, 38, 40, 42, 128, 130, 137, 184, 223n1; in relation to macropolitics, 88, 184–94. *See also* Gymnastics; Tactics of the self

Militancy, democratic, 10, 17, 31–36, 42, 125, 136–38, 192, 195

Military, 21, 24, 38–39, 47, 53, 61, 66, 69, 80, 89, 96, 172–73, 177

Millennium Bridge, London, 15, 82

Minorities, 194; minoritization of the world, 41, 53, 67, 126, 136–38, 171, 174; neoliberalism and, 21, 35, 53; pluralist assemblage of, 19, 78, 138, 178, 192, 195

Mirror neurons, 104–5, 121, 124, 213n6

Misplaced concreteness, fallacy of, 154, 218n8

Monotheism, 44, 46–7, 77, 138, 150, 155, 171

Mortality, 171–72, 174

Mutation, genetic, 13, 163; teleodynamism and, 86–87

Negative dialectics, 18, 141, 147

Neoconservatism, 22, 39

Neo-Kantianism, 98–100, 108, 119, 125, 135, 138

Neoliberalism, 13–14, 103, 126, 172, 177, 190, 195; biopolitics and, 53, 59; climate change and, 22–23, 61–62, 68–69, 136–37, 193; cosmology and, 6–7; crisis tendencies of, 40, 54, 93; democracy and, 54, 58–61, 195; desire for, 11, 22–25, 92–93, 189, 205–5n9; discipline

Neoliberalism (*continued*)

and, 7, 11, 20–21, 33, 35, 53–54, 58–59, 64, 67, 72–74, 96–97, 122; fascism and, 39–40; fragility of, 97; judicial system and, 21, 58–59, 62–63, 96; Keynesianism and, 7, 11, 22; moderate vs. radical versions of, 52–62, 80; nonhuman systems, and, 7, 10, 12, 117; policies of, 21–22; race and, 24, 63, 89, 95–97, 186; role performances and, 10, 68, 92–97, 172; security and, 21, 80, 86; self-organization and, 12, 31–32, 97; "subjective grip" of, 22–25, 117. *See also* Class; Democratic politics; Evangelical-neoliberal resonance machine; Friedman, Milton; Hayek, Friedrich; Ideology; Inequality; Labor unions; Laissez-faire; Markets; Media; Military; Minorities; State

Nettles, Meredith, 34

New Left, the, 40, 189

Newton, 6, 110, 122–23, 133–34, 143, 150, 156; collapse of Newtonian physics, 31, 152

Nietzsche, Friedrich, 18, 111, 141, 156, 163, 178, 187–88; aesthetic element of becoming and, 164–65, 169–70, 173; becoming and, 29–30, 107, 142, 150–52; double-entry approach of, 173–75; nonhuman processes and, 164–66, 169; periodic hesitation and, 134; nobility and, 169, 175; *ressentiment* and, 170, 173–75, 178; subjectivity and, 166; theodicy of, 173–75; transcendence and, 167, 169, 222n27; vitality and, 144–45; writing style of, 155. *See also* Cre-

ativity; Eternal return; Will to power

Noise, 18, 27, 152, 191, 224n9; creativity and, 13, 156, 192; markets and, 26, 92, 95; role performances and, 185, 190, 192; species evolution and, 13, 86–87; social movements and, 13, 91, 192; teleodynamism and, 92, 156

Nondiscursive systems, 26, 30, 205n9

Nonhuman systems: capitalism and, 7, 14, 26–30, 37, 67–68, 70, 149, 176, 205n9; causality and, 85, 88, 106, 114, 162; creativity and, 9–10, 18, 27, 31, 79, 150, 157, 160, 163–64; desires of, 29, 49; human entanglements with, 7, 13, 26–27, 31, 35, 47, 49–50, 142, 149–50, 163, 166, 174, 178, 204n4, 209n2, 224n9; Kant and, 16, 83, 99, 106–7, 111, 114, 117, 128, 159; markets and, 95–96, 118, 205n9; Marxism and, 32, 204n4; neoliberalism and, 7, 10, 12, 117; Nietzsche and, 164–66, 169; perceptual powers of, 29, 84–88; teleodynamism and, 85–88; Whitehead and, 169–70. *See also* Force fields

Nuclear power, 33, 36, 91

Ocean conveyor system, 28, 40, 46, 67, 83, 95–96, 141, 143, 154, 156, 160, 169, 172, 176

Occupy movement, 190, 194

Oedipus, 102, 139

Ontology, 120, 141, 218n9; ontocosmology, 9; ontopolitical perspective, 104–5, 218–19n11; speculative, 157. *See also* Cosmopolitical, the

Organism, 97, 101, 111; Kant and, 16,

83, 99, 106–7, 114, 128, 159; Nietzsche and, 164; perceptual powers of, 84–88; self-organizing, 8, 13, 58, 82, 85–88, 107, 159, 164; teleodynamism and, 85–88, 106; Whitehead and, 156, 158, 163

Original sin, 108–9, 128–29

Outside, an, 101; agency and, 145; force fields and, 30, 141, 191; transcendence and, 30, 222n27

Panagia, Davide, 170, 213n17

Passive syntheses, 104–5, 121, 124, 132, 213–14n6

Perception, 11, 46, 128, 161, 209n2, 213n17, 224n9; action-oriented modes of, 146, 171, 164; Nietzsche and, 164–65, 169–70; nonhuman powers of, 29, 84, 211n3; role performances and, 39, 185–88, 194

Periodic hesitation, 134–35, 185; pursuit of vitality and, 146

"Perpetual Peace," 116, 215n23

Plato, 122, 152

Pluralism, 78, 141, 175; deep, 99, 132, 224n4; ethos of, 139, 216n7; pluralist assemblage, 38, 41, 137, 175, 179, 188, 192, 216n7, 224n4; vitality and, 146–47, 195

Pluralization, politics of, 66–67, 94–95, 132, 146–47, 213n16, 216n7

Pluripotentiality, beyond the implicit, 74, 91. See also Incipience

Polanyi, Karl, 190–91, 207n23

Political economy, 14, 71, 88, 95, 194; as an assemblage, 13; becoming and, 29–30; climate change and, 30–31, 68; evangelical-neoliberal resonance machine and, 68; non-human processes and, 26–27, 30–32; Polanyi and, 191; role performances and, 188, 193; Sophoclean, 97

Post-Nietzscheanism, 141, 165

Postulates, Kantian, 16–17, 44, 101–4, 107–12, 114–20, 122–23, 127, 133, 136, 139, 159, 198, 214n17

Potentials, 157–58, 166, 222n34; co-existent, 153; eternal objects and, 161–62

"Powers of the false," 168

Practical wisdom, maxims of, 17, 102–3, 124–39

Preadaptations, 76, 89–90, 163, 168

Precarious Life, 208n2

Presumptive generosity, 132, 179; ethos of, 6, 133, 181

Problematic, a, 182; Kantian, 134; practical wisdom and, 126, 139. See also Assemblage

Process philosophy, 162, 176, 218n9. See also Becoming

Progress, 26, 107, 125, 130–31, 134, 136, 138, 146, 170; Kantian and, 16, 44, 111–12, 114–20, 139, 214–15n20, 215n23; Whitehead and, 162–63

Protean connectionism, 74, 154, 184, 211n23

Proust, 30, 144–45

Providence, belief in, 7, 47, 99, 101, 125, 133, 138, 149, 174; Augustine and, 109; Kant and, 103–4, 108, 111, 117–18, 120; markets and, 39, 92, 95

Quantum mechanics, 160, 164, 167, 169, 218n8; Bohr vs. Heisenberg, 153; Whitehead and, 123, 143, 150, 152–56

Race: Kant and, 115, 215n20; neoliberalism and, 24, 63, 89, 95–97, 186
Rancière, Jacques, 219–20n11
Rational choice theory, 72, 104
Rawls, John, 193, 219n11
Reason: instrumental, 98–99, 102, 103–5, 125, 138; practical, 17, 98–99, 102–5, 108–10, 111–12, 114, 119, 121–23, 125, 138; speculative, 98–99, 112, 119
Receptivity, 124; ethos of, 133; of the subject, 105, 121, 206n9
Reflexivity, 49, 73–76, 80; neoliberalism and, 94–96; practical wisdom and, 139; the will and, 128
Relativism, 137–38, 216n7
Religion within the Limits of Reason Alone, 105, 113
Resonance, 26, 40, 135, 172, 211n1; machine, 180, 194; role performances and, 182. *See also* Evangelical-neoliberal resonance machine
Responsibility, 46, 48, 71, 124, 127, 129–30, 181; Augustine and, 109, 113; ethos of, 17, 80, 133; Kant and, 113–14, 135
Ressentiment, 18, 39, 170, 173, 175, 177, 180, 204n4. *See also* Existential resentment
Roche, Paul, 216n32
Role performances: democratic politics and, 10–11, 19, 27, 37–40, 42, 95, 136–37, 181–95; experimentation with, 11, 19, 27, 38, 40, 42, 50, 129, 136, 181–90, 192–95; gender and, 183–84; macropolitics and, 184–90, 192–93; neoliberal, 10, 68, 92–97, 172; power and, 183, 185, 188

Romanticism, 141; Nietzsche and, 170
Romilly, Jacqueline de, 107–8

Sagan, Dorion, 85, 211n3
Secularism, 40, 47, 80, 136, 141, 149–50, 170–73, 186, 193; *ressentiment* and, 39, 177
Searching process, 8, 13, 15, 78, 92–93, 106, 156–58, 212n12; evolution and, 85–88; markets and, 89; vitality and, 142–43. *See also* Teleodynamism
Seer, 134–35, 173
Self-amplification, 15, 25, 40, 63, 82–83, 89, 154, 220n13; climate processes and, 33–35, 176; high-frequency trading and, 92; Kantian cultural induction and, 122; neoliberalism and, 94–97; role performances and, 194, 207n25
Self-interest, 103, 126, 131, 169, 179–80, 193; neoliberal formation of, 62, 70, 72, 93, 117–18
Self-organization, 12, 145, 154, 169; creativity and, 8–9, 25, 72, 87, 154, 157–58, 164–65; evolution and, 82, 84–85, 87–88, 94; Hayek and, 14–15, 55–58, 62, 66–68, 74; Kant and, 84, 106–7, 119, 128, 159; markets and, 12, 14–15, 25, 31–32, 54–56, 64–66, 81–83, 88–89, 92, 94, 97, 189; Nietzsche and, 164–65; nonhuman processes and, 7, 12, 25, 35, 106, 157; politics and, 194; powers of, 10, 14, 36, 26, 65, 68, 97, 178; social movements and, 66–67, 190; Whitehead and, 154, 157–58. *See also* Force fields; Teleodynamism

Serres, Michael, 102

Sexuality: role performance and, 184

Shaviro, Steven, 105–6

Shocks, 1–4, 6, 8, 25–26, 37, 45, 128, 132, 152, 177; creativity and, 26, 99, 159, 178, 205–6n9; "micro-shocks," 15; neoliberal tactic of, 54, 60, 209n2

Shock therapy, 99, 122, 139

Simmel, Georg, 23

"Slut walk," 190

Smith, Dan, 221–22n22

Social democracy: neoliberalism and, 22–23, 52; insufficiency of, 37

Social movements, 19, 26, 37–38, 80, 90–92, 137, 160, 167; climate change and, 69–70; creativity and, 14, 76, 80; pluralizing, 94–95; role performances and, 184, 187–94; self-organization and, 66–67, 160, 190; vitality and, 143

Sophocles, 47, 97, 124, 136, 139, 177, 213n1; cosmology of, 27, 36, 103, 108, 171–72; time and, 107–8, 139; tragic vision and, 101–2

Space: Whitehead and, 154–56

Speculative realism, 9, 77, 161, 176, 218n9

Spinoza, Baruch, 111, 209n2

Spirituality, 32, 41, 93, 100, 154, 172–73, 177, 181, 219n11; affinities of, 14, 68, 71, 119, 125; vs. belief, 47, 71, 176, 199; of cosmic gratitude, 175, 178; of existential resentment, 18, 39, 177–80; political economy and, 68–69, 154; mixture of resentment, hubris, and complacency, 177–80; pluralist, 195; of presumptive generosity, 6; Whitehead and, 175–76.

See also Ethos; "Spiritualization of enmity"

"Spiritualization of enmity," 169, 174, 176

Spontaneous orders: Hayek and, 56

State, the, 6, 46, 48, 191; cynicism and, 41, 182; democratic activism and, 11–12, 19, 26–27, 37–42, 67–69, 71, 78, 80, 131, 137, 176, 182, 184, 186, 190, 194–95; feminization of, 24; Friedman and, 52–54; Hayek and, 57–66, 70, 73–74; neoliberalism and, 7, 11–12, 14–15, 20–25, 30–33, 35–36, 38–41, 52–54, 57–66, 68, 89–90, 92, 96, 172, 189

Stonewall riots, 77–78

Subjectivity: and mirror neurons, 124; in nonhuman processes, 166–69; and tactics of the self, 121–24; Nietzsche and Whitehead on, 166–69

Sublime, the, 159; Kant and, 3, 17

Supreme Court, U.S., 63, 96, 189

Structuralism, 37, 189–90, 193

Sweetness of life, 76–77, 79, 101, 103, 124, 174, 181, 208n2

Symbiogenesis, 27, 81, 158

Tactics of the self, 128–30, 174; and Kantian gymnastics, 121–24. See also Mirror Neurons

Taylor, Charles, 217n7; exclusive humanism and, 48; fullness and, 18, 140–41, 147–48

Tea Party, 33, 78, 203n1, 224n8

Tectonic plates, 2, 28, 34, 40, 91, 172

Teleodynamism, 8, 15, 82–83, 106, 156, 171, 220n13; aesthetic element in, 158; autopoiesis and, 211–12n9;

Teleodynamism (*continued*)
creativity and, 85–87, 92, 156, 167;
evolution and, 86–88, 92; incipience and, 91; markets and, 88–89;
neoliberal ideology and, 92–94, 97;
vitality and, 142; Whitehead and,
158. *See also* Searching process
Theodicy: Nietzsche and, 173–75;
Voltaire and, 4, 177
Theogony, 100–102, 108, 120–21,
213n1. *See also* Hesiod
Thompson, Evan, 88, 161, 212n13,
221n21
Thought, 104, 120, 124, 126, 128, 155,
164–65; creativity and, 14, 16, 26,
75, 79, 85–86, 92, 98–99, 129, 144–
45, 160, 168, 174, 192; constraints
on, 108, 182; role performances
and, 186; vitality and, 143–44, 148
Thus Spoke Zarathustra, 168–69. *See
also* Nietzsche, Friedrich
Time, 60, 99, 120, 160, 171, 174; Bergson and, 156; chrono- , 30, 138, 141,
149, 156, 172; different scales of, 25,
28, 30–31, 107, 123, 154, 172; Hesiod
and, 107; Kant and, 99, 111; Newton
and, 152; Nietzsche and, 107, 174;
as "out of joint," 136; progressive,
8, 44, 48, 170; Sophocles and, 139;
untimely, 97, 134, 137, 186; Whitehead and, 107, 155–56
Time Regained, 144
Tipping points, 93, 128, 134, 188–89,
195; climate and, 67
Tragic, 103, 150; Kant and, 113, 117,
120; Nietzsche and, 173, 175; vision
of possibility, 107, 117, 133, 175–76,
181; vision of Sophocles, 101–2;
Whitehead and, 162

Transcendence, 18, 147, 222n27;
Nietzsche and, 30, 167–68, 175;
Taylor and, 141–42; Whitehead
and, 29
Transcendental arguments, 49, 110,
112, 118, 121–23, 131, 161, 164, 169,
214n6
Tsunamis, 1–3, 7, 23, 33, 36, 95, 132

Uexkull, Jakob von, 211n3
Uncertainty, 24, 62, 74, 146; cosmic,
109, 173; creativity and, 75–77;
experimental action and, 19, 37;
judgment and, 91; real, 9, 34, 76,
92, 134, 148; teleodynamism and,
88, 92
Unknowns, types of, 34
Unpredictability: vs. creativity, 157,
167

Vanishing points: one vs. two, 44
Vernant, Jeanne-Pierre, 102
Vibrations, 35, 82; creativity and, 143,
156, 162, 167–68; resonance and,
40; world of becoming and, 34
Vitality, 110; creativity and, 18, 79,
143–47; democracy and, 195; of
existence, 77, 79, 131, 143, 145–48,
174, 178, 181; fragility of, 145; fullness and, 140–48; pluralism and,
137, 147, 195; pursuit of, 18, 142–48;
spiritual, 173
Voltaire, 3–7, 171, 173
von Trier, Lars, 43, 208n1. *See also*
Melancholia

Wallerstein, Immanuel, 30, 193
Whitehead, Alfred North, 195,
218n9, 218n11, 222–23n34; aesthet-

ics and, 158–59, 165, 169–70; becoming and, 29, 107, 142, 150, 152,
159, 163–64; creativity and, 18, 123,
128, 143, 155–63, 167, 175; "eternal objects" and, 150, 161–64, 168,
175, 221n19, 222–23n34; God and,
29, 161–62, 168; Kant and, 105–6,
122–23; Newton and, 31, 122–23,
143, 152, 156; Nietzsche and, 155,
163–70, 175, 178, 222n27; quantum
mechanics and, 143, 150, 152–56,
164, 167; spirituality of, 175–76;
vitality and, 18, 143, 145, 148; writing style of, 155

White working class, 23–24, 89,
93–95, 117, 213n6
Will, 138, 171; Augustine and, 108–9,
113; creativity and, 129; as divided,
108–9, 113–14, 120, 128–29; as
emergent, 127–28, 137; Kant and,
107, 111–14, 120, 123; practical wisdom and, 17, 127–30, 133
Will to power, 164–66, 168–69, 175
Will to system, 126
World of becoming, 17, 27, 34, 38–39,
41, 94, 107, 125, 130–31, 133–35,
137–38, 141–42, 155, 165, 170–71,
185, 193. *See also* Becoming